Elizabeth Stansbury Kirkland

A Short History of English Literature for Young People

Elizabeth Stansbury Kirkland

A Short History of English Literature for Young People

ISBN/EAN: 9783743400276

Manufactured in Europe, USA, Canada, Australia, Japa

Cover: Foto ©ninafisch / pixelio.de

Manufactured and distributed by brebook publishing software (www.brebook.com)

Elizabeth Stansbury Kirkland

A Short History of English Literature for Young People

A SHORT

HISTORY OF ENGLISH LITERATURE

FOR

YOUNG PEOPLE

BY

MISS E. S. KIRKLAND

AUTHOR OF "A SHORT HISTORY OF ENGLAND," "A SHORT HISTORY OF FRANCE,"
"SIX LITTLE COOKS," "DORA'S HOUSEKEEPING," AND
"SPEECH AND MANNERS."

WITH ILLUSTRATIONS

CHICAGO
A. C. McCLURG & COMPANY
1892

PREFACE.

THIS volume is written as a companion to the "Short History of France" and "Short History of England," with which it forms a series. The study of literature calls for a knowledge of concurrent history. Half the value of acquaintance with writings is gone if the "setting" of each writer, as he appears in turn upon the pages, is not kept in sight. We need to know what influences were at work to make him what he was, and who were his contemporaries in literature, art, and government. On the other hand, to record an age without dwelling on its literature is to draw a face without the eyes. As John Morley puts it: "History tells us the deeds, but literature tells us the life of a nation."

In this history—in every history, short or long— a legion of worthy authors are crowded out; for it is impossible to tell everything (even in treating a single branch of a single subject), and we learn to exercise the self-denial involved in omissions. This task is a hard one, too, for it is far easier to tell everything than to pick and choose from the store. But experience teaches us that young people remember more when only a little is given them. A great array of facts appalls them with a sense of hopeless, endless toil.

"An attempt to introduce young people to the study of literature" would be a more descriptive title for the volume; but title-pages should leave something to the imagination. Our aim has been to achieve what Dr. Arnold describes when he says:

"The harvest gathered in the fields of the Past is brought home for the use of the Present."

E. S. K.

CHICAGO, October, 1892.

CONTENTS.

LIST OF ILLUSTRATIONS.

A SHORT
HISTORY OF ENGLISH LITERATURE

FOR

YOUNG PEOPLE.

CHAPTER I.

INTRODUCTORY.

FEW of us realize how much we owe to literature. From the moment when a little child first asks some one to tell him a story, to the time when the old man finds reading almost the only pleasure he has left, and really a solace for the loss of all the others; a large proportion of what makes life agreeable comes through those thoughts of men which have been embalmed in the written word and preserved for our benefit. He who first invented letters, who conceived the idea of making thoughts matured at one time and place, available at other times and places, was the greatest of benefactors. Since his invention it is said, and truly said, "Words are the only things that last forever."

It would be gratifying to be able to do anything toward encouraging and fostering in young people a real fondness for literature. By this is not meant what commonly passes for a love of reading, which is often nothing more than a desire to have a vacant mind entertained without the slightest trouble to itself. One who loves the best reading may be and possibly is a great reader; yet on the other hand, one may be a "great reader," as the words are often used, whose reading is a mere form of mental dissipation.

Reading, to do us any good, should be discriminative. We must learn to know why we prefer one author's style to another's; why the thoughts of the one seem to become a part of our own minds, while our eyes wander over the other with no sense of gratification. We must learn to appreciate the various kinds of imagery and take pleasure in books which minister to our sense of the beautiful. Our souls must be open to the lovely influences of poetry, and we must draw from it that inspiration which shall transfigure for us the prose of common life. We are all accustomed to the idea of the sprouting of seeds in the spring; but when Lowell writes:

> Every clod feels a stir of might,
>   An instinct within it which reaches and towers,
> And grasping blindly above it for light,
>   Climbs to a soul in grass and flowers,

the common event is glorified for us. No prose can express repose as does Tennyson's

> Music, that gentlier on the spirit lies
> Than tired eyelids upon tired eyes.

Whoever first applied the term "musical" to the sound of poetry, told in one word the secret of its charm. It is the music of the mind, and for this harmony our taste can be cultivated as well as for that made by instruments. Many nations have taken in verse their first literary steps, probably because, having no written works, they were obliged to trust to oral tradition, and rhythm helped them to remember the words. Homer's immortal epics were no doubt handed down by the voice of wandering minstrels for generations before they were committed to writing.

In reading and talking about literature, it is well for us to have a clear idea of what the word means. Not all that is written and printed comes under this head: All technical works — those peculiar to any art or science — all text-books, and nearly all that goes to fill the innumerable columns of the modern newspaper, should be excluded from it.

Besides the classes of books already mentioned, we can not, in the highest sense of the word, apply the name literature to books which are frivolous or intended merely for temporary amusement. Such books, doubtless, have their place; but do not let us confound them with what is enduring. There must be some appeal to the fancy, the imagination or the reflective part of man to give what we read a claim to this title; something tending to elevate the mind above material things, to warm the heart, to cultivate the taste, to inspire the imagination in order to bring what is written within its range. It is in this sense alone that we shall enter upon our acquaintance with literature.

Reading in its highest sense—not merely an amusement of the moment, which leaves no results except a craving for more dissipation of the same sort, but that which informs and elevates the mind while drawing out its fullest powers—this kind of reading is one of our purest enjoyments; and to make the most of it we must look carefully over the field spread out before us, and see how we can cultivate it to the best advantage.

The first classification that forces itself on our plan of work is the dividing of English literature into two parts; that which we can read as our own vernacular and that which we can not read except as we read a foreign tongue. To the latter division—what we can not read—belongs all that was written by our Anglo-Saxon forefathers before the middle of the fourteenth century. Until that time, all writing in England was in Latin except a few precious books written in Anglo-Saxon, which latter language some writers prefer to call Early English, and which is the rude, untutored beginning of our own language. A convenient division of English literature, made by a distinguished writer on the subject, arranges it in four periods, as follows: 1. Saxon-

English, or all that comes before the Norman Conquest;
2. Transitional English, or that from 1066 to about 1350,
during which time the two languages, Norman-French and
Anglo-Saxon, were gradually becoming fused into one; 3.
Early Modern English, from Chaucer to the writers of
Queen Elizabeth's time; 4. Modern English, from the
middle of the sixteenth century to our own day. After the
"transitional" period a secondary division is naturally made
by the close of a century, as it happens that each of the
centuries has a character of its own, differing from that
which precedes and that which follows it.

The earliest British writer whose name has come down
to us is Gildas, supposed to have been a Welsh monk of the
sixth century, who wrote in Latin a history of Britain from
the first invasion of Julius Cæsar to his own time. It is in
his book that we find the famous letter to the Roman consul in Gaul, begging for help against the unruly Scots and
Picts. Gildas was not an Englishman, for the Angles from
whom England takes its name had not yet arrived there;
but he was a Briton and belonged to the country, and, as
its first native writer must have a place in our literature.

CHAPTER II.

THE FIRST ANGLO-SAXON WRITERS.

BEFORE beginning on the systematic study of that
literature which we are to make our own by assimilation, we must take a hasty glance at the earlier
writers—those who wrote for the pleasure and benefit of
the people of their own times. And what a pleasure it was!
It is hard for us, to whom reading comes as naturally and
as easily as eating, to understand the eagerness with which
people who did not know Latin, and were therefore shut

out from the poetry and history in that language, welcomed the appearance in their narrow horizon of a poem which they could understand and commit to memory. It was like the lifting of a curtain toward the sunrise, or the introduction of a sixth sense which opened to them a new range of possibilities and made the world forever richer.

As we have said, the earliest form used by the Saxons, or English, as also by most other nations, was the poetical. The first poets did not employ rhyme, but their ears demanded rhythm, or the regular rise and fall of the voice at successive syllables; and to this they added what has been called "apt alliteration's artful aid." There were certain fixed rules for the latter, but it would not be profitable to spend time in learning them now, especially as the thing itself, in literature's advance in dignity and elegance, has been abandoned. Collier's "English Literature," gives an excellent example of it, which, though written nearly seven hundred years after the first English poem, will show the nature of this alliteration:

> *Ac* on a May Morwening   [*and*]
> On Malvern hills
> Me beFel a *Ferly,*   [*wonder*]
> Of Fairy me thought.
> I was Weary *for Wanderd*   [*with wandering*]
> And Went me to rest
> Under a *Brood* Bank   [*broad*]
> By a *Burn's* side;   [*brook*]
> And as I Lay Leaned,
> And Looked on the waters,
> I Slumbered into a Sleeping,
> It *Swayed* so *mury.*   [*sounded, murmuring*]

There is something touching in the glimpses we get of these old "men of letters," feeling their way dimly through the twilight, probably humbly fancying that the real glory and greatness of poetry and prose would always be, as it was then, in the sounding and ponderous measures and phrases of the classics. One wishes that some kind fairy might have whispered to them that the tree they were planting would, in a thousand years, throw all others into the shade; but there is no evidence that their thoughts ever soared so high.

Gildas wrote in Latin, and English literature, properly speaking, begins with Caedmon (pronounced Cadmon), who lived in the seventh century. He was a servant in Saint Hilda's monastery at Whitby, so little versed in the accomplishments of the day that he was not able to take his turn with the rest at singing to the harp which was passed from hand to hand after supper. Mortified at being unable to contribute his share to the general entertainment, he escaped to the stables (where it was his place that night to keep guard over the cattle), and there, overcome by vexation and loneliness, fell asleep. In his sleep these waking thoughts were continued in the form of a vision in which a heavenly visitor appeared to him saying, "Caedmon, sing!" "I can 't," said poor Caedmon, "that is why I came away!" "But you must sing to me," said the spirit. "What shall I sing?" asked the cowherd. "Sing the beginning of created things," was the reply, and a poetical version of the story of creation as told in the book of Genesis, passed through his dreaming mind, and was remembered by him when he awoke. The next morning he presented himself before the Abbess Hilda, to ask what use he should make of his new and wonderful gift of song. She, to test his power, gave him some portions of scripture to turn into verse, and when she found that the power was no transitory possession she persuaded him to embrace the religious life, that is, to become a monk. From that time he devoted himself to versifying different parts of the sacred writings, and his lines in the unlearned, common tongue, were for generations, the delight and solace of the pious monks of Whitby.

We give a few lines from the beginning of Caedmon's

poem, only substituting modern letters for some characters (th, etc.) peculiar to the Saxon :

Nu we sceolan herian	Now we shall praise
heofon-rices weard,	the guardian of heaven,
metodes mihte,	the might of the creator,
and his mod-ge-thone,	and his counsel,
wera wuldor fæder !	the glory-father of men !

The typical Saxon had two sides to his moral nature; and while he threw himself earnestly into the devotional frame of mind called forth by the strains of Caedmon, it can not be denied that he took the keenest delight in every thing that had to do with fighting. The story of Beowulf, the most ancient heroic poem in any Teutonic language, was written by some unknown hand in Germany long before an Anglo-Saxon poet, equally unknown, re-wrote it in his native tongue in England, late in the seventh century. The hero leaves his home among the Goths and sails to Denmark, where he frees a Danish chief from the attacks of a terrible fire-breathing monster named Grendel. Then he returns to his own country and rules in peace until his land is attacked by a hideous dragon whom he slays, but is himself killed by its fiery breath. The poem is intensely picturesque from its freshness and simplicity, while it owes very little to figures of speech. There are few similes, and the metaphors are of the most obvious kind; but the scene rises before us as if it were painted on canvas. We sit at the rudely-spread but abundant banquet, we hear the boastful talk of the warriors, and we see the desire for gain in the shape of plunder overtopping the love of glory. It seems, however, to have given both author and translator the purest pleasure to tell how its hero was able, after being dragged down into the den of a wicked she-fiend, to "let her soul out of its bone-house" or skeleton; in other words, put her to death. Homer has many ways of describing the parting between soul and body, but none more vivid than this.

Differing both from the lofty imagination of Caedmon and the warlike breathings of the author of Beowulf, are the hymns of Aldhelm, who was a young man when, in the seventh century, Caedmon died.

Aldhelm, at the age of sixteen, joined a monastery at Malmesbury, where the monks were so poor that they had not enough to eat.   In time he became its abbot, improved its material condition, and gathered about him a company of pure-minded and zealous young devotees, whom he inspired with his own enthusiasm.   His special gifts were for music and poetry, and King Alfred, who lived about two hundred years after him, thought him unequaled as a maker of English verse.*   It is said that on Sundays, when many persons from the country came into Malmesbury for trading purposes, he would station himself on the bridge and sing to them so sweetly that when the time came for service they would follow him into the church, putting off their business until the next day.   In Alfred's time people still remembered and sang the songs of Aldhelm; but unfortunately all the English ones are lost, and we have now left of his writing only some rather tame Latin verses.

While Caedmon was cultivating a new sense in the narrow understanding of his fellow-laborers, and when Aldhelm had just entered upon his work at Malmesbury,† an infant in arms was taking his first look at life; the lad who grew to be the great Bede, so wise, so good, and so revered as to have earned the title "Venerable."   We have become so much accustomed to coupling this epithet with the life of the saintly man, that we forget the fact of his ever having been otherwise than venerable.   He was devoted to the religious life from his childhood, being only seven years old when he was placed, late in the seventh

---

* This shows us that there were already other English verse-makers; of them no record or tradition gives the names or the words.

† The exact years of these occurrences are uncertain.

century, in the monastery at Wearmouth, in the bishopric of Durham. Although he became a man of great learning, he steadily refused every offer of a higher position than that of a simple monk; a pope in vain invited him to remain at Rome, whither he had gone on a visit, and his brethren at Wearmouth had no better success in trying to make him their abbot. A monk he was, and a monk he determined to remain, that he might have nothing to distract his mind from study and teaching. His pupils at Jarrow numbered at one time six hundred, and young men came from all parts of the kingdom to profit by his instructions.

His so-called "Ecclesiastical History of England" (most noted of his many works) was really a general history of his land, brought down to his own day, and is a storehouse of valuable information which no one else could have given. Forty-three other works—religious, scientific, and poetical—attest his industry, which ceased only with his life; and one of his young disciples, named Cuthbert, has left us a picture of his closing hours unsurpassable in its tender grace.*

* "When the morning appeared he ordered us to write with all speed what he had begun, and this done, there was one of us with him who said to him, 'Most dear master, there is still one chapter wanting; do you think it troublesome to be asked any more questions?' He answered, 'It is no trouble; take your pen and make ready and write fast.' Which he did, but at the ninth hour he said to me, 'I have some little articles of value in my chest, such as pepper, napkins, and incense; run quickly and bring the brethren to me, that I may distribute among them the gifts which God has bestowed on me.' Having said much more, he passed the day joyfully till the evening, and the lad above mentioned said, 'Dear master, there is yet one sentence not written.' He answered, 'Write quickly.' Soon after, the lad said, 'The sentence is now written.' He replied, 'It is well; you have said the truth. It is ended. Receive my head into your hands, for it is great satisfaction to me to sit facing my holy place where I was wont to pray.' And thus, on the pavement of his little cell, singing, 'Glory be to the Father, and to the Son, and to the Holy Ghost,' he breathed his last, and so departed to the heavenly kingdom."

CHAPTER III.

ALFRED AND OTHER SAXON WRITERS.

AFTER the death of the Venerable Bede and before the birth of Alfred, the next Saxon writer, two great scholars arose in England, whose writings made them famous all over Europe. These were Alcuin (735—804) and Erigena. As they lived abroad and wrote only in Latin, their works scarcely belong to English literature, but as they were Englishmen, we ought to know at least their names and something of their writings so far as they were of a national character.

The year of Bede's death is given as that of Alcuin's birth. He was born at York, which at that time was a centre of learning in England. He was the finest scholar of his age, and as such was invited by Charlemagne to make his home at the French court, where he spent the latter part of his life. His works are on the most varied subjects,—such as history, divinity, and exposition of the Scriptures, together with poems and an interesting series of letters to Charlemagne, who appreciated his value, and treated him with the greatest distinction.

The other noted English scholar, John Scotus Erigena, was probably a native of Ireland, and like Alcuin, passed much of his life in France; Charles the Bald, grandson of Charlemagne, being his patron. He was one of the boldest and most original thinkers of the middle ages, and at the time when he flourished, half a century later than Alcuin, had not his equal in Europe as a metaphysician. He had a ready wit, too, not dimmed by the subtleties of his metaphysical studies. One day the king asked him, at dinner, what was the difference between a Scot and a sot or fool. "Just the breadth of the table," answered Scotus.

With Alfred the Great (849—901), begins the true history of English prose. Bede made many translations into Saxon, but all this part of his work is lost; while we still have enough of Alfred's to show his vigorous style and his intense love of learning for its own sake. He was no scholarly recluse, enjoying literary work as a relaxation from royal state. Untiring activity alone enabled him to accomplish all the duties of a statesman, a general, a ruler and an author. His large mind desired instruction not only for himself but for all his subjects; and his life was spent in trying to encourage the study of letters among his ignorant people. Schools sprang up everywhere under his fostering care, and the centre of learning was transferred under him from the North to the South; from Whitby in Yorkshire to Winchester, not far from the English Channel, where, in his own court, he had a school which received his personal supervision. With all his claims to the rank of a scholar, he was absolutely free from vanity or pedantry. His noble simplicity bore the stamp of a mind above pettiness.

Alfred's work began, as was natural in an age whose possessions in the way of literature were so small, with translations. He rendered into English the "Universal History" of Orosius, a Latin writer of the fifth century; the "Consolations of Philosophy," written in the sixth century by Boëthius, the high-minded minister of Theodoric, who beguiled the long hours of his unjust imprisonment by recording his thoughts; Bede's "Ecclesiastical History" (really, as we have said, a history of Britain) written in Latin; and the " Pastoral Rule" of Gregory the Great, which Alfred called in Saxon "Gregory's Book on the Care of the Soul." Of his original works, not much remains beside his excellent code of laws. Of his " Manual," or hand-book, which would have been most valuable of all to us as showing his daily thoughts and habits, no copy is known to exist.

We must not think of King Alfred as working at his task

2

in   luxuriously furnished library, under the ligh of a softly shaded student-lamp. Cowper says, speaking of a three-legged stool,

> On such a stool immortal Alfred sat,
> And swayed the sceptre of his infant realms.

For the light, a single wax or tallow candle (possibly two, as he was a king) furnished the best that could be had ; and being without a clock, the methodical student caused his candles to be notched in divisons each of which would take an hour in burning, and thus he divided his time so as not to give to any one occupation more than its due proportion. One-third of the twenty-four hours, we are told, he gave to study and devotion, one-third to the business of his king-dom, while the remaining eight hours were all that he allotted to eating and amusement. Finding that the draughts in his too-well ventilated palace made the candles flame, he in-vented a lantern, in which thinly-shaved horn did the work of glass and prevented the candle from burning down too fast.   Nothing within the range of possibility was too great for him ; no worthy thing too small; and when he died, at fifty-two years old, worn out with hard work, he left a name which has ever since been revered by the millions in his country who know how to prize noble work done in a noble station.

A "Life of Alfred the Great," written in Latin by Asser, a learned monk contemporary with him, is the authority for many of the stories connected with this king, who made the monk his personal friend and preceptor.

An interesting writer of Saxon times, who flourished just a hundred years after King Alfred, as Alcuin had flourished a hundred years before him, was Alfric the Grammarian, who lived until the end of the tenth century. He wrote a lively little book to teach schoolboys Latin, which he put, in a quite modern fashion, into the form of a dialogue. He represents a number of pupils begging to be taught, who answer various questions as to their respective trades; in this way bringing before his pupils a large number of words used in common life, of which they learn the Latin equivalents almost as in a game. He also wrote, for the benefit of his boys, the first glossary, or partial dictionary, of Latin and English words. He followed in the footsteps of Bede by translating into English seven or eight books of the Bible.

Among the most curious and interesting of the literary monuments of England is the work known as the "Anglo-Saxon Chronicle," begun, no one knows when, and added to whenever there was something to say and somebody to say it, until the middle of the twelfth century. The old chronicle, with all its shortcomings and its credulity, is almost the only record we have of the century after Alfred's death. There are in existence six manuscripts of the chronicle, each enriched with such additions to the main story as would be most interesting to the monks of the particular monastery where it was copied. It is not difficult to imagine the gradual formation of one of these chronicles. When the first was begun, it would naturally contain all the scraps of tradition which had been handed down from one set of monks to another. Then as various events of the outside world came to their knowledge, these facts would be added in their order, together with such local items as belonged especially to the place where the record was made. This copy would then be sent to another monastery, would be copied out as far as it went, and would receive additions in its turn.

The "Anglo-Saxon Chronicle" does not, like many similar histories, begin at the Creation; it goes back only to a few centuries before the Christian era. After a time we arrive at Cæsar's conquest, and the record marches on, meagre and bare, through the Roman dominion, the frightful period of the Saxon invasions and the Heptarchy, the reign of Egbert, last Bretwalda and first king of all England, and, after a period of repose during the reign of Alfred, plunges again into discord and confusion, varied by blessed times of quiet, until the strong-handed and tyrannical Normans reopen the springs of national progress.

This chronicle brings us to the event of greatest importance to our language and literature: the conquest of England by William the Norman in 1066. Nor even then does it cease its curious life and fungus-like growth; but with the death of King Stephen, grandson of the conqueror, it comes to an abrupt end. Its last paragraph reads:

This year [1154] King Stephen died. . . And the King [Henry II] was received at Peterborough with great respect, and in full procession; so he was also at Ramsey, at Thorney, and at Spalding, and . . . .

What was intended to follow "and" will never be known, but we have not lost anything worth keeping. A new race of chroniclers arose to replace the rambling, irregular, straggling annalists of the early centuries, and their later accounts, though not always trustworthy, are more picturesque and varied than those of the humble monks who have been our authority up to the time of the first Plantagenet, Henry II.

This poor but precious chronicle, with its tale of disaster and oppression, creeps on, as we have seen, into Norman times, but the scholarship fostered by Alfred had dwindled under his illiterate successors, and in reading the story of those troubled years we wonder, not so much that England had not a brilliant literature, as that she had any at all. In the brief period of Danish rule there was an interval when a writer might have said his say undisturbed by the clash of arms, but the writer was not forthcoming; if we except the poem said to have been composed by King Canute when he and his warriors were rowing on the river Ouse, near the site of the old monastery at Ely:

Merie sungen the Muneches binnen Ely,
Tha Cnut ching reuther by;
Rotheth cnites ner the land,
And here ye thes Muneches sang.

Merrily sang the monks at Ely
When Canute the king rowed by;
Row, knights, near the land,
And hear ye the monks' song.

CHAPTER IV

ANGLO-NORMAN WRITERS.

WITH the Norman Conquest (1066), began a new era for England, in which its literature entered a new phase, influenced—yet never quite dominated—by a new language. The conquerors brought the love of letters, and the Anglo-Saxon mind, in which the capacity for literature had been almost dormant, slowly awoke to its enjoyment and production. The authors of the twelfth century wrote mostly in Latin. There were a host of them. John of Salisbury (1120–1182), the secretary of Thomas à Becket, satirized the frivolities of courtiers and the follies of the scholastic philosophers. Ordericus Vitalis (1075–1143) wrote an "Ecclesiastical History of England and Normandy," which tells more about the eleventh and twelfth centuries than any other work of the period. Then follows a group of writers who, under the general name of "old chroniclers," give, in a mixture of fact and fiction, the so-called annals of England from the age of fable to their own. The most important of these were William of Malmesbury, who wrote a "History of the Kings of England"; a painstaking work, authentic as far as his materials went; and Geoffrey of Monmouth, a Welsh monk whose vivid fancy led him to set forth, under the title of "History of the Britons," a romance which caused a plodding historian of the next century to assert that Geoffrey falsified the facts of history. We of the nineteenth century are disposed to be more charitable, and think that Geoffrey was only indulging his imagination for the amusement of his countrymen, as many a writer of romance has done since, without expecting to be taken literally. We owe to him the story of King Arthur and his Knights of the Round Table, and we should feel sorry to be without it; for, though we may not pin our faith to any one statement in it, we learn from it what our ancestors believed and enjoyed, and this knowledge has a historical value quite apart from the facts which the learned monk professed to relate.

Many chroniclers besides the two already mentioned divided with them the honor of writing, with more or less fidelity, the early history of their country. Of those who flourished in the twelfth century, the best known are Gerald of Wales, Henry of Huntingdon and Roger of Wendover. At this time the Saxon and Norman tongues existed side by side as spoken languages, while all the books which have come down to us were written either in Latin or Norman-French—far the larger proportion being in the former. Of the latter, the most interesting is the "Brut" (or Brutus) of Wace, an Anglo-Norman poet whose imagination seized upon the story told by Geoffrey of Monmouth, and reproduced it as a metrical romance of many hundred lines. Not to be outdone in patriotism, an English monk, Layamon, turned Wace's "Brut" into his own language, which may be called semi-Saxon, and thus produced the first English poem after the Conquest.

It was a great thing for England, this beginning of story-telling in the native tongue. Englishmen who could not understand neither the Latin of Geoffrey nor the French of Wace, were overjoyed at the opportunity of reading, in their own language, the story which had already become so famous; and the taste for fiction once acquired, the nation has advanced unceasingly in its fondness for this fascinating branch of literature.

To Walter Map or Mapes, England owes a debt only half-recognized, for his services in bringing together and harmonizing the Arthurian legends of Geoffrey of Monmouth and his brother chroniclers (or fabulists). From his pen came the story of the search for the Holy Grail, as we now know it, and the romance of Sir Galahad. To these he added various legends of what is called "The Arthurian Cycle," blending them so skillfully that they all seem parts of one story. This work was written in Norman-French. His satires against the clergy, in Latin, found eager readers both in and out of the monasteries. An addition to the literature of the same age, in the latter tongue, is the collection called "Gesta," a collection of wildly improbable stories which served to amuse the monks, and the few scholars who were not monks, in the interval of severer study.

It was in this same century, the twelfth, that we find the first traces of what afterward became so famous under the name of "Mysteries" and "Miracle Plays." These were an attempt to blend amusement with religious instruction. The first dealt only with Bible subjects; the second allowed the introduction of other matters, usually some incident in the lives of saints. Naturally, the two were often interwoven, and under the same general form continued to instruct and delight the illiterate until, in the sixteenth century, interludes and masques arose and led the way to the modern drama.

The only other purely literary work of the thirteenth century worthy of mention is the rhymed chronicle of Robert of Gloucester, written in what has been called "Transitional English"—a step between the semi-Saxon of the twelfth century and the later English of Chaucer's time.

With the thirteenth century, literature took a graver turn. Matthew Paris, who has been called the greatest of the old chroniclers, lived more than half through the century. Orm or Ormin, a monk (like most other writers during the same period), wrote in semi-Saxon English a paraphrase in verse of the church-service of each day, with the addition of a homily, or short sermon, also in verse.*

The greatest name of the thirteenth century, and one of the greatest in any century, belongs not to literature but to science. It is that of Roger Bacon (1214–94). He was born of a good family, was educated at Oxford, took holy orders, and afterward spent some years in Paris, where he acquired a great reputation for theological learning. Returning to Oxford he devoted himself to teaching and study, and entered the strict order of the Franciscans, who discouraged learning, as a luxury, and even denied him the use of pen and ink. Clement IV, hearing of his rare acquirements, sent him a command to write down his thoughts without regard to the rules of his order. Here a new difficulty arose. The Franciscans, vowed to poverty, had no money for writing-materials (in those days a serious expense for it was not till 1300 that paper began to supplant parchment), and Bacon's own family had been ruined

---

*A quotation will serve to show the change in spelling between the thirteenth century and our own.

> Thiss bocc is nemmnedd Orrmulum,
> Forrthi thatt Ormin it wrohhte.

> This book is named Ormulum
> Because that Orm it wrote.

The object of doubling the final consonant occurring after a vowel, was apparently to serve as a guide to the pronunciation of the words by strangers, especially those of the Gallic race, which is prone to leave such consonants unpronounced.

in the "Barons' Wars" of Henry III. To supply this want would cost him not less than sixty pounds, equivalent to more than a thousand dollars of our money now. Loans were obtained from friends, and with almost incredible industry, Bacon wrote, within a year and a half, his "Opus Majus" (great work) and two minor works, which summed up the study of a lifetime. He urged upon men the study of nature herself as a means of understanding her processes; and, as has been said, laid the foundations of that great system which afterward took form in the mind of the second Bacon; the Lord Chancellor of James I.

CHAPTER V.

THE FOURTEENTH CENTURY.

ON entering the fourteenth century we must be prepared for a long step in advance. Before treating of Chaucer, the "day-star" of English poetry, and his contemporaries, we must mention some of lesser note. Robert de Brunne wrote a religious poem called "Hand-lynge Sinne," and translated some rhyming French chronicles. Laurence Minot made war-songs, celebrating the victories of Edward III. in France. Richard Rolle, "the Hermit of Hampole," whose life has in it an element of romance, wrote "The Pricke of Conscience." He had a strong leaning to the "religious life" and, knowing that his aspirations toward it would not be favored by his family, he begged from his sister two gowns, a white and a gray, which he fashioned as well as he could into a monkish dress, and from that time lived a life of retirement and devotion. Having satisfied his friends of his sanity, he was allowed to spend his years in a cell not connected with any monastery, and then became one of the busiest writers of the age.

A sentence or two from Rolle's explanation of his own style will be found interesting as illustrating some of the principles of transition by which the cumbrous old language was approaching the form we now use:

> I seke no straunge Ynglis, but lightest and comunest & swilk is moste lyk unto the Latyne, so that thai that knawes noght the Latyne, be the Ynglis may com to many Latyne wordis. In the translacion I feloghe the letter als-mekille as I may, and ther [where] I fynd no propre Ynglis, I feloghe the wit [sense] of the wordis, so that thai that schulen rede it them thar not drede erryng.

It is probably at this date—the first half of the fourteenth century—that the first miracle-plays were written in English. These were the work of Ralph Higden, a monk, who afterward wrote in Latin a "Polychronicon," or summary of general history, of great repute in its day, and still interesting as bringing to a close the long series of "chronicles," which were destined to be replaced, a hundred years later, by the first attempts at history.

We have now arrived at the great period of early modern English; the language as it remained, without great alteration, until the time of Elizabeth (the age of Spenser and Shakspeare), after which the translation of the Bible, under James I., may be said to have fixed it in its present form.

It is not easy to assign exact dates to the early works of the fourteenth century, for, as books were not then printed but copied by hand and circulated in that form, there was not the publishers' practice of dating them on the title-page.

For many years the honor of having written the first English book was assigned to Sir John Mandeville, under which name a most interesting book of travels was given to the world. The writer professes to have spent thirty-four years in visiting the various countries of Asia, making a détour into Egypt in the course of his wanderings. The marvels he relates are enough to make one's hair stand on end; though he often puts in a discreet remark to the effect that he did not see these things himself, but only had them from others. Until comparatively late years, writers on literature no more thought of doubting the existence of Mandeville than that of Chaucer. There is, however, a tendency to dethrone this long-venerated idol, and to think the work a clever compilation of some writer who never saw Palestine or China, but made up his account from the reports of others. Be this as it may, the result is a most entertaining book, written in fourteenth-century English and illustrated with wood-cuts dating evidently from the infancy of the art. If one takes the trouble to learn only a few score words and become familiar with the antiquated spelling, the travels of Sir John will be found well worth reading. If any spice of humor existed in the author it is carefully concealed, for he is as grave as a judge in his narrations; but we can extract abundance of fun for ourselves out of the quaint recitals, and must always feel grateful to the laborious author or compiler.

Here is a specimen of his "boke," spelling and all:

The gret King hathe every day 50 fair Damyseles, that serven him everemore at his Mete. And whan he is at the Table, thei bryngen him hys Mete 5 and 5 to gedre. And in bryngynge hire Servyse, thei syngen a Song. And after that, thei kutten his Mete and putten it in his Mouthe; for he touchethe no thing ne handlethe nought, but holdethe evere more his Hondes before him, upon the Table. For he hath so longe Nayles that he may take no thing ne handle no thing. For the Noblesse of that Contree is to have long Nayles and to make hem growen alle ways to ben as longe as men may. And there ben manye in that Contree, that han hyse Nayles so longe that they envyronne alle the Hond: and that is gret Noblesse. And the Noblesse of the Women is for to have smale Feet and litille; and therefore anon as thei ben born, thei leet bynde hire Feet so streyte, that thei may not growen half as nature wolde.

A vivid picture of the growth of our language from Saxon to Norman-English can best be had by transcribing some of the familiar words of the Lord's Prayer as they were written in successive centuries:

A.D. 700.   Thu ure Fader, the eart on heofenum,
              Si thin noman gehalgod,
              Cume thin rike,   [reich, kingdom—German]
              Si thin Willa on eorthan twa on hoefenum;
              Syle us todag orne dægwanlican hlaf [loaf], etc.

A.D. 1120.   Ure Fader in Heven rich,
              Thy name be halyed ever lich.
              Thou bring us thy michel bliese
              Als bit in Heven y doe
              Evear in yearth bin it alsoe.
              That holy bread that lasteth ay,
              Thou send us this ilke day; etc.

A.D. 1380.   Our Fadir that art in hevenys;
              Halewid be thi name,
              Thi kyngdom come to,
              Be thi wil done in erthe as in hevene.
              Give to us this day oure breede oure othir
                  substaunce; etc.

Somewhat later than Mandeville's work appeared "The Vision of Piers Plowman," a remarkable poem written by William Langland, who seems to have been intended for the church but to have passed into secular life, for we hear of his wife Kitte and his daughter Calote. The poet represents himself as having fallen asleep among the Malvern Hills, and there having a series of visions (for there are several wakings), in which he describes the life and manners of the poor classes of England, and declaims bitterly against the corrupt lives of the monks and the extortions of the begging friars. In one place he makes a singular prophecy which was fulfilled in the sixteenth century in the attack of Henry VIII. on the monasteries. He warns the monks that the time will come when they

Shall have a knock of [from] a king, and incurable the wound.

A greater name than Langland's is that of John Wycliffe

(1324–84), who may be called the first English protestant, from his earnest protesting against the abuses and corruptions prevailing in the church of Rome, which was still, as its name of Catholic implies, the universal church of Christendom. Milton, writing three hundred years later, says of him that he was "honoured of God to be the first preacher of a general reformation to all Europe." Poetically, he is spoken of as "the morning star of the Reformation."

Wycliffe's great work is his translation of the Bible into English. Full of faults and inaccuracies, it was yet the unsealing of a fountain of living waters to the unlearned mass of his countrymen, who were thirsting for a better knowledge of the source of their belief than could be obtained from listening to the sermons of friars or seeing the performance of miracle plays. Of the earlier partial translations of the Scriptures the language had already become as antiquated as the language of Piers Plowman is to us; and nothing like a version of the whole had ever been attempted.

Of Wycliffe's work as a reformer and a theologian, our limits do not allow us to speak. Political and religious dissatisfaction often go hand in hand, and the same party which was engaged in opposition to the king was prominent in favoring the opinions of the Lollards, as Wycliffe's followers (for some reason now unknown) were called. The doctrines preached by him caused him to be accused of heresy, but he had powerful supporters, and, although the objectionable books were publicly burned, no penalty was inflicted on him personally, except that he was expelled from the University of Oxford. He retired to the little church of Lutterworth, where the carved pulpit from which he preached may still be seen; and there, alternating his work among his flock with the writing of theological works and tracts in strong, nervous English, he remained until successive strokes of paralysis obliged him to give up his labors.

In the last year of his life, he was summoned to appear before the Pope at Rome, but he disregarded the summons, and in 1384, death found him in his quiet parsonage. This was ninety-nine years before the birth of that other great reformer, Martin Luther. Forty years later, the malice and violence of the enemies of reformation caused his bones to be disinterred, burned to ashes, and scattered into a little brook; but the seeds which he had sowed in men's minds, though lying dormant for many years, germinated when the nation awoke to fresh life at the call of Luther. As Fuller, the church historian, puts it, writing some centuries later: "Thus the brook conveyed his ashes to Avon, Avon into Severn, Severn into the narrow seas [Bristol Channel], they into the main ocean; and thus the ashes of Wycliffe are the emblem of his doctrine, which now is dispersed the world over."

> The Avon to the Severn runs,
>   The Severn to the sea,
> And Wycliffe's dust shall spread abroad
>   Wide as the waters be.

A few verses from Wycliffe's translation of the Bible, given below, show how far the English of his time was from that of our day. It was English, however, and not Norman-French or semi-Saxon; and with some little labor we can pick out its meaning.

As it is writun in Ysaie, the prophete, Lo! I send myn angel before thi face, that schal make thi weye redy before thee.

John was in desert baptisynge, and preaching the baptysm of penaunce, into remiscioun of synnes.

And alle men of Jerusalem wenten out to him and al the cuntree of Judee; and weren baptisid of him in the flood of Jordan, knowleching her synnes.—St. Mark, ch. i.

The name most commonly coupled with Chaucer's is that of John Gower (1320–1408), his contemporary, who survived him eight years. Gower was also a poet, but so far inferior to Chaucer that his works are now read only for their antiquarian interest, and not, like Chaucer's, for the pleasure they give us. In his day he was much read, for then books were few. His principal work is the "Confessio Amantis" —Confession of a Lover—which he wrote at the request of King Richard II., grandson and successor of Edward III. The king and the poet met one another in their boats on the Thames (then used as the great highway or thoroughfare of London), and Richard invited his friend into the royal barge for a little talk. "Book some new thing," said he, "into which book I myself may often look." The result was a poem of some 30,000 lines, written in English ; Gower's previous writings having been mainly in French or Latin. Gower lived to a great age, and passed the last eight years of his life in total blindness. He had a strong personal friendship for Chaucer, who in his turn calls him "the moral Gower"—a name which has ever since clung to him.

Gower's French work, a religious poem which probably gave rise to this epithet, is lost. His principal Latin work, "Vox Clamantis," is a satire on the vices and follies of the age, wherein the king is not spared, a circumstance which, by a side-light, throws credit on Richard for continuing his friendship with the poet.

John de Trevisa, a Cornish clergyman, translated Ralph Higden's "Polychronicon." In this translation he tells us that he avoids the "old and ancient English," so that the people of his time can understand it ; and in another hundred years, when Caxton prints this translation, we read that he finds it necessary to re-write the "rude and old English ; that is, certain words which in these days be neither used nor understood." So times change, and language changes with them.

Although the list is closed of Chaucer's English contemporaries, there remains the name of a Scottish writer, who died some years before him. John Barbour (1320–94) was the author of a long poem called "The Bruce," describing the deeds of that hero, who lived about half a century before he wrote. Barbour held an office in the church and was a man of scholarly education; he was also a zealous patriot, and did full justice to the character and exploits of Robert Bruce, while his own soul was on fire with the thought of Scottish liberty and independence. He writes from the heart:

> Ah, Freedom is a noble thing;
> Freedom makes man to have liking;
> Freedom all solace to man gives;
> He lives at ease who freely lives.

CHAPTER VI.

GEOFFREY CHAUCER.

CHAUCER was unquestionably the greatest writer of his time. Unlike the others, he had no especial lesson to teach or particular view to inculcate. He wrote purely for pleasure and because he could not help it; all his wisdom, fun, pathos, sweet poetic tenderness, love of nature, and clever insight into human character had to come out in words. The feeling that he was making something to live that never lived before, gives the joyous tone running through his work, and produces the effect of bubbling over. He was the first great English story-teller; and when we remember with what eagerness works of fiction are read even in our advanced age, we can not wonder that the people of the fourteenth century, living in the childhood of the new civilization and having little besides the frivolous French *fabliaux* or the inventions of Geoffrey of Monmouth to satisfy their intellectual hunger, should have seized upon the food offered to their imaginations in the picturesque tales of Chaucer. This would account for his popularity in his own and the following century, but he

JOHN WYCLIFFE.

ias kept his place for five hundred years only because he had that to say which will command the ear of humanity at all times—a representation of human nature as it is, given by one who sees by intuition into the very heart of things. The music of his verse, his wit, his humor, his delightful photographing of the foibles of his characters as well as of their good qualities and their outward appearance, his delicate discrimination, his way of raising everything, by the magic of his touch, above the sphere of commonplace—all help to mark his work with the stamp of genius. The verdict of the centuries is justified.

No certainty exists as to the date of Geoffrey Chaucer's birth; some biographers giving it as 1328, while others place it as late as 1340. He was the son of John Chaucer, a vintner or wine-seller, and was born in London. It is beyond question that he had a good education, probably at one of the great universities. Both Oxford (founded in the eleventh century) and Cambridge (twelfth century) claim him as a student, though on shadowy grounds. He came early into royal favor; how, one can not say, but he is mentioned as belonging to the household of Lionel, Duke of Clarence, King Edward III.'s third son. At a later time, he accompanied the king himself to France and was there taken prisoner and ransomed by Edward for the sum of £16. Soon after this we hear of his first ventures in poetry. At this time he was much impressed by French models, and his early poems, "The Court of Love," "The Book of the Duchess Blanche," and others, show strong traces of French influence. He also translated, or rather imitated, a favorite French poem of the time called "The Romaunt of the Rose." The Duchess Blanche was the first wife of John of Gaunt, Duke of Lancaster, son of Edward III. and Chaucer's life-long patron and friend.

Chaucer's wife, Philippa Roet, was the sister of the Duke's third wife; so we see that though the poet's parentage was

3

humble, his own qualities made him the associate of princes. After his marriage, he was repeatedly employed by the king on diplomatic missions to Italy, and the works produced during this period are said to be in his second, or Italian, manner. The best known of these are, "Troilus and Cressida," "The Assembly of Fowls," and "The House of Fame." At the time of Chaucer's first visit to Italy, the poet Petrarch was still living, and a passage in the "Canterbury Tales" leads us to suppose that our poet may have seen him there.

He had pensions, wardships, offices of various kinds, and "grants," in other words, gifts, which made him a prosperous man. He was now at the summit of his fortunes, and we enter upon the study of his third and best period, the English, to which all his noblest works belong. A few only of these can be mentioned here; the dainty apologue of "The Flower and the Leaf," the longer poem called "A Legend of Good Women," the "Dream," and, last and best, the "Canterbury Tales." Our young people, who have so much to read, can not perhaps spare the time to make a full study of Chaucer; but they should by all means make acquaintance with the Prologue to this immortal work.

The "Canterbury Tales" are told by a company of people assembled to make a pilgrimage to the shrine of St. Thomas à Becket at Canterbury; and as this is something which interests all classes of people from the king to the beggar, the poet finds opportunity to introduce into his story a variety of characters, occupying different social positions. The action of the story includes a long ride on horseback, which furnishes us with fresh, breezy out-door life, and active exercise. It was fitting, almost inevitable, that Chaucer should lay the main scene of his story in the open air. He was, above all things, a lover of nature. We think of him and his fellow-travellers (for it is hard to realize that they made the pilgrimage only in the poet's imagination), always as on the wing — never as having arrived at their destination or even as being assembled at the Tabard Inn before setting out. Mrs. Browning says that all the railroads that may intersect the earth forever can not hush the "tramp, tramp," of their horses' feet.

One always forms some mental portrait of a favorite writer, and it is pleasant to be able to compare this with the statements of those who knew him. As to Chaucer's personal appearance we have more testimony than is usual in regard to those of a long-past time. He was, like King David, "of a ruddy countenance," with the fair hair of the typical Saxon; not tall, and, late in life, inclining to be stout, for he himself intimates that he was "no poppet to embrace." All agree in ascribing to him that air of courtesy and good-breeding which is acquired by familiarity with the best society; and he tells us that at the time of writing his "Canterbury Tales" he had contracted a habit of walking along with his eyes fixed on the ground, for which he is good-naturedly rallied by one of his companions. Other writers of his time and that immediately succeeding him refer to him as their "dear master," their "reverend father"; and it is to the enthusiasm of his fellow-poet, Occleve, that we owe the beautiful miniature portrait of him which may still be seen at Oxford.

If men should have suddenly to choose the one English poem which should survive, all others to be at once destroyed; a very large number of voices would doubtless be raised in favor of the "Canterbury Tales." And if the nineteenth-century reader can spare time but for one book of all written in English before the Elizabethan age, he may take the same immortal work, sure of finding himself better instructed than if he had read all the others and left that out.

This great achievement distinguishes the fourteenth century from its fellows. It was the period of the waking up of the English mind to a condition of full life and vigor; of the assimilation of the Saxon and Norman elements of the language, and of its substantial victory over the Latin as the medium for the interchange of thought among all classes and its transmission to future ages.

Chaucer, toward the end of his life, saw the greater part of his income withdrawn (upon the retiring of his patron John of Gaunt, "time-honored Lancaster"), but afterward Fortune again smiled and he ended his days in comfort. He died at Westminster (now part of London), in a house near the abbey and not far from the place which Caxton made memorable by his printing-press. One of Chaucer's biographers says that his house was removed to make way for Henry the Seventh's chapel. If this be true it adds one more to the associations which make that honored spot so dear to our hearts and our imaginations. It is all ours as well as England's. The English back of 1776 are our fellow-countrymen, and when we gained our independence we did not abandon our heritage.

CHAPTER VII.

WRITERS OF THE FIFTEENTH CENTURY.

THE fifteenth century has been well called a period of going backward. No great English writers flourished in it; even the victories of Henry V. brought out no poet burning to perpetuate the glory of his country in spirit-stirring verse; and the dreary Wars of the Roses seem effectually to have crushed whatever desire for literary fame might lurk in the hearts of those who held the pen. In all ages, however, there are persons who must write, as birds must sing; and of the few whom this turbulent century has to boast we must take those whose writings have been thought most worthy of preservation.

John Lydgate (1375—1460), a poet of the next generation after Chaucer's, was originally a monk at the monastery of Bury St. Edmunds; and being well read in such history and literature as were then accessible to English students, he turned into English verse many a tale of ancient date, preferring always the lives of the saints. A catalogue of two hundred and fifty works, of which "The Falls ot Princes" is the best known, attests his prodigious industry. His satire of "The London Lyckpenny" is very curious and interesting from the picture it gives of the streets of London at that day.* Lydgate had traveled in Italy, and was looked up to as first among the literary men of his generation. It is said that he taught the young men who came to study with him how to make rhymes, an accomplishment which, fortunately perhaps for us, they seem to have failed to practise.

The name of Thomas Occleve (born 1368) is generally coupled with that of Lydgate, but it is merely an assoc'a-tion in point of time, for Occleve's rhymes are almost without interest. He, like Gower and Lydgate, avows himself a disciple of Chaucer, and is proud to disclaim any attempt at originality. He says that Chaucer would willingly have taught him, and adds, "but I was dull and learned little or nothing."

Of a very different cast is our next writer, to whom, though born in Scotland, we are proud to give a high place

---

* Then unto London I did me hie,
    Of all the land it beareth the price;
"Hot peascods!" one began to cry,
    "Strawberry ripe, and cherries in the rise!" [on the stem]
One bade me come near and buy some spice;
    Pepper and saffron they 'gan me beed; [offer]
But for lack of money I might not speed, etc.

among English poets.   King James I. of Scotland (1394–1437), captured when a lad nine years old from the Scottish ship which was conveying him to France that he might be safe from the clutches of his murderous uncle, the Duke of Albany, passed the next nineteen years of his life in captivity in England, where he was educated in all things as became a king's son, heir to a neighboring throne.

Prince James (who became nominally king within a year after his capture) was transferred, after a detention in various other strongholds, to Windsor Castle, where, looking out of the window one summer morning, he saw his fate in the Lady Joanna Beaufort, daughter of the Earl of Somerset and niece of the famous Cardinal Beaufort.   To this lady he addressed his longest poem, "The King's Quhair,"* in which he begins by bewailing his loneliness in his solitary room at Windsor, and goes on to describe how he looked out of the window and saw

> The fairest and the freshest youngë flower

that he had ever seen in his life; this being his metaphor for the lovely girl who was walking in the garden.†

Released from captivity soon after the accession of Henry VI., he married his lady-love, and the two went to Scotland with every prospect of a long and happy life.   The tragic close of this life—James's assassination by the lawless

---

* Book; hence our word "quire."

† The description of the poet's first sight of his lady-love closes thus:

> And when she walked had a little thraw [way],
>   Under the sweete greene boughis bent,
> Her fair, fresh face, as white as any snaw,
>   She turned has, and forth her wayis went.
> But tho [then] began mine aches and my torment,
>   To see her part and follow I na might;
> Methought the day was turned into night.

In the epilogue to his poem, King James acknowledges his obligations to three English poets—Chaucer, Gower, and Lydgate.

nobles whom he had ruled justly but too strictly—throws a shadow over our recollections of the brilliant poet, who was worthy of a different fate. The tender beauty of his one love-poem—the only verses which can be with certainty attributed to him—makes us marvel that a flower so sweet could grow in a soil so stony and so barren as the war-shattered reigns of Henrys IV. and V.

Two other Scottish poets contribute to the literature of the early fifteenth century: Andrew Wyntoun, who wrote a rhymed history of Scotland, and one Henry the Minstrel, commonly called "Blind Harry," having been blind from birth. The latter produced a long poem on William Wallace, the Scottish hero, and earned his bread by reciting or chanting it to his own accompaniment on the harp. Neither of these show any great poetic talent.

A writer of more merit was Robert Henryson, a schoolmaster of Dunfermline, who lived in a later part of the fifteenth century (1425–1506), and is considered one of the best Scottish poets of his time. He was the first to write a purely pastoral poem, and versified Æsop's fables with sweetness and skill. The dates of his life are uncertain.

The list of prose-writers in this century is also very small. The first in point of time is Reginald Pecock, an English bishop of great learning and piety, who by his independence of thought and moderateness of speech made himself disliked both by the clergy and their opponents, the Lollards. A few words of Bishop Pecock's, copied literally, illustrate the state of our language in the middle of the fifteenth century, the days of Columbus's boyhood:

Fro eeldist daies contynueli hiderto men weren woned [wont] forto speke and write her [their] wordis not oonli in treuthe, but also therwith togidere forto speke and write tho wordis in sum gaynes and bewte [gayness and beauty].

The thought set forth is, that style of expression must be observed as well as truth of assertion; and a quaint illustration which he appends shows that good style in other matters is also coming in vogue. It reads:

Euen rizt as menn fro eeldist daies hiderto weren woned not oonli forto ete her mete, but also therewith forto ete her mete in deliciose [delicate] maner.

It may be here remarked that one of the characteristic traits showing the chaotic state of the English tongue up to within some three hundred years, is the utter irregularity in the spelling of words. Spelling in Chaucer's day was entirely arbitrary and unsettled, and the same writer spelt the same word in two or three different ways on the same page. Bullokar's "Booke at Large for the Amendment of Orthography for English Speech" (1580) is almost the first attempt to bring order out of this chaos.

Some of Pecock's ideas not agreeing with those of the church of Rome, he was deposed from his bishopric and sent to Thorney Abbey, where, shut up in a private room, forbidden ever again to touch pen and ink, and limited to the Bible and three or four books of devotion as his companions, the unfortunate man vanishes from sight.

Sir John Fortescue, a learned lawyer and chief-justice of England, wrote a spirited work on "The Difference between an Absolute and Limited Monarchy," in which he draws a comparison highly favorable to England as contrasted with the despotism of France. He makes out an excellent case for his own country, though it is by some very odd illustrations. He says that the Englishman, if he be poor and sees another man having riches which he may take from him by force, will not fail to do so; and this—so runs the inference —proves conclusively that the English are the bravest nation in the world, and one that will not stand oppression.

Among the valuable bequests of the fifteenth century to its modern successors, is the curious collection of letters from and to the Paston family, which by great good fortune have been preserved while most of the correspondence of that date is lost beyond recall. There are more than a thousand of these letters, ranging in date from 1424 to 1506, including everything, from a school-boy's epistle asking for a little pocket-money, a pair of new trousers, and permission to come home at Christmas for the vacation, to those discussing important affairs of state, or telling some piece of public news which has since become a matter of history. Successive Sir John Pastons correspond with high officials, and through the long struggle with France and the confused incidents of the War of the Roses we catch many glimpses of domestic life. Lady Paston, the wife of the first Sir John, sends a rather hard-hearted letter to her son's school-master, desiring that he will whip the boy soundly if he needs it, which his mother evidently thinks will be the case.

What small progress had been made toward modern English, even as late as 1454, will be seen by a sentence from one of the "Paston Letters" of that date:

And where as it pleasyd yowr Lordship to dyrecte your letter to me for a maryage for my por suster to a jantylman of your knowleth, in cas she wer not maryd; forsothe, my Lord, she is not maryd, ne insurid to noman, etc.

We meet in this century our first English female author, Dame Juliana Berners, a prioress, who wrote both in prose and verse on hunting and hawking.

At the same time flourished the first "poet-laureate to the king," John Kaye, appointed to that office by Edward IV., who was a patron of literature. Of Kaye's poetic achievements nothing remains, so we may suppose that they were not of a high order; being probably limited to perfunctory rhymes on the king's doings. The title of laureate was then conferred by the universities on any poet who could make verses according to the rules of rhetoric, the wearer of the title receiving a laurel wreath. If, in addition to this distinction, he was allowed to teach boys, he was publicly presented with a rod and ferule. "The king's poet-laureate" was a distinct title, and was soon dropped, not to be revived until toward the end of the sixteenth century.

CHAPTER VIII.

CAXTON AND MALORY.

 GLORIOUS name now comes to the front—that of William Caxton, through whose zeal and industry the first printing-press was set up in England. It is a long stride from the manuscripts of Chaucer to the printed pages of Caxton. The world was waking and would be wide awake a few years later, when Columbus should have stretched out his daring hand. Three great innovations came into full vigor during this fifteenth century: gunpowder, the mariner's compass, and, greatest of all, the printing-press, which empowered all men to make their own the knowledge of the past ages.

William Caxton, who brought the first printing-press to England, was an author as well as a printer. He was born among the woods of Kent, a shady place better fitted to give good fibre, mental and bodily, than to provide "book-learning." He was apprenticed to a silk-merchant, and traveled extensively on the continent in pursuit of his silk-business; and when one finds that he secured the friendship and patronage of Margaret Plantagenet (sister to Edward IV.) when she went to Burgundy as wife of Charles the Bold, we are prone to fancy that silks and satins at bargain-counter prices paved the way to her womanly favor. Before this time, he had begun translating from the French an old "History of Troy"; but lacking confidence both in his half-learned French and his half-forgotten English, he laid aside the work; and it was long afterward that his lady mistress, hearing about the fragment, asked to see it, and by judicious praise and criticism encouraged him to finish it; and its simple, pretty story is best told in his own note on its publication:

Forasmuch as age creepeth on me daily, and feebleth all the bodie, and also because I have promised divers gentlemen, my friends, to address to them, as hastily as I might, this said book, therefore I have practised and learned at my great charge and expense, to ordain this said book in print, after the manner and form as ye may here see; and it is not written with pen and ink, as other books be, but imprinted to the end that all men may have them at once.

There were in Europe already many printing-houses, and Caxton went from one town to another, learning in each what was to be learned. It was at Cologne that he finished his "History of Troy," and it is probable that it was there printed and bound. None of his earlier works are dated—he little thought what interest we should feel in them—but it is generally believed that the first book printed in England was his own translation from the French of "The Game and Play of Chess." This he says he finished on the last day of March in 1474. No division of labor lightened and speeded his task; he was author, ink-maker, compositor, proof-reader, pressman, folder, binder, publisher, and book-agent.

The following copy of one of his placards shows that only the form and not the spirit of advertising has changed in these four hundred years:

If it please any man, spiritual or temporal, to buy any Salisbury Church service-books, emprinted after the form of this present letter, which be well and truly correct, let him come to Westminster, to the almonry at the red pale, and he shall have them good there.

Like all the world's benefactors, William Caxton "builded better than he knew." He printed, published, and sold many volumes of which even the names are forgotten;

although every authentic issue from his press is now worth its weight in gold.   There are Caxton societies, having for their sole end and aim the finding out every item, great or small, connected with his life or works; and by them the libraries and even the business records of every place he is known to have lived in have been ransacked.

Among the books printed on Caxton's press was one by an almost unknown writer, Sir Thomas Malory, of whom little has come down to us except his name.   The book is the " Birth, Life, and Acts of King Arthur," now commonly called "Morte d' Arthur" or "The Death of Arthur." Humble and unpretending as was its introduction to the world, it is safe to say that it will be read as long as the English language is spoken.   Sir Walter Scott says of it: " It is the best prose romance the English language can boast."   Southey said that there was no book except "The Faëry Queen," which he had read so often or with such deep interest.   A later writer declares it to be as truly the epic of the English mind as the Iliad was of the Greek.

"Morte d' Arthur" was written a hundred years before Sir Philip Sidney's prose romance, "Arcadia"; and the reasons why the latter is so much better known to us (by name, at least) are, first, Sir Philip, the flower of chivalry, is so interesting himself that everything he did seems encircled with a halo; and second, when Malory's long poem came out, the mass of the people were only just learning (under the impulse of the new art of printing) to read.   As to the court, the fine folks of Queen Elizabeth's day loved to read of the doings of lords and ladies like themselves; and such were the characters in "Arcadia."   They cared nothing for impossible old wizards practising magical arts, or even for knights-errant doing impossible deeds of valor and knightliness.   Perhaps the same spirit still exists, and it is that which impels the generality of readers to turn from all improbabilities and revel in the character-painting and realistic details so popular in our day.

Yet do cultivated people appreciate these strange, wild dramas of unreal life; and the way in which our poets have made use of Malory's pages shows us that they, at least, perceive their merit as a fountain of picturesque romance. They gave the names, characters, events, and even dialogues for Tennyson's "Idyls of the King," and his exquisite shorter poems, "Sir Galahad," "The Holy Grail," and "The Passing of Arthur." A few other sheaves from the same great planting are Spenser's "Faëry Queen," Drayton's "Polyolbion," and the first English tragic drama, Sir Thomas Buckhurst's "Ferrex and Porrex"; beside a host of smaller themes.

King Arthur seems to have been the last of the British heroes who, in the fifth and sixth centuries, tried to defend their island and the race of Britons, first against the Scots and Picts, and last against the Saxons, whom the indiscreet Britons had called in to help them oppose their first enemies. Our earliest connected account of these mythical personages and their magical adventures comes through Geoffrey of Monmouth, already noted in treating of the twelfth century. Geoffrey professes to have gathered his information from "an ancient manuscript" found in Brittany, and gravely tells historians who may come after him to say what they please regarding the Saxons, but not to venture upon any remarks touching the kings of the Britons, since they have not *that book* in the British language which Walter, archdeacon of Oxford, brought out of Brittany. Regarding "that book," William of Newbury, writing in the next century, says that "Considering how saucily and shamelessly Geoffrey lied throughout," he advises all "to trust the Venerable Bede, whose wisdom and sincerity are beyond doubt. . . . . Then that fabler, Geoffrey, with his fables, shall be straightway spat out by us all."

The excellent William of Newbury knew no distinction between imaginative writing and "saucy and shameless" lying, for prose-fiction was scarcely yet naturalized in England. The explanation given by Caxton of the motives which led him to print this work of Malory's is as curious as anything else in the book:

After I had accomplished and finished divers histories, as well of contemplation as of other historical and worldly acts of great conquerors and princes, and also certain books of ensamples and doctrine, many noble and divers gentlemen of this realm of England came and demanded me many and oft-times wherefore that I had not made to be printed the noble history of the Holy Grail and of the most renowned Christian king, the best and worthiest of all, King Arthur, which ought most to be remembered amongst us Englishmen before all other Christian kings. . . . And, for to pass the time, this book shall be pleasant to read in; but for to give faith and belief that all is true that is contained herein, ye be at your liberty: but all is written for our doctrine [instruction] and for to beware that we fall not into vice nor sin, but exercise and follow virtue.

The fact is that Malory did not go directly to Geoffrey of Monmouth for his tales, but wove them out of several French "Arturian romances," some being earlier than Geoffrey's chronicle, but all bearing on the doings of the mighty king, with the stately knights, graceful ladies, and scheming wizards of the old romance. These pass before us: their loves and hates, their quarrels and reconciliations, their good deeds and their bad, all make a stately panorama, with witchcraft and enchantment serving for background, as did the interference of the gods in the Homeric scheme.

The young prince Arthur is required, after the death of his father, to prove his royal blood by drawing out a sword, fixed by magic in a stone. No other human hand has been able to stir this weapon, but the anointed youth draws it forth as easily as he would a knife from a cheese.

The enchanter Merlin, the deathless wizard whom, centuries later, Walter Scott finds still inhabiting a lighted tomb (see his "Last Minstrel"), is ever at Arthur's hand to guide and guard him; and when he comes to grief, it is always through going contrary to the sorcerer's counsel. Merlin warns Arthur not to marry Guenever; and it is the bad conduct of Queen Guenever and the treachery of his most trusted friend that ruins his home.

His life has been a failure. The hated Saxons whom he hoped to drive ignominiously from the land of Britain have prevailed against him. Worn out, not so much by age as by grief and disappointment, he meets death in battle. Having a mortal wound, he withdraws a space to die, attended only by his faithful knight, Sir Bedever. His last care is for his magic sword Excalibur. The scene as portrayed by Tennyson in "The Passing of Arthur" is one of the most thrilling and touching in the entire realm of romance. The casting of the mighty blade afar over the bosom of the lake, its being seized before it touches the water by an arm thrust forth to draw it down, and the death of the ancient hero at the same moment, seem to mark at once the end of a life, of an entire world of enchantment, of an empire and even of a race of men; for the ancient Briton has now no place among the nations, except as his blood may survive among the Welsh and Cornishmen, and across the channel, whither fled a few fugitives who gave its name to Brittany in France.

CHAPTER IX.

THE TRANSITION PERIOD.

IN leaving the somewhat barren fifteenth century for the rich and abounding sixteenth, our notice is attracted by a group of poets who belong to both. The first of these, John Skelton (1460-1529), was a writer of great spirit and of considerable learning, to the latter of which attributes we have Caxton's testimony when he says of him that he had translated from the Latin :

Not in rude and olde langage, but in polysshed and ornate terms craftely, as he that hath redde Vyrgyle, Ovyde, Tullye, and all the other noble poets and oratours, to me unknowen. And also he hath redde the nine muses, and understand theyr musicalle scyences, and to whom of theym each scyence is appropred. I suppose he hath dronken of Elycon's well.

Skelton was "laurel-crowned," not only at the English university, but also at Louvain, in Flanders. He became a priest, but did not on that account restrain his fearless pen, which satirized coarsely and without mercy the follies of the court, the oppression of the poor, the exactions of the church, and the pride and haughtiness of Cardinal Wolsey. During the early years of the sixteenth century, Skelton was in favor at court (being tutor to Prince Henry, afterward Henry VIII.), and also enjoyed the patronage of Wolsey; but after his satire, "Colin Clout" and "Why come ye not to court?" the great prelate's friendship turned to enmity, and the poet was forced to take sanctuary in Westminister, where he died.*

The next three names in this "transitional literature"

---

* The peculiarities of Skelton's style may be shown by a quotation from his elegy on the death of " Phyllyp Sparrow," a favorite bird killed by a cat:

> O cat of carlyshe [churlish] kinde,
> The fynde was in thy mynde,
> When thou my byrde untwyned!
> I wold thou haddest been blynde!
> The leopardes sauvage,
> The lyons in theyr rage,
> Myght catche the' in theyr pawes,
> And gnawe the' in theyr jawes!
> The serpentes of Lybany [Libya]
> Myght stynge the' venymously!
> The dragones with theyr tongues
> Might poison thy lyver & longes! etc.

belong to Scotland. The first of these, William Dunbar (1460-1520), was thought by Sir Walter Scott to be the greatest of all Scottish poets, and has been called "the Chaucer of the North." He began life as a Franciscan friar, and begged his bread from door to door, preaching as he went. Afterward, finding this kind of life for him full of hypocrisy, he laid aside his friar's gown and was employed on diplomatic service for the king (James IV. of Scotland), and in this way visited many foreign countries. He received a small pension from the king, and although he groans, as did Spenser at a later period, over the necessity of securing support by servility, the income thus gained enabled him to devote his days to literature. His most famous works are "The Thistle and the Rose," a graceful wedding-song upon the marriage of King James IV. with Margaret Tudor, sister of Henry VIII.; "The Golden Terge" (targe, target or shield), an allegorical poem; and a coarse but vigorous satire, "The Dance of the Seven Deadly Sins." Dunbar is supposed to have died about 1530.

Gavin (or Gawain) Douglas (1475-1522), son of "Archibald Bell-the-Cat" who appears in such picturesque guise in Scott's "Marmion," was born at a somewhat later date than either of the two last mentioned. He entered the church and became bishop of Dunkeld. He is best known for the first translation into English verse of Virgil's "Æneid." This work was finished just after the battle of Flodden, in which two of the poet's brothers were killed. He died in London of the plague in 1521.

Sir David Lindsay, who lived from about 1490 to 1555, is the third of the famous Scottish trio. He was a bold satirist and, belonging himself to the governing class, his denunciations of the corruption prevailing in it are the more striking. The young prince, afterward James V. of Scotland, was placed in his care from the hour of his birth; and in Lindsay's earnest appeal to the king for right and justice

4

for others, he touchingly reminds him of this. He tells him, in his poem of "Lindsay's Dream," how tenderly he carried him in his arms till he began to gang (walk), wrapped him up warmly in bed and told him old stories.*

Now, he says, he will tell him a new story, and under the usual guise of an allegory he sets forth the tyranny of the great over the humble, and pictures the misery that had come upon the people from the neglect of their king, their natural protector. All this, however, had little effect on a young man who had been trained from infancy by those about him to self-indulgence and disregard of his people's rights. Sir David Lindsay has been called the poet of the Scottish Reformation, and undoubtedly did much toward encouraging that change by the force of his verse.

> Still is thy name in high account,
> And still thy verse has charms,
> Sir David Lindsay of the Mount,
> Lord Lion King at Arms.†   —WALTER SCOTT.

Writers of lesser note during this same period (covering the end of the fifteenth and the beginning of the sixteenth centuries) were Alexander Barclay (died 1552), whose "Ship of Fools" gained him some credit in its day; and Stephen Hawes, who wrote a dull poem called "The Pastime of Pleasure," and several others; all of small value.

To the same century belong the fine old ballads collected by Bishop Percy at a later time, and including such poems as "Chevy Chase," "The Nut-Brown Maid," and many others which, being learned by rote and repeated from one generation to another, helped to make the dull hours of the ignorant less dreary, and to infuse a spirit of refinement

---

* Quhen thou was young, I bure the in myne arm,
  Full tenderlie, tyll thou begouth to gang,
  And in thyne bed oft happit the full warme.

† Head of the Herald's College in Scotland.

into their coarse and sordid lives. It is of one of these that Sir Philip Sidney writes: "I never heard the old song of 'Percie and Douglas' that I found not my heart moved more than with the sound of a trumpet."

With the reign of Henry VIII. we begin upon the true sixteenth-century literature. The names of Sir Thomas Wyatt and Lord Surrey in poetry, and Sir Thomas More and William Tyndale in prose, stamp the first half of this century with their own peculiar mark; not of greatness like that of the Elizabethian period, but of an emerging from the confused language of the Middle Ages into a style and manner now accepted as the beginning of modern literature.

Sir Thomas Wyatt (1503-42), called "The Elder" to distinguish him from a son who was executed for being concerned in a rebellion against Queen Mary, leads, in point of time, the writers of his century. His name is linked with that of his fellow-poet, Lord Surrey, who, though fourteen years younger than himself, was his intimate friend and fellow-worker. Surrey acknowledges the elder poet as his "master," and some ten years after his death their works were published in the same volume, Surrey's being placed first, probably from respect to his higher rank. To the two together belongs the distinction of raising English verse to a loftier place in the matter of melody and rhythm than it had ever known before. Both had spent much time in Italy, and become inspired with the musical literature of that country; Wyatt was the first to introduce into English verse the true Italian sonnet, though that honor has often been given to Lord Surrey, who also used the new measure. Wyatt's sonnets, however, conform more exactly to the requirements of the Italian model, which is very strict in its rules. His poems are all short, and abound in grace and tenderness, though marred by the "conceits" or affectations which at that time were thought indispensable to fine writing.

Wyatt's history is an interesting and in some respects a romantic one. Born in the higher circles of society, he graduated from Cambridge University as Bachelor of Arts at the age of fifteen, was accomplished in all that makes a gentleman, and grew into great favor with the king, Henry VIII., the latter employing him more than once as an ambassador. He was knighted by his royal master, and with the exception of a short interval when he was out of favor on account of his friendship for Anne Boleyn, he stood high in Henry's regard as long as he lived.

The name of Henry Howard, Earl of Surrey, brings before us a young nobleman belonging to one of the proudest families of England, brought up on terms of intimacy with members of the king's household and known for his courtly grace and his many accomplishments. Like Wyatt, he did much to improve English poetry, and first introduced into it the form now known as blank (unrhymed) verse, which was to be made exquisite by Shakespeare and majestic by Milton.

Surrey's love-songs and sonnets contain much praise of the "fair Geraldine," who can not be certainly identified with any lady of the day, and may have been only a child whose beauty captivated his imagination.

Surrey's life had a tragic close. Being related by blood to the king, he rather unwisely, though with authority granted by the Herald's College, had the royal coat of arms quartered with his own. He had done this for years without objection from any one, when suddenly the jealous tyrant, who was now suffering under a frightful disease which made him more savage than ever, issued orders for the execution not only of Lord Surrey, but of his father, the Duke of Norfolk, pretending that this assumption meant that they might lay claim to his throne after his death. Surrey's was the last death-warrant issued by Henry VIII.—not signed by him, for his bloated fingers

could no longer hold a pen. The hand of the dying
tyrant was held while he made some mark that would
connect more closely the infamy of the deed with his
name.

The young, the gallant, the enlightened poet laid his
head on the block, just as his destroyer was gasping out
in agony the last hours of a misspent life; while Norfolk,
whose death-warrant was for some reason delayed, was
spared to linger in prison through the six years of Edward
VI.'s reign, dying soon after he had regained his liberty.

The following is one of Surrey's best sonnets:

> The *soote* seson, that bud & bloom forth brings,   [*sweet*]
> With green hath clad the hill, and eke the vale;
> The nightingale, with feathers new she sings;
> The turtle to her *make* hath told her tale;   [*mate*]
> The hart hath hung his old head on the pale,
> The buck in brake his winter coat he flings;
> The fishes flete with new repairèd scale;
> The adder, all her slough away she flings;
> The swift swallow pursueth the flies *smale*;   [*small*]
> The busy bee her honey now she *mings*;   [*mingles*]
> Winter is worn that was the flowers' bale.
> And thus I see among these pleasant things
> Each care decays, and yet my sorrow springs.

CHAPTER X.

SIR THOMAS MORE AND OTHER WRITERS.

IF Lord Surrey was the typical man of *belles lettres*
(polite literature), of his time, Sir Thomas More
(1478-1535), was the type of the statesman, the
patriot, the incorruptible judge. No man has left a purer
record. From a child his wit and love of study caused
him to be singled out from his companions for the delight
of his elders, and as he grew to manhood he still kept up
his high standard. At the age of ten he was placed in

the household of Cardinal Morton (who figures in Shakespeare's "Richard III." as Bishop of Ely), and enlivened with his childish vivacity the staid circle, seated around the Cardinal's table.

"Whoever liveth to try it," said the old prelate, who was an octogenarian when young More's pranks pleased his guests, "shall see this child here waiting at table, prove a notable and rare man." And so he did. His father allowed him to enter the university, but, finding that Thomas was throwing himself heartily into the study of Greek, removed him before he had taken his degree, and made him finish his studies elsewhere. The study of Greek was then only beginning to be introduced into the great English colleges. After the capture of Constantinople by the Turks (1453), many Eastern monasteries were broken up, and the monks and students, driven out and dispersed through Western Europe, carried with them their precious Greek manuscripts and the enthusiasm which saw in the Greek language an object worthy of devoted study.

The elder More's disapprobation arose, not from narrow-mindedness, but from a natural conservatism which shrank from seeing his son waste time on what he considered a new-fangled notion. The youth, however, had already gained so good a knowledge of the new-old language that its stores of thought were a help to him all his life.

In England the names of Grocyn, Colet, and Linacre are connected with the effort to make this noble tongue known to English students; and with them was joined the great Dutch scholar, Erasmus, the friend and fellow-religionist of Luther, who could not fail to become likewise the friend of Thomas More.

At twenty-one, More entered Parliament, where he opposed the marriage-portion proposed for the king's daughters and was imprisoned and heavily fined in consequence. Later he gained great distinction as a lawyer.

The circumstances of his marriage are characteristic of his generosity and easy temper. A certain friend of his who had three grown-up daughters, signified to More that he would like to bestow one of them upon him in marriage. More consented and chose the second, who is said to have been the prettiest of the three; but when he understood that it would be unpleasant to the older sister to have a younger one preferred to herself, he gave up his own wishes and took the eldest. She rewarded him by making an affectionate wife, and he caused her to be instructed in literature and other things, especially in music, of which he was very fond. She died a few years after her marriage, and his second choice (not one of those three sisters) was less fortunate, the new wife proving both ignorant and shrewish. Still his sunny good temper was never disturbed, and he took great comfort with his children, particularly with his daughter Margaret, who afterward became Mrs. Roper. She was like him in mind and character, and the friendship between them is one of the most beautiful recorded in history.

More's devotion to business did not bar him from literary pursuits, which, indeed, were more natural to him. His first work, "The Life and Death of King Edward V.," is unfinished, but is interesting because the material for it must have come largely from his old patron, Cardinal Morton, who was a friend to the poor little king, and narrowly escaped the fate of many others who stood in the way of Richard III.

A man of More's ability could not long remain in a private station, and we find the king employing him in diplomacy, and adding one office to another until he was made Lord High Chancellor. It was during the intervals of his many and various missions to foreign countries that he wrote "Utopia," a work of such originality that it has given a new word to our language, and we call any scheme which seems too lofty to be carried out, Utopian. The word itself is taken from a Greek one meaning nowhere, and the book attempts a description of an ideal life under a perfect government. Some of More's advanced theories have been adopted by the students of political economy in our own day; others are impracticable, but all breathe the same love of equal justice and respect for the rights of all which distinguished More through life.

One anecdote showing the shrewdness of the chief-justice is more amusing to us than it was to his wife, who was then Lady More, her husband having been knighted by the king. Some one had given her a little dog which had been stolen from a poor woman, though this was of course unknown to the lady. The first owner came before Sir Thomas and claimed the animal, which Lady More was unwilling to give up. More was equal to the occasion. He bade his wife stand at one end of the long hall and the claimant at the other. Then each was to call the dog and abide the consequences. The experiment resulted in favor of the poor woman, the little dog running to her as soon as he heard her voice. Sir Thomas, to gratify his wife, bought the dog from its owner with a piece of gold, and she went on her way rejoicing.

It was, unfortunately for public honesty, a general custom for the judges of that day to take gifts from suitors, either before or after judgment had been rendered. To this practice, More sternly refused to conform, and several anecdotes are told of the ingenious methods by which the parties to suits tried to evade his determination. One lady, after he had given a decision in her favor, sent him a pair of gloves filled with gold angels to the amount of about $1,000 of our money. More accepted the gloves but sent back the money, saying he could not refuse a lady's present but did not like the lining.

One of More's most striking traits was the rapidity with

which he disposed of the cases brought before him as
lord chancellor. On one occasion he was told that there
were no more cases upon the docket; whereupon a wit
wrote:

> When More sometime chancellor had been,
> No *more* suits did remain;
> The same shall never *more* be seen,
> Till *More* be there again.

Lord Campbell, in his "Lives of the Lord Chancellors,"
says that the same thing has never happened since that
time.

Sir Thomas More was a conscientious Catholic, even
carrying his zeal so far as to aid in the persecution of
heretics. He was also intensely loyal to his king; but
when the latter loyalty interfered with that to his church
and his conscience, he did not hesitate for a moment.
When Henry VIII., who burnt men when they did not
believe in the doctrines of the church, chose to declare
himself its head in England; More, with others as unflinch-
ing as himself, denied the king's right to such supremacy,
and after a farcical trial was convicted of high treason and
suffered death at the block. He never lost his cheerfulness
nor his humor. When the lieutenant of the tower apolo-
gized for the poor fare he was forced to give him, More
replied that he found no fault with it, but when he did,
the officer was at liberty to thrust him out at once. When
he mounted the scaffold, being then somewhat infirm, he
asked the warden to help him up. "When I come down,"
said he, "I can shift for myself." On kneeling down to
receive the stroke he put his long white beard out of the
way, saying to himself, "Pity that should be cut; it has
never committed treason." After his death, his head was
placed on London bridge, according to the custom of the
time; and his daughter Margaret Roper bribed the keeper
of the bridge to let it fall into her hands as she was rowed

in a boat underneath. This beloved head she always kept in her own apartment, and died clasping it to her breast in a fit of delirium.*

No new translation of the Bible had been made for about a hundred and fifty years, when William Tyndale (1484–1536), an English clergyman who had long before declared that he wished an English Bible might be in the hands of every ploughboy in the country, finished his version of the New Testament (1525). He had been obliged to do it in secrecy and under constant dread of detection, for he was one of the followers of Luther, and therefore liable to the penalties of heresy. Hunted from place to place, he still persevered in his work, and from time to time rendered other parts of the Scriptures into his native tongue. The language of Wycliffe's version had become obsolete, and was therefore out of the reach of the common people. Tyndale's possessed a force and purity which made his translation rank among the best specimens of English in his time.

Knowing himself to be unsafe in England, he took refuge in Flanders; but the enmity of the king pursued him there, and through Henry's urgency he was apprehended at Brussels, and strangled at Vilvoorde, near Brussels; his body being afterward burnt to ashes. His last words were: "Lord, open the king of England's eyes!"

Miles Coverdale (1487–1568) made a version of the whole Bible, printed ten years after Tyndale's translation of the New Testament, which does not differ from it widely in diction. Coverdale was the first to separate from the body of the Old Testament the books known as Apocrypha (rejected matter), and place them separately at the end.

From this time, for the next twenty years, repeated versions appeared, which were often only revisions of the

---

* See Tennyson's "Dream of Fair Women."

previous ones; and by the time Queen Elizabeth had been ten years on the throne (1668), the Bible was, or might be, in the hands of every one who knew how to read.

The remaining writers of this period need only a few words. Robert Fabyan and Edward Hall wrote chronicles of English history, of more or less accuracy. Lord Berners, at the request of Henry VIII., translated Froissart's chronicle into English. John Leland (1500–52), the first professional antiquarian, made it his business to collect as much as he could of the vast mass of historical material lying unrecognized and in danger of destruction in town-halls, cathedrals, and castles. To further this object he traveled over England, describing minutely all the places he visited; his description of these journeys is called "Leland's Itinerary." He was a man of prodigious industry and enthusiasm, and overworked his brain, being insane during the last two years of his life.

Sir Thomas Elyot is noted as being the first English writer on education. In his treatise called "The Governor," he condemns the practice of allowing "cruel and irascible schoolmasters" to have unlimited power over the helpless children committed to their care, and recommends a discipline reasonable, yet firm. He was a physician, and wrote a professional work called "The Castle of Health," which was much admired.

Among the writers of the time must be included King Henry VIII., who wrote, early in his reign, a book in Latin against Luther, entitled "The Seven Sacraments." For this service to the church, the pope bestowed on him formally the title of "Defender of the Faith," which has been borne by his royal descendants ever since.*

Henry VIII. did much greater service to literature by

---

* "Fidei Defensor," abbreviated "Fid. Def.," may still be found on some English coins.

the encouragement he gave to literary men than by his own contributions to letters. He gave John Leland the title of "King's Antiquary," and supported him while he was making his researches; he sent Roger Ascham abroad to pursue his studies, and took care that Sir Thomas Elyot was supported while he was writing books for the instruction of his countrymen. We have already mentioned the translation of Froissart, made by Lord Berners at his request. This last work, being "chronicles"—pictures of the times—and being written with simple-hearted faithfulness, marks almost an era in literature. Men speak of "the time of Froissart." Even its translation into English was a noteworthy event. One simple, thoughtless remark has become classic, noting as it does the impression made on the Frenchman's mind by the Englishman. He says of some whom he met, "They took their pleasure sadly, after their fashion."

The drama now began to assume a form somewhat different from that of the old "Mysteries" and "Miracle Plays." A new kind of dramas called "Moralities" came into vogue, having for their characters personages representing the virtues and vices in a sort of allegory. Next came the "Interlude," a short play resembling a farce, and full of the rough jokes suited to the coarse taste of the times. In one of these interludes, for instance, called "The Four P's," there is a dispute between a Pedler, a Palmer, a Pardoner, and a 'Poticary, as to which can tell the greatest lie. Each tries to outdo the other; until at last the Pardoner says he never saw a woman out of temper, and is declared winner. John Heywood was the most famous writer of interludes.

The first English comedy was written by Nicholas Udall (1505–56), and belongs to this same half-century. It is called "Ralph Royster Doyster," and gives a picture of life in London. It was followed a few years later by "Gammer Gurton's Needle," by John Still, afterward a bishop, in which the characters are rustics of the humble sort, and the humor is of a lower order than that of Udall's play. Such was the preparation for the full development of English drama in the plays of Shakespeare, whose birth took place only a few years later.

Udall was head-master at Eton school, and "Ralph Royster Doyster" is supposed to have been written to be acted by his boys. One of these boys was Thomas Tusser, author of a poem called "Five Hundred Points of Good Husbandry," and he shows up the methods of Udall as follows:

> From Paul's I went to Eton sent,
> To learn straightways the Latin phrase,
> Where fifty-three stripes given to me
> At once I had.
> For fault but small, or none at all,
> It came to pass that beat I was;
> See, Udall, see, the mercy of thee
> To me, poor lad.

CHAPTER XI.

EARLY ELIZABETHAN PERIOD.

AS has been noticed by an eminent writer on English literature, the most splendid authors of Elizabeth's reign were not born until just about the time when that reign began. The era of greatness, therefore, for this period, does not begin until the Virgin Queen had been for some twenty-five years seated upon the throne, and we must first turn our thoughts to some of the minor lights which served to usher in the day.

A name which brings up a train of gentle and kindly thoughts is that of Roger Ascham (1515–68), the tutor of Queen Elizabeth, and friend of Lady Jane Grey. To a sweetness of nature which nothing ever embittered, he added refinement, uprightness, and a tireless devotion to study. His father belonged to the humbler walks of life, but his own education was of the best, a kind friend putting everything in his power, from his earliest school-boy days to his graduation at Cambridge University. Living in the reigns of four sovereigns (Henry VIII. and his three children — Edward, Mary and Elizabeth), he found favor and employment under all. Henry granted him a pension which enabled him to travel in Italy for the completion of his education; Edward appointed him tutor to his half-sister Elizabeth (his penmanship was so beautiful that he had the honor of instructing the princess that accomplishment); he was Latin secretary to Queen Mary, in spite of his being a protestant; and he was in Queen Elizabeth's service, in different capacities, until his death; upon which occasion the thrifty queen remarked that she would rather have lost £10,000 than Master Ascham. His first. book, "Toxophilus," was written to encourage the practice of archery, which he considered the most elegant, healthful and improving sport that a gentleman could engage in. He rendered his country a service by writing in English instead of Latin, and had the manliness to defend what he knew to be an unfashionable course. His apology in the preface for using his own language shows how that noble tongue had been neglected by other native writers:

As for the Latin or Greek tongue, everything is so excellently done in them that none can do better; in the English tongue, everything in a manner so mean, both for the manner and handling, that no man can do worse. He that will write well in any tongue must follow the counsel of Aristotle: to speak as the common people do, to think as wise men do, so that every man may understand him and the judgment of wise men allow [approve] him. Many English writers have not done so, but using strange words, as Latin, French and Italian, do make all things dark and hard.

Ascham's next published work was a "Report of the

affairs of Germany and the Emperor Charles his Court,"
for which his position as secretary of the ambassador to
that country gave him good opportunities. But the book
most interesting to us is his "Schoolmaster," in which
he pleads lovingly for kindness and discretion in the
treatment of young learners, in opposition to the brutal
severity then exercised, and suggests a method of teaching the ancient languages as we now teach children the
modern, which is pronounced by Dr. Johnson to be
"perhaps the best advice ever given for the study of
languages." How greatly Ascham had at heart the good
of both pupil and teacher may be gathered from some
words in the "Schoolmaster":

It is pity that commonly more care is had, and that among very
wise men, to find out a cunning man for their horse than a cunning
man for their children. To the one they will gladly give a stipend of
200 crowns by the year, and loth to offer the other 200 shillings. God
that sitteth in heaven laugheth their choice to scorn, and rewardeth
their liberality as it should; for he suffereth them to have tame and
well-ordered horse, but wild and unfortunate children.

Thomas Wilson (1524–81), a contemporary of Ascham's,
was the first English critic. He wrote a "System of Rhetoric
and Logic," in which he strongly advises simplicity of
language, and condemns the "strange inkhorn terms"
which the writers of his time mistook for elegance. "He
that cometh lately out of France," he says, satirically,
"will talk French-English and never blush at the matter."
Sir John Harington, a godson of Queen Elizabeth, and
himself a poet (he was the translator of Ariosto), apparently bore no good will to the critics. He wrote several
epigrams, one of which runs as follows:

> The readers and the hearers like my books,
> But yet some writers can not them digest ;
> But what care I? for when I make a feast,
> I would my guests should praise it, not the cooks.

Another of his epigrams is worth quoting:

> Treason doth never prosper; what's the reason?
> For if it prosper none dare call it treason.

The first metrical version of the Psalms was made by Sternold and Hopkins in the reign of Edward VI. A favorable specimen of the work is to be found in the versification of part of Psalm XVIII.:

> The Lord descended from above, and bowed the heavens most high,
>   And underneath his feet he cast the darkness of the sky;
> On cherub and on seraphim full royally he rode,
>   And on the wings of mighty winds came flying all abroad.

The earliest English anthology (a collection of poems or poetical selections from various authors) was called "Tottel's Miscellany" (1657). This helped to make verse familiar to the mass of the nation, who were perhaps hardly yet educated up to the enjoyment of the best poetry, though they fully appreciated the interludes and comedies which, on the stage, appealed to the eye as well as to the mind.

The name which seems more nearly than any other to be a connecting link between the beginning and end of the sixteenth century is that of Thomas Sackville (1536-1608), afterward Lord Buckhurst and later, Earl of Dorset. He is known to us by any one of the three names, though the first two seem more especially devoted to him. Like More and Ascham he received a university education, and like the former was elected to parliament at twenty-one. He studied law, and the first English tragedy, "Gorboduc," was written by him in connection with Thomas Norton, to entertain the lawyers and students of the Inner Temple.* Sackville, it is said, wrote the best parts of this.

The plot in this first English tragedy begins like that of Shakespeare's "King Lear." Gorboduc, a British king,

---

* The building in London where law-courts were held and where students pursued the study of the law.

divides his kingdom during his lifetime between his two sons, Ferrex and Porrex. (The latter names afterward gave a title to the play.) The younger kills the elder, whereupon the mother, in revenge, kills the younger. The people in revenge for such cruelty, rebel, and kill both father and mother. The nobility, to avenge the death of the king, kill the rebels and then the kingdom falls into a most dismal state of civil war from which it has not emerged when the play concludes.

Sackville's fame as a poet, however, rests not on "Gorboduc," which is interesting principally as being the forerunner of that brilliant series of productions known as the modern drama, but on the remarkable fragment which forms the "Induction" (Introduction) to the "Mirrour for Magistrates." Magistrates, in this sense, means rulers—great persons—and the poem was intended to show to such, as in a glass, their own possible fate, by reminding them of the misfortunes of those who came before them. The poet descends into the regions of the dead under the guidance of an allegorical personage called Sorrow, and is met by fearful shapes representing Remorse, Fear, Revenge, Misery, Old Age, Famine, War, and others; each described with a few bold touches which individualize the character and make it stand before you as in a painting. After the description of all this wretchedness, the poet's intention was to portray the fate of those of olden times whose greatness had not preserved them from woe or downfall, but he finished only the stanzas on Henry, Duke of Buckingham—Richard III.'s Buckingham—whom the king first (according to Shakespeare) through ingratitude maddened and drove to treason and then beheaded.

Sackville also wrote sonnets, called by an admiring contemporary "poems finely sauced," but of these none remain. In the "Mirrour for Magistrates" the following stanza describing Famine is notable:

5

> But, oh, the doleful sight that then we see!
> We turned our look, and on the other side
> A grisly shape of Famine wrought we see,
> With greedy looks, and gaping mouth, that cried
> And roared for meat [food] as she would there have died,
> Her body thin and bare as any bone,
> Whereto was left naught but the case alone.

But Sackville was too useful a man to be allowed to spend his life in making poetry or writing dramas. When the "Mirrour for Magistrates" had reached its first historic character he abandoned it to take part in active political life, and from that time was in constant occupation as a statesman, surviving Queen Elizabeth and her generation, and dying (1608) in a good old age, at the council-table of King James I.

A poet of high repute in his day, and whose writings are still interesting as heralding the appearance of the brilliant group which has made the age of Queen Elizabeth so famous, is George Gascoigne (1555–77). His "Steele Glasse" is a clever satire on the vices and follies of men, and is the first long poem, not dramatic, written in blank verse.

John Davies (1570–1626), knighted in the reign of James I. and so known to us by the name of Sir John, wrote in Queen Elizabeth's time a reflective poem dedicated to her with the title, "Nosce Teipsum" (Know Thyself). This is interesting as giving the first example of what was afterward called the "heroic quatrain"—four ten-syllable lines with alternate rhymes. Davies had been wild in his youth, but reformed after some sharp discipline from the Queen, and ended his life as a prosperous lawyer. One of his quatrains refers in the following terms to the discipline which had taught him discretion:

> This mistress lately plucked me by the ear,
> And many a golden lesson hath me taught;
> Hath made my senses quick and reason clear;
> Reformed my will and rectified my thought.

Of religious writing, there was much during this transition period. Besides Tyndale's and Coverdale's translations of the Scriptures, there were four others, namely: a new version, known as "Matthew's Bible," edited by John Rogers (1505-55), the first martyr in Queen Mary's cruel reign; an "authorized version" prepared by command of Henry VIII. and superintended by Archbishop Cranmer, known as "The Great Bible;" the "Geneva Bible," translated at that city by Englishmen, in which the present division of the text into verses first appeared; and finally the "Bishops' Bible," that translation made in the reign of Queen Elizabeth in response to an address offered during the joyful ceremonies attending her coronation; which prayed that she would "liberate some prisoners who had been shut up in an unknown tongue;" namely the four Evangelists and St. Paul.* The book of Common Prayer, prepared by Cranmer, was published nearly in its present form during the reign of Edward VI.

Of the many religious and theological writers of England during the reign of Henry VIII. the best known is Bishop Latimer (1491-1555), a bold and energetic preacher who suffered martyrdom in Queen Mary's reign. Some idea of his force of expression may be obtained from a sentence in one of his sermons in which he upbraids his hearers for their frivolity: "you velvet-coats, you upskips, you hodipoles, you doddipecks!" He also reproved the women for "laying out their hair in tussocks and tufts." His words to his brother martyr Ridley, as they stood waiting for the fire to be lighted, have become one of the war-cries in the fight for freedom of thought. He said, "Be of good comfort, Master Ridley, and play the man! We shall this day light such a candle, by God's grace, in England, as shall never be put out."

---

* It is said that the ready-witted queen aptly parried the request by answering that it would be well first to ask those prisoners whether or no they desired liberation.

The great preacher of the Reformation in Scotland was John Knox (1505–71). After several years of preaching in various places, he settled at Geneva in Switzerland, where he, in the last year of Queen Mary's reign, published anonymously his "First Blast of the Trumpet against the Monstrous Regiment of Women." The three Marys of England and Scotland furnished the text of this book: Mary of England, Mary Queen of Scots, and Mary of Guise, the Scottish queen's mother and widow of James V. The next year Knox went to Scotland, where he preached and wrote with incessant energy against the Church of Rome. His last work was the history of the Reformation in Scotland.

While Knox was preaching in Scotland, John Fox (1517–87), issued in England his famous "Book of Martyrs," describing the persecutions under Queen Mary. This book may not be relied on for correctness, but though lacking truth as to details, it presents a vivid picture of the horrors of the time. Bishop Burnet ("History of the Reformation"), says that having compared those Acts and Monuments with the records, he had never been able to discover any errors or prevarications in them, but the utmost fidelity and exactness.

The most famous Greek scholar of the sixteenth century was Sir John Cheke (1514–57), of Cambridge University. The most famous Latin scholar was George Buchanan, a Scottish writer celebrated for the elegance and purity of his classic style. He was tutor to King James VI. of Scotland (afterward James I. of England), the son of Mary Queen of Scots and of her murdered husband, Lord Darnley.

CHAPTER XII.

MISCELLANEOUS WRITERS.

THE age of Elizabeth was rich in translations. Among the many poets who undertook this kind of work may be mentioned especially Sir John Harington (1561–1612), who has been already named, translator of Ariosto's "Orlando Furioso;" Edward Fairfax, who rendered into musical English verse Tasso's "Jerusalem to the verses of the French contemporary poet, Du Bartas; and, greatest of all, George Chapman, translator of Homer.

In respect to history, England owes a debt of gratitude to the indefatigable antiquarian, John Stow (1525–1605), who rescued from oblivion many priceless memorials of older times which were perishing by neglect or given up to wanton destruction. The tales told by eye-witnesses of the wilful waste of precious manuscripts on the suppression of the monasteries by Henry VIII. and the consequent scattering of their treasures, almost defy belief, and remind us of the story about the Caliph Omar and the Alexandrian Library.

Stow was the son of a humble tailor and was brought up to his father's trade; but his zeal for collecting antiquities was such that everything else gave way to it. He had some well-to-do friends, who helped him to live during the forty years in which he was composing his "History of England," a work now lost; but he outlived them all, and in his last days was forced to apply to King James for a license to beg "in churches or other places." His "Survey of London," a work on which all succeeding descriptions of the city have been based, was published during his life-time, as were also some condensations made by himself from his history.

More fortunate than Stow was John Speed (1550–1619), also a tailor's son and a zealous antiquarian. His "History of Great Britain," in which he presumed to doubt Brute the Trojan, and to cast grave discredit upon Albion the giant, was gladly received by students of history, and he found no difficulty in securing abundant appreciation of his labors.

William Camden (1551–1623), a man of great learning and of high position among students, was likewise inspired with a desire to search out the past, and, as Speed puts it, "blew away sixty kings with one blast." Camden's reputation for scholarship stood so high that he was selected by Lord Burleigh as the fittest person to write the "Annals of Queen Elizabeth." For this purpose the Lord Treasurer put at his disposal a great mass of state papers, over which Camden labored for eighteen years, in the intervals of other employment, before it was ready for the press. The principle on which he wrote may be inferred from his favorite extract from Polybius:

Take from history why, how, and to what end a thing hath been done, and whether the thing done hath been according to reason; and whatsoever is else will rather be an idle sport than a profitable instruction; for the present it may delight, but for the future it can not profit.

Ralph (or Raphael) Holinshed was another painstaking and laborious chronicler of the time, from whose pages Shakespeare drew largely in writing Macbeth and other plays founded on English history. Richard Grafton's Chronicle, published earlier, is not considered very valuable, being mostly patchwork from other writers.

In the stirring times of adventure, travellers naturally had their share of literary interest. A "Discourse" by Sir Humphrey Gilbert (1539–83), on the possibility of a northwest passage to China, was published (without his knowledge) by Gascoigne, the poet already mentioned; but the prince of geographers in the sixteenth century was Richard Hakluyt

(1553-1616), whose book entitled "The Principal Navigations, Voyages, Traffics and Discoveries of the English Nation," perpetuates his name. He also translated books of travel from the Spanish.

Hakluyt's work was continued in the next century by Samuel Purchas (1577-1628), who published his researches under the name of "Purchas his Pilgrimage." Several books of a similar kind followed, one at least of which was founded on manuscripts left him by Hakluyt.

Having thus passed in review various writings which have special interests for their motive power, we return to literature proper, of which the function is to entertain and elevate, and not, except incidentally, to instruct or exhort.

Of the writers characteristic of Elizabeth's reign the first to be considered is John Lyly, author of "Euphues," a singular book which, under the mask of much ingenious playfulness and plotting, strives to reform and make serious the foppish youth of England. To effect this Lyly adopted a style full of quaint conceits and far-fetched allusions, which became the fashion among courtly people, and continued to influence, far into the next century, the style of those who wrote merely to please. "To talk euphuism" became an accomplishment. A writer of the century says, "that beauty in court that could not parley euphuism was as little regarded as she which now there speaks not French." Lyly reminded the rich and fashionable that "it is not great manors, but good manners, that make the gentleman,"—a phrase appropriate in all ages.

Shakespeare ridiculed euphuism in the character of Armado, a boastful fellow in "Love's Labour's Lost," and Sir Walter Scott has made it amusingly absurd in the mouth of Sir Piercie Shafton, in his novel of "The Monastery."

Lyly had all the fame he wanted, but little profit. He depended on patronage and, one would think, with reason, since the rich and great were vying with each other in following the fashion he had set them; but we find him writing to Queen Elizabeth in this doleful strain:

Thirteene years your highnes servant, but yet nothing; twenty freinds, that though they saye they wil be sure, I find them sure to be slowe. A thousand hopes, but all nothing; a hundred promises, but yet nothing. Thus casting vpp the inventory of my friends, hopes, promises and tymes, the summa totalis amounteth to iust nothing. My last will is shorter than mine invencion; but three legacies,— patience to my creditors, melancholie without measure to my friends, and beggerie without shame to my family.

Lyly was also a dramatist of considerable merit. His most graceful play is "Campaspe."

Next in order comes the "mirror of knighthood"—the courtier, the soldier, the man of letters, the *gentleman*—so fondly mourned in his own times and remembered in all times—Sir Philip Sidney (1554-86). There have been others as noble, as gentle, as brave; but few had Sidney's advantage of combining with these qualities such literary ability as· will carry down a name for centuries among the ranks of a country's most distinguished authors.

Everything was done for Sidney's education that wealth and affection could furnish. After having gone through the usual course of intellectual training in England, he lived for a while in Paris, where he chose only the best and loftiest society. Being driven from that city by the massacre of St. Bartholomew, he travelled elsewhere on the continent, and brought home with him an added knowledge of other lands, united with a knowledge of men's hearts and motives which strengthened his ability to help direct the affairs of state. With this journey, which closed when he was twenty-one year's old, Sidney's education may be considered finished. On his return to England he sprang into such sudden popularity as few men of his age have enjoyed. His fine manners, grace of carriage and personal beauty, together with elegant accomplishments and a playful wit, made him the observed of all observers. Queen Elizabeth instantly received him with the highest favor and used jokingly to call him her Philip, as distinguished from the Pope's Philip—Philip II. of Spain, who had for a few disastrous years been the husband of her sister Mary. When he was three-and-twenty she entrusted him with a difficult and delicate mission to the Emperor of Germany. When he returned he was received by the queen with warm commendations. She was more than satisfied with the manner in which he had carried out her wishes, appointed him to the coveted office of cup-bearer, and gave him a lock of her hair. The great queen knew how to appreciate good sense and manly worth, especially when they were united to personal attractions.

It was now his turn to bestow favors as well as to receive them. People of all ranks flocked to the open doors of the youth of wealth and position, and the dedications of books, poems, etc. which he received were almost innumerable. About this time his friend Gabriel Harvey made him acquainted with the poet Edmund Spenser, and thus was formed a friendship honorable to both. Spenser passed many happy hours with his friend at Sidney's country seat of Penshurst in Kent, and the two pursued together those studies in which their souls delighted.

Sidney's principal literary work, the " Arcadia," he composed for his sister's pleasure, and called it "The Countess of Pembroke's Arcadia." It is a prose-poem, where the characters are lords and ladies living in the country and enjoying its pleasures, without laying aside the elegance and refinement of courtly life. The moral tone is the highest possible, and the characters discourse to one another on topics both lofty and deep. It is to this romance that we owe the noble phrase, "They are never alone who are accompanied by noble thoughts." The story is, to our modern taste, tedious, and some of the " conceits " far-fetched and labored ; but these were the faults of the age. Many beautiful passages can be selected from the "Arcadia," and Cowper has expressed no more than the truth when he speaks of "Sidney, warbler of poetic prose."

A work more in accord with modern ideas is the "Apologie for Poetrie," in which Sidney (who was knighted by Queen Elizabeth in 1583 and must henceforth be called Sir Philip) warmly defended his favorite art against the attacks of the Puritan, Stephen Gosson, who wrote a book called "The School of Abuse" against plays and poetry, thinking the one mischievous, the other at least useless. Sidney's answer is the first piece of modern literary criticism, and is written in clear, readable English, while he especially condemns the affectations in language common at that time, and makes the shrewd remark, "It is not rhyming that maketh the poet, no more than a long gown maketh an advocate."

Sidney's poetry consists mostly of sonnets, written to a lady whom he calls Stella (a star), while he figures himself under the name of Astrophel (lover of a star). The Stella of his muse is supposed to have been Lady Penelope Devereux, daughter of his old friend the Earl of Essex. His own wife was a daughter of Elizabeth's minister, Sir Francis Walsingham. The sonnets are graceful and musical, and in each one there is some pleasing thought or quaint conceit. In one of them occurs the well-known expression, addressed to himself when he did not know what to say, "Fool! Look into thine heart and write!" His fame, however, rests upon his prose, which was beyond that of any other English writer up to his time.

While Sidney was thus amusing his leisure hours with literature, he was at the same time busy with public affairs, and was from time to time employed in the queen's service. He wished to go with Drake on one of his enterprises against the West Indies. He had made all of his preparations secretly, for fear of being forbidden, when Drake sent a hint of his intentions to the queen, who laid her commands on him to stay where he was, saying she could not afford to risk "the jewel of her times" in such an enterprise. He was bitterly disappointed, and Elizabeth consoled him, as far as she could, by making him governor of Flushing, in the Netherlands, a town which was to be the basis of operations against Spain. The Earl of Leicester, Queen Elizabeth's favorite and Sidney's uncle, was military governor of the Netherlands, and Sidney joined him there hoping for a brilliant campaign.

There is little more to tell. In an ill-planned and rash expedition against Zutphen, in Holland, Sir Philip, whose generosity had made him take off his cuishes and give them to an old officer whom he observed to be without them, was wounded in the thigh and carried off the field to die after a few weeks of acute suffering. His well-known action on the battle-field need not be repeated here; * it belongs to history and is repeated wherever knightly generosity and self-sacrifice need an illustrious example.

We have spoken of Sidney as the first literary critic. A writer of the same period, George Puttenham (ancestor, no doubt of the modern Putnams), wrote an elaborate work called "The Arte of English Poesie," in which he says that his aim is "to help the courtiers and the gentle-women of the court to write good poetrie, that the art may become vulgar to all Englishmen's use." We see here the old and literal meaning of "vulgar" —i.e., common to all. This explanation is interesting as showing the interest felt by the fine ladies and gentlemen of Queen Elizabeth's reign in the comparatively new art of "poetrie." They had not yet quite emerged from the feeling that writing was not an occupation for fine court people, but should be left to

---

* See "A Short History of England," page 234.

the lower class.   Neither Sir Philip Sidney's "Arcadia," nor his "Defense of Poesie" was published during his life-time. Queen Elizabeth, whose active mind made her desire to do a little of everything, wrote some verses about the trouble Mary, Queen of Scots was giving her; and was the first to apply to that much-discussed person the felicitous phrase: "The daughter of debate."

CHAPTER XIII.

SPENSER AND LESSER WRITERS.

THE four men who rank highest among English poets of past centuries are unquestionably Chaucer, Spenser, Shakespeare, and Milton. We have already made some study of Chaucer, who died in 1400, and from whose life those of Spenser and Shakespeare are separated by an interval of more than two hundred years, while Milton comes some fifty years later.

It was a pretty conceit of the time to call Spenser "The Sunrise" as Chaucer had been called "The Day-Star" of English poetry.   Edmund Spenser was born (it is supposed) in 1553, the year in which Queen Mary came to the throne. His early career, and the story of the last sad months of his life are shrouded in obscurity; but of the time in which his work was done we have details quite full considering that he wrote no letters that have been preserved, and had no Boswell.   His friends have left on record many proofs of their love and admiration, but the little home-touches which would show his domestic life are wanting.

Spenser was always the man of letters and the friend of men of letters.   His one point of contact with every-day life seems to be his faithful secretaryship to the military governor of Ireland.   Like many poets before and since, he began his work by translating from foreign tongues into his own. His first original production was "The Shepherd's Calendar," containing twelve eclogues or pastoral poems; in which he assumes the name of Colin Clout, which he used afterward, in various works, in speaking of himself. He was in temper and disposition a Puritan and was recognized as such by the chiefs of the Puritan party; they seeing in his allegory a purpose to forward the glory of God as interpreted by their ideas.

Spenser was appointed — probably through Sidney's influence—private secretary to Lord Grey de Wilton, who went to Ireland as Lord Deputy of that distracted and unhappy country. There he wrote his only prose work, "A view of the present State of Ireland." In this we do not find, as we might expect from his nature, a gentle and merciful policy recommended in dealing with the savage islanders. The opinion he expresses of the native Irish coincides with the brutal saying setting forth the views held by certain western frontiersmen concerning the American savage; namely: "A good Indian is a dead Indian."

It was in the intervals of his work as secretary to the Lord Deputy, that he wrote the first three books of the "Faërie Queen." He was living in Kilcolman Castle, an abode which had been assigned to him from the confiscated estate of the Earl of Desmond, in a lovely spot on the bank of the picturesque river Mulla. Raleigh visited him there and heard him read part of the "Faërie Queen"; and on the strength of his admiration for its wonderful beauty and interest, prevailed on its author to go back to England with him, to "push his fortune at court." Nothing came of it—nothing except the often-quoted stanza of fine vituperation directed against patronage, which in these days is represented by "office-seeking":

> Full little knowest thou, that hast not tried,
> What hell it is in suing long to bide:

> To lose good days that might be better spent;
> To waste long nights in pensive discontent;
> To speed today, to be put back tomorrow;
> To feed on hope, to pine with fear and sorrow;
> To have thy Prince's grace, yet want her peers';
> To have thy asking, yet wait many years;
> To fret thy soul with crosses and with cares;
> To eat thy heart with comfortless despairs;
> To fawn, to crouch, to wait, to ride, to run,
> To spend, to give, to want, to be undone.
> Unhappy wight, born to disastrous end,
> That doth his life in so long tendance spend!

The world of Elizabeth's time was quick to recognize the quality of the "Faërie Queen," and to bestow on it that praise to which no writer is indifferent. The great critic Hallam says of it that it became at once "the delight of every accomplished gentleman, the model of every poet, the solace of every scholar." Probably no poem ever took the literary and social world so completely by storm; with the possible exception of Byron's "Childe Harold." Spenser wrote a gay, spirited account of his trip, "Colin Clout's Come Home Again," in which, in his assumed character of a shepherd, Colin tells how Raleigh, shepherd of the ocean, caused him to "wend with him, his Cynthia for to see." In Cynthia one recognizes Elizabeth, who was sun, moon, and stars to her admiring courtiers. He describes England, the queen herself, many celebrated persons in public life, and some living poets. Among the latter he introduces Shakespeare, whose name, he says, like himself, doth heroically sound.

Between the publication of the first three books of the "Faërie Queen" in 1590, and the next three in 1596, he married; and at this time we have his epithalamium and eighty-eight sonnets or "amoretti," as love-songs were then called. We can not doubt that he had a happy home, for every allusion—and there are many—which his verses make to the joys of an ideal family circle, gives the impression that Spenser's was one which satisfied all his heart's desires. But the peaceful, gentle, dutiful, poetic course of his life was doomed to feel a terrible, heartrending blow; a catastrophe which perhaps caused or hastened its ending. A bloody rebellion broke out in Ireland, and Kilcolman Castle was naturally a main point of attack. It was carried "by storm," a phrase of war which means that all within was at the mere mercy of the stormers, whereas a capitulation without final assault carries terms of mitigation of the horrors of defeat. It was sacked and burned, with circumstances from which the imagination shrinks in horror. Spencer with his wife and two sons escaped during the tumult; but, according to a tradition which is generally accepted as truthful, an infant child perished by violence or by fire.

If, as is supposed, Spenser had been occupied during the last preceding years in writing the remaining six books planned in the scheme of the "Faërie Queen," the precious lines were lost in the catastrophe. We have only the first six. The silence of despair seems to have come upon the grand and gentle poet; and even his friends have left no sign whereby to do more than guess at the closing scene. He died in 1599, it is said, of a broken heart. His bones were laid (by his own request) in Westminster Abbey, near to those of "Father Chaucer," where his tomb may still be seen in the sacred "Poets' Corner."

The plan of the "Faërie Queen" included twelve books, displaying the twelve moral virtues. The six he treated were holiness, temperance, purity, friendship, justice, and courtesy. He even speaks, in his preface, of twelve other books, to treat the twelve "political virtues," whatever that may mean—probably loyalty to the powers that be, whether worthy or otherwise; battle-courage in whatever cause; unquestioning adherence to the established faith, etc.; such being the ideal of good citizenship in Spenser's age and station.

Doubtless the volumes grew in bulk, in the writing, beyond the author's original idea of length; for even the six books finished are of a voluminousness going far beyond our latter-day standard. Spenser's use of language was so lavish—though so admirable—as to lead us to think of the modern slur which finds expression in the epithet "wordy."

Yet this would be a flagrant injustice when applied to so great a work as Spenser's. It has been well said that he created not only his characters but the very ground they stand on; his scene is independent of all time and space; he has nothing to do with history or geography; the whole world of imagination is his theatre of action. We must indeed imbibe some drop of his spirit before we are capable of flying with its flight; that done, he lifts us to the skies and, like a true Merlin, carries us whither he will.

Popular laziness has led to popular neglect of the "Faërie Queen." Men look at the splendid structure as a beautiful edifice of labyrinth, wherein they enter not for fear of losing their clue and wandering whither they know not. Hazlitt says: "Some persons look at the allegory as if they thought it would bite them. . . . This is very idle. If they do not meddle with the allegory, the allegory will not meddle with them." In truth the gorgeous descriptions, the plaintive tenderness, the exquisite adaptation of sound to sense, are themselves "a thing of beauty and a joy forever," while the portrayal of the loathsomeness of sin and the beauty of holiness; the tales of adventure, so thrilling that one almost loses breath in the reading; all these have their worth quite outside any allegorical unity which served the poet as a thread whereon to string his gems of thought.

Among the poets of lesser note in Spenser's time was William Warner, whose "Albion's England" is a lively poetical history of England from the Deluge (!) down to Warner's own time. It is not a great poem, but it is full of incidents,

EDMUND SPENSER.

true or imagined, and was very popular in its day. Toward
the end of the century, Samuel Daniel—"well-languaged
Daniel," as he was called in his own time—wrote a "History of the Civil Wars between York and Lancaster," in
smooth but not very interesting verse. A better poem, in
the form of a dialogue in defence of learning, is his "Mu-
sophilus." A third poet, whose writings show more power
than those of the two last mentioned, and who outlived
them both, is Michael Drayton (1563-1631), author of the
"Polyolbion." This is a long poem about England, with
a little of everything in it; antiquities, minute descriptions
of places, legends, scraps of information of all sorts. The
poem takes a sort of ramble over England, photographing
the scenery (in words) and picking up whatever the writer
thought would be of interest to his readers. We find it
tedious now, and it had little success even in its own day,
for by that time (1613) Spenser and Shakespeare and Ben
Jonson had raised the standard of poetry and given its aims
a new direction, and the many thousand verses of the
"Polyolbion" (Professor Tyler says that the word means
" Many-ways-happy ") were out of date; something to be
admired, but not read. Drayton wrote many years earlier,
a poem called "The Barons' Wars."

When we are asked to name the author whose prose shed
most glory on the sixteenth century, we answer without a
moment's hesitation, Richard Hooker (1554–1600). He
was born in 1553—within the lustrum* which gave birth to
Spenser, Sidney and Raleigh, the decade which produced
Bacon, Daniel and Drayton, and eleven years before the
birth-year of Shakespeare and Marlowe. It was an age of
great men, and Hooker's name stands out among the rest
as the writer of the best English his country produced.
Hooker's personal history is interesting. Born of poor par-

---

* A period of five years.

6

ents, he showed early so remarkable an aptitude for study that he was sent to Oxford by the assistance of friends among the clergy, and rewarded their kindness by becoming one of the most learned men of his time. After finishing his university course, he became a clergyman of the Church of England and soon afterward committed the great mistake of his life. We have the account in the words of his biographer, Isaac Walton, who says that when Hooker arrived in London from Oxford, wet and weary, he was received with so much kindness by his landlady that he thought himself bound in conscience to believe all she said.

She persuaded him that as he was of a weak constitution he ought to have a wife that would take care of him and perhaps thus prolong his life, and he, being too simple-minded to suspect deceit, authorized her to select one for him. The person she chose was her own daughter, described by Walton as a "silly, clownish woman and withal a mere Xantippe," whom Hooker was too honorable to reject, feeling himself committed to the marriage. This foolish, unmannerly and ill-tempered person made his life wretched, and the whole story is told in the narrative given by two college friends who went to visit him. They found him—the scholar, the rector, the gentleman—tending sheep with a volume of Horace in his hand; and when the scene was transferred to his house, his wife called him away from his friends to rock the cradle while she went about some other business. The account goes on to say that they received little entertainment except from his conversation, and the whole situation was so depressing that they returned to the inn instead of finishing their visit.

His greatest work was "The Laws of Ecclesiastical Polity" —a defence of the system of the Church of England. This is admired, even by those who do not agree with the author's sentiments, for his power of thought and beautifully clear method of arrangement. His discreet and orderly character and conduct and his faultless literary judgment have earned for him the name of "The Judicious Hooker."

CHAPTER XIV.

ELIZABETHAN DRAMATIC PERIOD.

HE modern English drama, after its first appearance in the comedies of "Ralph Royster Doyster" and "Gammer Gurton's Needle," and the tragedy "Gorboduc," grew rapidly. The craving for amusement which had called up these entertainments demanded more, and a host of writers sprang up to meet the want. The theatres of the sixteenth century had little in common with the superbly-decorated buildings in which modern lovers of the drama assemble to see their favorite performances. They had indeed passed the stage when the players acted their parts in temporary sheds, set up in some inn-yard, to be pulled down as soon as the play was over. But the first permanent theatre opened in London, the Blackfriars —so called from the part of the city where it stood—was simply a round wooden wall without a roof,* at one side of which was the stage, covered with thatch, so that players' clothes might not be spoiled. For the safety of the spectator's finery no provision was made.

The other appointments were in keeping with these arrangements. A rough gallery, high enough to clear the heads of the actors, ran across the back of the stage, serving the purpose of a castle-wall, a balcony or a high window,

---

* This explains the expression in one of the preludes to Shakespear's "Henry V.":

Or may we cram
Within this wooden O, the very casques
That did affright the air at Agincourt.

and to this the characters mounted when their turns came to speak from those lofty eminences. The audience was never in doubt as to the spot where the action was supposed to take place, for the name of the town, castle or forest was painted on a board hung in full view. The scenery was of a description that would not be tolerated now in a tenth-rate theatre. Shabby, faded draperies, absurd expedients for the suggestion of thrones, banquets, camps, forests, rocks, seas, ships, etc., these (without side-scenes, flies, or traps) were the stage-fittings of those simple-hearted times; and in spite of the smallness of the stage, part of its space was given up to favored nobles, gallants and others who sat, stood and walked about to the serious inconvenience of the performers. In truth no well-dressed and decent person of either sex could venture into the "pit" with its crowd of low, ribald boors. It was well that this "pit" was roofless, for otherwise the air would have been pestilential. Even so it was polluted beyond description.*

The performance began at one o'clock in the day and was over by four; and when the play was going on, the fumes of ale and tobacco filled the space, while conversation—that is, shouting and quarrelling, mingled with card-playing—went on unchecked.

Time wore on and things began to change for the better; and as the taste of the age did not allow ladies to enter the play-house, the plays sometimes took place in the hall of some nobleman's house, where the players were rewarded

---

* The social position of the player was in keeping with the character of the play-house. As late as the fourteenth year of Queen Elizabeth's reign (1572, when Shakespeare was eight years old), an act was passed "for the punishment of vagabonds," which included in this class "common players in interludes, and minstrals, not belonging to any baron of this realm." And by statute of 1597, the punishment of the "vagabond" was "to be stripped naked from the waist up, whipped till bloody, and sent from parish to parish to the place of his birth."

with a few pence apiece and a supper. All female parts were played by boys, the sense of decorum at that day not allowing women thus to exhibit themselves in public.

The earlier Elizabethan dramatists, though noted in their day, are little more than names to us now, for there is not in their plays that world-wide applicability to human nature which makes the works of Shakespeare so real to us. In their time, however, they had great popularity. Among them may be named Lodge, Peele, Lyly (author of "Euphues"), Kyd, Nash and Greene, the last of whom is remembered as much for the misfortunes brought upon him by his own indiscretion and self-indulgence as for the merit in his works. He is said to have been the first person in England who actually made his living (or tried to make it) by writing, and to have died of want. The latter may not be literally true; but we have his own word for it that he wasted his substance in riotous living, and was indebted to the charity of a poor shoemaker for a roof to die under. Shortly before his death he wrote to his long-forsaken wife concerning a bond for ten pounds which he had given the shoemaker:

Doll, I charge thee, by the love of your youth and by my soules rest, that thou wilt see this man paide; for if hee and his wife had not succoured me, I had died in the streets.

Greene has earned most attention in a curious way. He had some quarrel with Shakespeare, and wrote a bitter attack on him, calling him a plagiarist, and one strutting in the plumes of his betters!

All sixteenth-century writers who had not means of their own, were supported up to this time (so far as our records go) either by pensions, public offices or private liberality; or else like Shakespeare, they made their living in other ways than by the pen; often as actors. But the sad truth is that the money earned by the dramatists of that age was spent at the tavern and in low company.

Improvidence and recklessness seem to have been the characteristics of the brotherhood.

Christopher Marlowe (1564–93) was the son of a shoemaker. Like many other dramatic writers of the time, he received a university education; probably by the assistance of some well-to-do friend who discerned his genius. He was the first to venture on a play composed entirely in blank verse, the authors before him having written their dramas in rhyme, or in prose, or in a mixture of the two.

Marlowe's plays, which are all tragedies, are noted for their power of depicting intense passion and suffering. The first was "Tamburlaine the Great,"* which was followed by "The Life and Death of Doctor Faustus" (the subject made immortal in Goethe's "Faust"), "The Jew of Malta," and "Edward the Second." The malignant passions are depicted by him with terrible power. He lost his life at the age of twenty-nine in a tavern brawl; a waiter 'whom he was attacking seizing Marlowe's dagger and turning it upon its owner. The point entered his eye, and he died soon afterward of the wound.

Here, if we followed strict chronological order, the name of Shakespeare should come in; but as it is necessary to give him a chapter to himself, we will finish the list of those who are classed together as Elizabethan dramatists, reserving his life and writings for separate consideration.

It is not generally known that among the authors of Elizabeth's reign were many novelists, whose works are no longer of interest to us, having been thrown out of sight by the greater dramatic brilliancy then dawning. A Frenchman, M. Jusserand, has written an entertaining book on this subject, in which, beside the well-known romances of Sidney and Lyly, he enumerates those of a dozen other authors, giving sketches of their plots and specimens of

---

* The same person as " Timour the Tartar."

their style. The book is translated into English by Elizabeth Lee.

"Oh, Rare Ben Jonson!" Such is the phrase which we are accustomed to associate with the idea of the dramatist who comes next after Shakespeare in the estimation of literary critics. Some friend gave a stone-cutter eighteen pence to cut it on a slab in the wall near his tomb (he was buried upright), and there it will remain, probably, until Westminster Abbey is spoken of as a thing that was; like its neighbor, St. Margaret's churchyard.

Jonson (1573–1637) seems to have been marked out in his early years for the contradictions of fate.. His father, a clergyman, died at about the time of his birth, and his mother afterward married a bricklayer, who took him from the university, where the kindness of friends had placed him, and set him to handling the trowel. This not being to his taste, he ran away and enlisted in the war against Spain in the Netherlands, a few years after Sir Philip Sidney met his death upon the field of Zutphen. In the army he saw the rudest form of life, and its effects were visible all through his career in a certain disposition to *swaggering* and boastfulness, and a roughness of manner which never left him.

Returning to England penniless, he studied for a short time at Cambridge, but being forced to do something to earn his living, he took up the trade (for such it was considered in those days) of actor, at the same time assisting established playwrights in writing their dramas. On the stage he was a failure, and when one reads the description of his huge, ungainly figure, his heavy features and his awkward gait, the result of his histrionic efforts is not surprising. Disappointed in this means of making money, he set out in earnest to write dramas; and at the age of twenty-two had already made his mark in stage literature. He had also killed another actor in a duel; and, having written something disrespectful about the Scotch, was in danger of having his right hand chopped off, according to the fashion of those days, by the Scottish king, James I. (of England). Nothing came of it, however, and his mother cheered him by showing him some poison she had prepared for him in case the sentence had been carried out.

Jonson wrote both comedies and tragedies, beginning with the first. "Every Man in his Humor" contains characters—Captain Bobadil, for instance—which are used as types to this day. It is interesting to find the name of William Shakespeare cast as an actor in the first performance of this comedy. "The Alchemist" has the character of Sir Epicure Mammon, whose peculiarities are indicated in his name. Only two other comedies are reckoned as first-rate, "Volpone, or the Fox," and "The Silent Woman." His tragedies are "Catiline" and "Sejanus"—dark, cruel, and terrible as the periods of Roman history in which the scenes are respectively laid.

For many years Jonson lived a chequered life. He was made poet-laureate—the first of an unbroken series which has continued down to the present time—and received a pension; but he could not keep out of quarrels, and had a miserable controversy with some of his brother dramatists which embittered his life and kept him always in an ill-humor. During his easy years he composed many court masques—a kind of spectacular play much in request by the rich and great, and well paid for. These were the rollicking years when much time was spent at the "Mermaid"; a favorite tavern frequented by the wits of the day, at which met the "Mermaid Club" (said to have been founded by Sir Walter Raleigh), where Shakespeare, too, was among the guests.

The closing years of Jonson's life were very dreary ones. Always in debt (for, like many of his brother poets, he had little self-denial), tormented by painful illness, and yet still obliged to work in order to support himself, he toiled on after his pen had lost its vigor and his works were no longer welcomed. Still he had good friends who did what could be done to cheer his declining days. He survived his friend Shakespeare more than twenty years.

Jonson was, like all the best dramatists, a poet as well as a play-writer. Some exquisite songs are scattered through his plays, and at the time of his death he was engaged on a pastoral play called "The Sad Shepherd," which shows that the poetic faculty had not deserted him, though he could no longer write plays which pleased the public. His prose criticisms are forcible and expressed in good English.

There is reason to believe that all the great play-writers of Shakespeare's day were familiarly acquainted with each other; but at that time there were no "interviewers," nor was it thought decorous—perhaps not interesting—to report private conversations and convivial gatherings. A single glimpse of the social life of the age reaches us through Thomas Fuller (of whose own writings we shall hear later), and who wrote thus in 1662, forty-six years after the death of Shakespeare and twenty-five after that of Jonson. He is speaking of Shakespeare:

> Many were the wit combats between him and Ben Jonson; which two I behold like a Spanish great galleon and an English man-of-war. Master Johnson, like the former, was built far higher in learning; solid, but slow in his performances. Shakespeare, with the English man-of-war, lesser in bulk but lighter in sailing, could turn with all tides, tack about, and take advantage of all winds by the quickness of his wit and invention.

Such a word-picture as this is worth volumes of conjecture.

After Shakespeare and Ben Jonson, the next place is generally conceded to Francis Beaumont (1584-1616), and John Fletcher (1579-1625), two dramatists who wrote together and formed the first recorded literary partnership. Fletcher outlived his co-laborer, and wrote many plays alone, both after Beaumont's death and during the time of their joint production; but the idea of such a friendship is so pleasant to dwell upon that the first thought of either brings up the name of the other. Their works, like those of all the playwrights of the time, were very unequal; they contain passages of beautiful poetry intermixed with much that is tame and flat; and their characters, beside being grossly immoral, are untrue to nature. The style, also, is more artificial than that of either Shakespeare or Jonson. Of their joint works the most original is "The Knight of the Burning Pestle," the first English burlesque, intended as a travesty of the high-flown romances of the period, as the "Don Quixote" of Cervantes ridiculed them as they existed in Spanish literature. Of their serious works, the most important is "The Two Noble Kinsmen." Among Fletcher's individual plays, "The Faithful Shepherdess" may be especially mentioned.

Some beautiful songs are given as the joint work of the companion poets, though they were probably the work of Fletcher alone. As an example, see the "Song to Melancholy," beginning "Hence, all ye vain delights," and closing with the oft-quoted line:

> Nothing's so dainty sweet as lovely melancholy.

Of the remaining dramatists of this rich and full period, we can give little more than the names. Philip Massinger wrote many plays, of which one, "A New Way to Pay Old Debts," is played to this day. John Webster excelled in representing the horrible, in such plays as "The Duchess of Malfi." A long list of contemporary writers follows, the chief of whom are Middleton, Dekker, Marston, Ford, Chapman (the translator of Homer), and Shirley. The last named, although only seven years old at the time of Queen Elizabeth's death, is reckoned among the Elizabethan poets. He has not the force and originality of the earlier ones, but possesses more refinement. Better known than his dramas is his beautiful poem beginning:

> The glories of our earth and state
> Are shadows, not substantial things.

Shirley espoused the king's part in the great civil war, and afterward, when his dramas failed to support him, philosophically took up school-teaching for a living. The Restoration did not mend his fortune. His home was burned in the great fire of London (1666), and soon afterward his wife and he died on the same day. And so ended the Elizabethan dramatists.

CHAPTER XV.

WILLIAM SHAKESPEARE.

THERE has probably never been another man about whom so much has been thought, written, and said, of whom we really know so little as we do of Shakespeare. To the people of his own time he was not the great man he appears to us; he was simply first an inferior actor, then one of the proprietors of one of the theatres in London, then the writer of dramas, more or less popular, and of a few poems. No one, therefore, thought it worth while to collect and treasure up anecdotes about him, or to make out a connected story of his life. It was reserved for later ages to discover his vast knowledge of human nature, his wide sympathies, his artistic skill, his wonderful power of depicting character ; and also as we can not help suspecting, to find sometimes in his works a meaning of which the poet was himself unconscious. He often wrote, no doubt, "better than he knew," and we have the benefit of it.

William Shakespeare was born at Stratford-on-Avon,

in Warwickshire, in April, 1564. The exact day is not known; but as his baptism is recorded as taking place on the 26th, it has been found convenient to assume that he was born on April 23d, St. George's Day, which was also the day of his death. His father, John Shakespeare, is variously stated to have been a butcher, a wool-comber, and a glover. Perhaps he was all three, as the occupations might have been easily combined. The maiden name of Mistress Shakespeare was Mary Arden. She came of what is called in England "a good family," meaning one which could trace back its descent through several generations. We know nothing further about her, but as it is generally acknowledged that sons inherit the brains of their mothers, we are disposed to think well of Mary Arden.

Of Shakespeare's education, we know little except from the indications afforded in his writings that he was a man of wide reading. He was undoubtedly taught at the grammar school in Stratford; one of those foundations or restorations of Edward VI. to which the England of that century was so deeply indebted. Ben Jonson says of him that he had "small Latin and less Greek," but Jonson was rather proud of his own scholarship and probably had a higher standard than was generally accepted in that age. Of Greek, Shakespeare may well have been ignorant; but Latin, taught at every grammar school (often at the expense of English), must almost necessarily have been among his pursuits. His father, who had been made a prosperous man by his marriage with Mary Arden, became deeply entangled in debt when William was about fourteen years old, and this occasioned his removal from school at an earlier age than that at which the sons of well-to-do persons usually left it. Where or how the son picked up the great variety of knowledge shown in his writings, we do not know; but it is probable that, like most geniuses, he occupied himself with many topics. His great acquaintance with technical law-terms gives rise to the supposition that he studied in a lawyer's office. Aubrey, a gossipy writer of the seventeenth century, says that he taught school, which in itself is a means of learning. In some way or other, he certainly obtained an acquaintance with several sciences, with history, and with the romance-literature of his own country, France, and Italy. His Roman plays show that he knew Plutarch. We imagine him to have been, like Scott, an omniverous reader, and to have possessed a memory which held with a tenacious grasp whatever was committed to it.

A tradition, as vague and unsubstantial as such things usually are, represents Shakespeare in his youth as joining with some other wild young fellows in stealing deer from the park of Sir Thomas Lucy, a neighboring magistrate who, as is said, had the offender arrested and prosecuted. The story is not more improbable than that of George Washington and the cherry-tree; and some disrespectful verses, addressed to the knight by the alleged criminal, certainly imply that Shakespeare had a grudge against Lucy to pay off.

At the age of eighteen the future poet married Anne Hathaway, the daughter of a "substantial yeoman" living at Shottery, a village about a mile distant from Stratford. Of her, as of the mother of Shakespeare, we know little, except that she was nearly eight years older than her husband, he being but eighteen at the time of his marriage. Four years afterward, we hear of him in London, in connection with the theatre; and from this time to that of his final retirement to his native village, his life is cast among dramatists and literary men generally. Tradition tells us that he at first made a few pence by holding the horses of the gallants who frequented the theatre. If he did, it was not long before he found other work to do. We hear of him as first adapting plays to the stage, then producing some of his own; making a living as stage manager and constantly advancing in prosperity until he became part-owner, first of the Blackfriars theatre and afterward of the Globe. He was an actor, too, during the first part of his career; a very poor one probably, as we hear that the ghost in "Hamlet," and Adam in "As You Like It" were his favorite parts. By all together, however, he earned a handsome competence, being the first man of letters in England who did so; and this was due, not to his writings, but to the sums paid for admissions to the Globe theatre. For companions, he had the leading writers of his day, and never lacked for good company. The queen, who was very fond of amusements, enjoyed seeing his plays acted, and on at least one occasion suggested a subject to him. Not only actors, but to some extent dramatists also, were then considered an inferior class, being placed below the level of tradesmen. Our author, therefore, did not have access to what was considered "the best society"—namely, the court circle; but the friendship of great men for one another does not depend upon rank or riches.

No manuscript of Shakespeare's is known to be in existence, nor even any scrap of his hand-writing except four extremely rough and dissimilar signatures appended to the four pages of his will. The document was executed during his last illness and the only explanation of the existence of such scrawls from the hand of a practised writer is the suggestion that they are made either by a hand in the extremity of illness or by one held and guided by another hand. This circumstance has been seized upon by those who deny to Shakespeare the authorship of the plays bearing his name, as a support to their unbelief; as has also been the fact that in this will, though directing the disposition of his "second-best bed," etc., he makes no mention of his ownership of any plays, in manuscript or otherwise, albeit many of the greatest dramas were not printed until six years after his death. But the world believes that the immortal work could not, falsely, have passed as his for centuries, unchallenged; and that the difficulties urged against that belief are trivial.*

Shakespeare's first published work was the poem of "Venus and Adonis," dedicated to his young friend Lord Southampton. The poem enjoys the high praise of great critics; but at this day it is valueless to the general reader from its length, its rambling nature and the coarseness of its plot. Several of his plays had been acted before this time, but it was for the interest of the managers that new plays should not be published, for fear of lessening the popular interest in them, or having them "pirated" by other theatres. It is not within the scope of the present "Short History" to discuss the order in which the plays of Shakespeare were written, nor the genuineness of those the authorship of which is questioned. It is enough to say that they may be broadly divided into comedies, tragedies, and histories, or historical plays; though in several cases the drama may be described by more than one of these terms. To the first class belong "As You Like It," "Much Ado About Nothing," "The Merchant of Venice," "The Winter's Tale," "Twelfth Night," "A Midsummer Night's Dream" and "The Tempest," with others of minor note. To the second, "King Lear," "Othello," "Hamlet" and "Macbeth," together with the romantic mediæval drama of "Romeo and Juliet." To the third, the Roman plays of "Coriolanus," "Julius Cæsar" and "Antony and Cleopatra"; the legendary British play of "Cymbeline," and that wonderful series of scenes from English history beginning with

---

* The slur of Greene (already mentioned) calling Shakespeare a plagiarist and "one strutting in the plumes of his betters," also affords an argument to many who maintain that Bacon wrote the best of the plays called Shakespeare's, and was debarred by his lofty station from acknowledging their authorship.

"King John" and ending with "King Henry the Eighth." The latter have been justly described as one great drama, of which "King John" shall be the prologue; the eight intermediate plays, so wonderfully dovetailed together and reaching from "Richard the Second" to "Richard the Third," the acts; and "Henry the Eighth" the epilogue. For such a drama we do not wonder that the author desired

> A kingdom for a stage, princes to act,
> And monarchs to behold the swelling scene.

The best preparation for thoroughly enjoying and profiting by Shakespeare's historical plays, is a good knowledge of the period in which the action is laid. A great general once said that all the English history he knew was learned from Shakespeare; but if this was literally true his knowledge must have begun late and ended early, had many gaps in it, and been often incorrect. A poet or a dramatist does not profess to give the literal truth of history. He uses its facts as far as they serve his purpose; he transforms them by the magic of his imagination from dry statistics into living, breathing realities; but there his province ends. The student should first make himself acquainted with history as it happened, and then forever fix it in his mind by giving himself up to the charm with which it is invested by the genius of the dramatist.

Beside the poem already mentioned, Shakespeare wrote "The Lover's Complaint," some poems in a collection called "The Passionate Pilgrim," and one hundred and fifty-four sonnets, or rather short poems of fourteen lines, mostly on the subject of friendship. Much controversy has arisen in regard to the person to whom these sonnets were addressed, but it would not be profitable to detail it here. Many of them are very beautiful.

Shakespeare remained in London, visiting his home at Stratford perhaps yearly, perhaps more frequently, until 1612, when he retired to the place of his birth to spend the

WILLIAM SHAKESPEARE.

four years of life that yet remained to him. Of his life in London we have only an occasional gleam in the writings of his contemporaries. One of these said, in a book called "Wit's Treasury," published in 1598, when the poet was thirty-five years old, that William Shakespeare was the chief living poet and dramatist of England. Spenser called him:

> The man whom nature's self hath made,
> To mock herself, and truth to imitate.

Ben Johnson, who knew him well, called him:

> Soul of the age;
> The applause, delight and wonder of our stage:

and names him "The Sweet Swan of Avon," saying that he was "not for a day, but for all time." Milton, outdoing the rest in hyperbole, closes the poem addressed to him thus:

> Then thou, our fancy of itself bereaving,
> Dost make us marble with too much conceiving;
> And so sepulchred, in such pomp dost lie,
> That kings, for such a tomb would wish to die.

To collect what has been written about Shakespeare since his own time would be to make, as has been well said, not a volume, but a library. The whole reading world has combined to do homage to his greatness.

Shakespeare retired to his native town a rich man for those days, bought a handsome residence called the New Place, and—we may imagine, for nobody knows—lived the free-and-easy life of a country squire. His only son, Hamnet, died at eleven years old. This son and Judith, his twin sister, were named after a baker and his wife, Hamnet and Judith Sadler. An older daughter, Susanna, and his daughter Judith, survived him. Both were married and left children, but the family died out before the end of the century.

The old house in Henley street where the poet was born has been wisely bought and preserved by the British

7

government, and is still the resort of pilgrims from all quarters of the world. The "New Place," a handsome house and grounds where he spent his latter years, fell into the hands of a vandal who, not wishing to live in it, pulled it down that he might not have to pay the taxes on it. Westminster Abbey has a monument to Shakespeare, but his dust lies beneath the pavement of the parish church at Stratford-on-Avon, with the well-known lines carved on the stone:

> Good friend, for Iesus' sake, forbeare
> To digg the dust enclosed heare.
> Blest be ye man yt spares these stones,
> And curst be he yt moves my bones. *

These words may be the expression of a wish expressed during the poet's lifetime, but can scarcely be received as the product of his muse.

CHAPTER XVI.

RALEIGH. BACON.

BEFORE passing on to the literature which belongs wholly to the seventeenth century, we must go back to the two great prose-writers whose lives were spent almost equally in the sixteenth and seventeenth, although their writings place them in very different categories. These are Walter Raleigh and Francis Bacon.

Of the many-sided Raleigh (1552–1618), the "Shepherd of the Ocean," as Spenser quaintly calls him, we can give but a few details, sufficient, it is hoped, to induce the young reader to seek the records of that brilliant life in larger works. He came from an old, though not a noble

---

* The letter in the Saxon alphabet which represents the sound of "th" is nearly identical with our letter "y."

family; was early brought to the notice of the queen,* and lived for many years in the full splendor of prosperity. His adventurous spirit sent him more than once to the New World, where he founded two separate colonies, neither of which became permanent. The members of the first, poor and starving, were rescued and taken back to England by Captain Francis Drake; those of the second were supposed to have fallen under the Indian tomahawk, for no trace of them could be found when, three years after their settlement, a ship was sent to seek them out. It was Raleigh who gave to the Atlantic coast the name of Virginia, in honor of his royal mistress, the Virgin Queen; and it was he, as is reported, who first brought to the knowledge of English people the useful potato and the soothing tobacco plant. Raleigh impoverished himself in these expeditions, but by prudence and careful husbanding of his resources and the help of grants from the queen, he became again possessed of ample means. His subsequent career was as varied as his early one. He commanded a land-force at the time of the Spanish Armada; he joined various expeditions against the Spaniards, always gaining laurels and often solid plunder; he explored the Orinoco River and wrote a brilliant account of the wonders of South America, and he continued during Elizabeth's reign to be the recipient of her bounties.

After James I.'s accession (1603), Raleigh's affairs took a different turn. He had enemies at court, made such, perhaps, by his arrogance and ostentation while standing high in the favor of the great queen; and he was accused of being concerned in a plot to dethrone James I., the Scottish king so much disliked by the English people, and place Lady Arabella Stuart, cousin of James, on the throne

---

* The famous story of Raleigh's throwing his rich cloak down over a muddy place in the path for the queen to step upon, is used by Sir Walter Scott in "Kenilworth," chapter XV.

in his stead. A base wretch whom Raleigh had befriended swore away his life, and a capital sentence, which seems to us most unjust and uncalled for by the evidence, was pronounced against him. He was then committed to the Tower, where he lay for twelve years in prison, and employed himself in writing his most extensive work, "The History of the World." The subject was too large for any man, and Raleigh began as if he were to have a hundred years to work upon it. One follows him through one hundred and forty pages before he leaves the Garden of Eden, and many superfluous questions are discussed which have no interest for us. Still, there are passages of great beauty, and it would be hard to find a finer apostrophe to Death than that which closes the volume:

Oh, eloquent, just and mighty Death! whom none can advise, thou hast persuaded; what none hath dared, thou hast done; and whom all the world has flattered, thou hast only cast out of the world and despised: thou hast drawn together all the far-stretched greatness, all the pride, cruelty, and ambition of man, and covered it all over with these two narrow words: *Hic jacet.*

Sir Walter is best known to us as a prose-writer, but he was also the author of several graceful poems, which show that he had poetic talent of no common sort. Of these "The Nymph's Reply"—an answer to Marlowe's "Come live with me and be my love"—is the most esteemed. Another called "The Lye" is full of spirit.

During his long imprisonment his wife was allowed to be with him, and Prince Henry, James's oldest son, often visited him. In the thirteenth year of his imprisonment he told the king of a gold mine in South America which he could probably obtain for his majesty. James at once released him, without, however, pardoning him, and Raleigh set out for the Orinoco with the old sentence still hanging over his head. The expedition was unsuccessful; Raleigh's oldest son was killed in an action against the Spaniards;

the gold mine was not reached, and he returned a disappointed and practically a ruined man. This mean-souled king was at that time anxious for friendship with Spain; and when the Spanish ambassador demanded the death of Raleigh, James tried at first to find some excuse for his prosecution in the circumstances of the alleged offence. As that could not be done without revealing his own share in the matter, he ordered the soldier, author, statesman, to be executed on the old unproved charge of treason—a lasting shame to the memory of James the First. Raleigh met death bravely and philosophically.

With respect and interest amounting almost to awe, we come to the consideration of a man of mighty mind; Francis Bacon (1561–1626). The first question usually asked by young people on reaching this name is, "Was he a relative of Roger Bacon?" Probably not. Roger Bacon, the first English scientific writer, lived and died a monk, and was, therefore, childless; and though the second great Bacon may have had some remote relationship with the first through what is called collateral descent, there is no connection traceable between them.

Sir Nicholas Bacon, the father of Francis, was Queen Elizabeth's Lord Keeper of the Great Seal, a post of high responsibility and honor, which office he held for twenty years. That he did not lack the quickness of wit which was possessed by so many of Elizabeth's courtiers, is shown by his answer when the queen remarked that his house was too little for him. "Not so, Madam," he replied; "your majesty has made me too great for my house." And as a pendant to this we may quote the answer of Francis to the queen when he was about eight years old. "How old are you, my little man?" she inquired. To which the future courtier promptly replied, "Just two years younger than your majesty's happy reign." The queen used to call him, in jest, her little Lord Keeper.

Of course Francis was finely educated. He is said to have taken a dislike to Aristotle (or rather to the Aristotelian system) at school; a fact worth remembering when we come to study his own system. He left college at sixteen, and accompanied the English ambassador, Sir Amyas Paulet, to Paris, in order to be trained as a diplomatist. When he had been there about two years, his father died, having neglected to make any provision for him (Francis was the younger son of a second wife), and at eighteen he was obliged to return to England and seek some means of supporting himself. He selected the law, and after the necessary study was admitted to practise. He was soon elected to parliament, in which body he sat for several years, and on one occasion warmly opposed a measure on which the queen had set her heart. This displeased her, and the next-year, when the office of attorney-general fell vacant and Bacon was an applicant for the post, she decided to give it to Sir Edward Coke, author of the famous law-commentary now called "Coke upon Littleton." The Earl of Essex, Queen Elizabeth's favorite after the death of Leicester, urged her to grant his suit, and when his efforts proved fruitless, gave Bacon, to console him for his disappointment, the beautiful estate called Twickenham Park which he afterward sold for a large sum.

It is sad to be obliged to mention here that failing which was the cause of all Bacon's subsequent misfortunes, and ended in his downfall—his extravagance. He lived constantly beyond his means, and of course ran in debt, and the result was that he was continually harassed by demands which he could not meet, and which still did not prevent him from indulging in new expenditures.

In 1596, when Bacon was thirty-five years old, he was given the office of Queen's Counsel, a position both important and lucrative.

Before the end of the century, Bacon published ten of

those essays which are known wherever the English language is read. They are crowded with thought, expressed in strong though not always elegant English. In diction, Hooker was his superior, but in variety of range and depth of thought, Bacon was excelled by no man of his century.

The man who wrote "Reading maketh a full man; conference [conversation] a ready man, and writing an exact man," enriched our language with a sentence on which a volume might be written without exhausting its meaning. In his preface he hopes that these essays "will come home to men's business and bosoms." A collection of his apophthegms (short, pithy sentences into which a great deal of meaning is compressed) is valuable reading for young and old. " A man that is young in years may be old in honor, if he have lost no time." "Some books are to be tasted, others to be swallowed, and some few to be chewed and digested." Again, "Men fear death, as children fear to go in the dark." "Revenge is a kind of wild justice." "He that hath wife and children hath given hostages to fortune." Hallam, one of the best authorities on English classics, remarks, "It would be derogatory to a man of the slightest claim to polite letters, were he unacquainted with the 'Essays' of Bacon."

Bacon wrote also a philosophical romance entitled "The New Atlantis," and a "Life of Henry VIII.," in which the first attempt is made in English literature to write history according to the modern conception of it—that it should be so written as to show the development of the people of a nation; not merely the acts of its kings and warriors.

Among the charges brought against Bacon is that of ingratitude, because it was his business, as Queen's Counsel, to prosecute his friend Essex for treason (1601). This does not, however, seem just. Essex was a man so rash, so headstrong, that it was impossible for any friend to influence him for good or to save him from the consequences of his folly; and during the trial, Bacon dealt as gently with him as he could. When it was over and he was commanded to prepare a statement of the case, he used so much moderation toward Essex that the queen exclaimed angrily, "I see old love is not soon forgotten!"

With the accession of James I. (1603), Bacon's fortunes improved. He was knighted, with some three hundred others, and became Sir Francis. He was married in the same year. Later he was appointed to various offices in the gift of the crown, reaching the highest when he was made Lord Chancellor (1618). He was created successively Baron Verulam and Viscount St. Albans, and just at this point, when he had attained to a position so proud that it seems as if he could have desired nothing further, he became a disgraced and ruined man.

No one, probably, could have been more surprised than was Francis Bacon, Viscount St. Albans and Lord Chancellor of England when he was suddenly accused of having accepted money from a litigant while a suit was in progress —in other words, taken a bribe. Many departments of the government were notoriously corrupt, and the taking of bribes had grown to be so much a matter of course that it seemed almost like the regular order of things. Bacon had not done this to any great extent, and had not always given judgment in favor of the person who thus tried to corrupt him; but he had enemies who pushed the charges against him, and the public, having a general impression that things were going amiss, demanded a scape-goat. Bacon could not deny the facts, although he asserted his innocence of any evil intention; and a sentence of terrible severity was passed upon him. He was condemned to a fine of £40,000, to be imprisoned during the king's pleasure, to be dismissed from all his offices, deprived of the power of sitting in parliament, and forbidden to come within the limits of the court. A more dreadful, sudden fall, short of a death sentence, has seldom been witnessed. The crushing penalty was carried out only in part. The king remitted the fine and released Bacon from imprisonment, and after a time he was allowed again to come within the verge of the court; but he never again held any office or sat in parliament. Perhaps nowhere in human history has the folly of living beyond one's means received such a signal rebuke. Large as had been his income, his immeasurable extravagance had gone beyond it, and like an overbalanced tower the great structure fell in ruins.

He retired into private life, and employed his remaining time in prosecuting investigations in science, in adding to the number of his admirable "Essays," and in carrying on toward perfection the vast system of philosophy that had for many years engrossed his attention in the intervals of other business which alone was enough to exhaust all the strength of even the greatest of his fellow-men of any age or race.

His death, which occurred five years after his downfall and one year after Charles I. came to the throne, was brought about directly by his devotion to scientific research. It had come into his mind that perhaps meats might be preserved by being kept cold—in those days refrigerators had not been dreamed of—and he determined to try the effects of stuffing a fowl with snow. Impatient to make the experiment, he stopped his carriage at a cottage by the roadside, bought his fowl, and stood on the cold, damp ground to see that his directions were carried out. This brought on a sudden chill, and instead of going home, he drove to the house of his friend, the Earl of Arundel, which happened to be near by. Here his illness rapidly increased, and in a few days he breathed his last (1626), congratulating himself that the snow experiment had succeeded "excellent well."

Bacon's aims in his literary and philosophical work were always of the noblest. A touching passage in his will says, "My name and memory I leave to foreign nations, and to mine own country after some time has passed over." He was right in judging that time would soften the remembrance of his faults among his countrymen, and that his real greatness would be remembered and cherished by them.

It is not possible here to give an account of his services to science, or to explain his philosophy farther than to say that it is a mistake to suppose that Bacon invented or discovered any new system. He attempted only to show the correct method of making investigations; and adopted and advocated (though he did not originate) the "inductive" as opposed to the "deductive" system: That is, the plan of taking known facts as a starting point and thence working backward toward a cause, instead of assuming a cause and seeking for conclusions which should follow in logical sequence. It may be called the system based on experiment and experience instead of on speculation. Since his time this has been called the "Baconian" method in contradistinction to the "Aristotelian;" seeing that Aristotle* started with certain postulates or syllogisms, whence followed endless metaphysical discussions, barren of benefit to the race, while Bacon turned his attention to the arts and sciences which might benefit mankind and expand the realm of knowledge to embrace the earth beneath and the universe around us.

---

* It is not to be supposed that Aristotle did not also employ observation and induction as a necessary part of his system.

CHAPTER XVII.

SEVENTEENTH CENTURY.   MISCELLANEOUS ESSAYISTS.

E may now fairly leave the sixteenth century behind, and enter on that which is not inferior to it in strength; and, in variety, even excels it.   In the seventeenth century we have Shakespeare still with us for sixteen years and Bacon for twenty-six.   Milton was the contemporary of Shakespeare for eight years, and Dryden closes the century.

In naming the writers of the seventeenth century, we must not omit the prince of pedants, King James I., who followed Queen Elizabeth (1603–25).   The king honestly considered himself the wisest man in his dominions.   His poetry (or rather rhymes), his criticism, and his theological disquisitions, have ceased to interest us.   Only one of his works, "A Counterblast to Tobacco," is at all amusing, and of that most persons know only one sentence; that in which the fragrant weed, not being to the king's taste, is described as "loathsome to the eye, hateful to the nose, harmful to the brain, and injurious to the lungs." *

The language of Queen Elizabeth's time had already grown antiquated, and the scholarship of the early translators of the Bible was open to question; so King James ordered a new translation made, which is known to us as the "Authorized Version," and is still in use.   This was finished in 1611, and in English Bibles one reads even now the dedication "To the most high and mighty prince James, By the grace of God King of Great Britain, France, and Ireland, Defender of the Faith," etc.   This translation

---

* This sentence is full of tautology (repetition), seeing that *loathsome* and *hateful* mean the same thing, and so do *harmful* and *injurious*.

was meant to be final; but in our own day a "Revised Version" of the Bible has been issued (finished in 1884), which, while it is superior in correctness to the one of King James's time, has not as yet taken hold of the hearts of English-speaking readers bound up in love and reverence for the earlier one.

Two distinguished theological writers of this period, excelling all others of their time in knowledge of church-history and of early Christian writers, were Launcelot Andrews (1555-1626), Bishop of Winchester, and James Usher (1580-1656), Archbishop of Armagh in Ireland. The former was one of the translators of King James's "Authorized Version;" the latter formed a "Chronology of the Bible" which held its ground for two hundred years.

The most generally learned man in England in the first half of the seventeenth century was probably John Selden (1584-1654), lawyer, statesman and author. Of his many writings, the most curious is the "Mare Clausum" (Closed Sea), in which he claims the exclusive right of the English to the ocean for a certain distance around England. After his death his secretary published, from recollections of his conversations, a volume called "Selden's Table-Talk."

An author who has hardly received his due share of attention is James Howell, a Welshman (1590-1666), the author of many works now obsolete, and of the first collection of English letters intended by their author for the press. Howell was a great traveller, and has left in his "Letters" and his "Instructions for Foreign Travel," a series of pictures of the European life of that day, full of acute observation and interesting as bringing up comparisons with our own time.

To go back to the great prose-writers whose names adorn the first part of the seventeenth century, those of most note who come after Bacon and Raleigh and were contemporary with Milton, are Isaac Walton, Thomas Fuller, Jeremy

Taylor and Sir Thomas Browne; each distinguished by special excellence in his own department. Of these Walton was born the first and lived the longest, dying at the age of ninety.

The lives of all these men embrace the period of the Civil War, the great events which led to it and those which followed it. It was a time of religious, intellectual and political upheaval, and while some writers (Milton, Bunyan, etc.) show the deepest and most enduring marks of the moral turmoil about them, one wonders that the others could have lived and written and not shown greater traces of its influence—sometimes quite ignoring it.

Isaak Walton (1593–1683) kept a linen-draper's shop in London until he was past fifty years old, then retired to the country to spend the rest of his life in the enjoyment of nature and of the society of men of letters, who found him a delightful companion. At sixty, he gave to the world his "Complete Angler," a book in which fishing as a fine art furnishes only the foundation for a series of exquisite pictures of rural life and scenery, quaint bits of old-world learning, tender moralizing, and daintily graceful reflections on all sorts of subjects such as might come into his head while sitting with a rod in his hand by the side of some lovely rippling brook, with the summer breeze making music among the leaves overhead, and the air filled with delicious odors.

A second work of Walton's, in a different strain but equally charming, is the "Lives" of five of his friends; the poet Donne, Sir Henry Wotton, Richard Hooker, the saintly George Herbert, and Bishop Sanderson. The last of these, a learned and excellent divine, would not be known to us in literature but for Walton's sketch of his life; the others we have already been interested in. In these lives, the transparent simplicity of Walton's style engages our admiration; and the gentle reverence with which he handles the memory of his dead friends is both touching and instructive.

Thomas Fuller (1608–61) is called the "Church Historian," the title of the work by which he first became known being "The Church History of Britain, from the Birth of Christ to the year 1648." The most popular of his works is his "History of the Worthies of England;" a book in which he not only deals with the personal memoirs of noted men, but takes the opportunity of scattering through it all sorts of information—historical, botanical, architectural and antiquarian—of the counties where they happened to live.

The epithets "quaint" and "witty" are those most often connected with his name. He wrote at a time when the fiercest passions were aroused by the difficult relations between church and state; but he never loses his good-humored gayety, or for a moment becomes ill-natured in his partisanship. He was a clergyman of the Church of England, and as such was the object of some persecution in the civil war. Being driven from his pulpit he became a chaplain in the royal army and on one occasion, being left in charge of a castle garrison which was attacked by the Roundheads, drove away the besiegers with loss.

Beside the two books mentioned, Fuller wrote many others, all full of droll conceits, earnest piety, a shrewd knowledge of the world and an unfailing kindness of disposition.

Among the many learned divines of the time we are now considering, Jeremy Taylor (1613–67) is perhaps the only one whose purely religious works continue to be read and even studied in our own day. He is called "the poet among preachers." His rich fancy, eloquence and imagination add a charm to his writings which attracts those who might be insensible to his deep and fervent piety. This ornateness is carried even to a fault, and sometimes seems to weary the imagination by over-stimulating it; but Taylor succeeds in enchaining the attention of his reader, and mingles many grains of profound thought with the lighter and more fanciful exuberance of his pages. His books on "Holy Living" and "Holy Dying" are still closet-companions to many a pious mind which finds nourishment and gratification in his discourses.

Taylor had to suffer even more heavily for his loyalty to the king than did Fuller. From being a favorite and successful preacher he suddenly found himself, on account of the Civil War, without a living, and like Fuller became a chaplain and took an active share in the operations of the army. His rectory having been sequestrated by Parliament he retired to Wales and occupied himself in school-teaching. Here he married a lady with some property, and gave up his teaching, but was occupied industriously with his pen. He was too prominent not to be a mark for Puritan resentment, and repeatedly suffered fines and imprisonment in consequence. He took charge of a small parish in Ireland, and after the restoration was made Bishop of Dromore. He did not find this an easy or tranquil position, for the Irish Catholics about him were as bitterly opposed as the Puritans to the Established Church; and after seven years of toil he died, at the age of fifty-five.

Among Taylor's many books on the subject of religion, the one most widely known in his own time was "The Liberty of Prophesying," a most eloquent plea for toleration in religion. "Prophesying" is here used in the sense of "preaching," which meaning we often find given to it in the Bible.

William Prynne (1600–69) is famous not so much for his literary achievements as for the misfortunes which sprang from them. He was a Puritan of the Puritans, and published a book called "Histrio-Mastix," directed against theatrical performances of every description. For this book he was sentenced by the Star Chamber (1632–3) to pay a fine of £5,000; to be expelled from the University of Oxford and the legal society to which he belonged; to stand twice in the pillory, each time losing an ear; and to be imprisoned. Aftei being released he published other writings still more violent, and judged libelous by the court, which then pronounced sentence of another fine equal to the first, in addition to which he was to be branded on both cheeks, have the remainder of his ears (spared by the mercy of the first hangman) shaved off, and be imprisoned for life.

Still more ill-fated was Dr. Alexander Leighton, a Scottish clergyman who, for writing against episcopacy, received the same punishment as Prynne, besides having his nose slit and being whipped from Newgate to Tyburn. Both these men were released by the Long Parliament, and received such reparation as was possible, Prynne ending his life in the public service under Charles II.

Among the prose-writers of this time should be mentioned the name of Robert Burton (1576–1640), whose "Anatomy of Melancholy" is found to be really an antidote for melancholy, by virtue of the fine wit and wisdom with which it adorns that dreary-sounding subject. It is full of curious learning, drawn from books which few men even read; and some later writers are accused of stealing their aphorisms and witticisms from its pages. Burton himself was subject to fits of melancholy, to relieve which, it is said, he wrote his famous book. It became a great favorite with the readers of his day. A short extract may give some idea of its lighter style:

A painter's shop, a flowery meadow, is not so gracious an aspect in Nature's storehouse as a young maid, *nubilis puella*, that looks for a husband; or a young man that is her suitor; composed look, composed gait, clothes, gestures, actions all composed; all the graces, elegancies in the world are in her face. . . . They are beyond all measure coy, nice and too curious on a sudden. . . . . No sooner doth a young man see his sweetheart coming but he smugs

FRANCIS BACON.

up himself, pulls up his cloak now fallen about his shoulders, ties his garters, points, sets his band, cuffs, slicks his hair, twires his beard, etc.

It was in the seventeenth century that the delightful form of literature known as the essay became a recognized means of expressing the writer's ideas on some particular subject, in a shorter fashion than by a treatise, or entire book. It seems to have occurred first to Bacon thus to set down in few words his thoughts on topics of general interest, and he was followed by many others, the most notable of whom, in the period we are now discussing, was Sir Thomas Browne (1605–82). He was a highly-taught essayist in the paths of science. He was a botanist, mineralogist, mathematician, horticulturist, philologist and linguist. These deep themes so fully occupied his mind that though he lived in the times of the Rebellion, the Commonwealth and the Restoration, one reads his calm and labored paragraphs finding no marks of consciousness that his king was brought to the block, a Protector placed in control of all England, the order of things again upset, and finally another king enthroned at Westminster. Yet he was no self-inclosed Dryasdust, for he possessed a fresh and racy quality of mind and power of expression that give almost the charm of romance to his writings and make them readable even now, after the lapse of two hundred years. No scientific fact is too high for his discourse, and none too small. Neither is his clear view confined to things about him; it also can discern what is to come; for in an essay entitled "A prophecy concerning the future state of several nations" he predicts that America will be the seat of the "Fifth Empire," the Assyrian, the Persian, the Macedonian and the Roman being the first four.

The essay of that day was very far from being what it later became and still is; a polished and perfected jewel of thought, an edifice of words built up to set forth a

8

certain fact or opinion in its best and completest shape. It was of old more what its name implies, an effort or experiment, a throwing together of suggestions for the reader to arrange and digest. Sir Thomas Browne's essays were of this character, and he generally managed to say something which is still worth reading, though it must be admitted that the grains of wheat are often buried in a rather large heap of chaff. In the days of the Charleses and Cromwell, readers were used to solid discussions on politics and religion, and what we should call dry and tedious histories; while science was almost unknown as a topic for popular treatment. So it comes that sundry crude and absurd notions of existing things prevailed; and Browne's best-known book was "Pseudoxia Epidemica," or inquiries into vulgar (popular) errors. Among those he exposes is the notion "That an elephant hath no joints; and that, being unable to lie down, it sleepeth against a tree; which the hunters observing, do saw the tree almost in two; whereon the beast leaning, by the fall of the tree falls also down itself and is able to rise no more and so is easily taken." This and other pardonable errors of fact the learned doctor voluminously refutes by quotations from the classics and otherwise.

Among such "old gray-headed errors" (as Sir Thomas himself puts it) is also the notion that a man becomes dumb if a wolf sees him before he sees the wolf. He suggests that this may spring from "a vehement fear, which produceth obmutescence." Another is the alarm felt at the ticking of the "death-watch." He describes the harmless little insect and says that he that could explain the phenomenon would extinguish "many cold sweats in grandmothers and nurses."

But alas! The learned doctor himself discards and ridicules the idea that the earth moves while the sun stands still! This may remind us of the fact that even after the earth was admitted to be a round ball, many years elapsed before its relations with the other heavenly bodies were understood.

The fondness of the learned for making words out of the Latin and Greek, which marked (among countless others) · Milton himself in that century and Johnson in the next, is highly exemplified in Browne. They have a certain interest in that they show how in the formation of our tongue, words were thrown upon the current to sink or swim as their nature and degree of usefulness might decide. It was not till a full century afterward that the protest arose which turned men's taste back to Chaucer as "the well of English undefiled," and gauged the worth of a writer's style not by its classicality but by its tendency to the old English idiom.

CHAPTER XVIII.

EARLY SEVENTEENTH-CENTURY POETS.

T is time now to take up the poets whose names are identified with the first half of the seventeenth century, which brings up the period to the execution of Charles I. and the establishment of the Commonwealth. None of them, if we except Milton, whose earlier poems were written at this time, can be called great; though much of their work is pleasing, abounding in fancy, and distinguished for smoothness of rhythm; yet often marred by quaint and affected diction. Some of this class of writers have received the inappropriate name of metaphysical poets —not because the science of the mind occupied their attention in any way, but because their far-fetched "conceits" came from the intellect and not from the heart. The earliest and one of the most noted of these was John Donne (1573–1631), whose verses, in spite of awkward disfigurement caused by straining after effect, show some poetic feeling. His satires, the best known of his works, are coarse and vigorous, and were much admired in their day. Donne's personal history is more interesting than his poetry. He fell in love with the daughter of Sir George More and married her without her father's consent, whereupon Sir George took her away from him and caused Donne and the friend who had given the bride away, to be thrown into prison. They were soon released, but Donne was obliged to have recourse to a long and expensive lawsuit to get his wife again, and for some years they were on the verge of starvation. A kind friend gave them a home and it would seem that the poet's family was welcome everywhere, for at a later time, when they were in distress, another friend insisted that Donne with his wife and their eleven children should live at his house. Donne went abroad with his patron, and during his absence he and his wife wrote each other every day. After some years of estrangement, Mrs. Donne's father was reconciled to the marriage, and made his daughter and her husband an allowance, which the latter voluntarily relinquished after his wife's death.

Donne had long been importuned, by the king and others who knew his talents, to enter the church. He hesitated from fear of unfitness, but at last yielded and became a "fashionable" preacher. From this time he lived in comfort.

His poems are unequal in merit. One of the most charming of his many love-songs is that addressed to his wife when she pleaded against his leaving her to travel on the continent. It begins:

> Sweetest love, I do not go for weariness of thee,
> Nor in hope the world can show a fitter love for me.

Though Shakespeare still lies at Stratford where he was originally buried, he has a monument in the crowded "Poet's Corner" of Westminster Abbey; and Donne, in a fanciful plea for room in the sacred corner for the bones of the greatest of poets, penned these touching lines of appeal that the elder tenants should make place for their later brother:

> Renownèd Chaucer, lie a thought more nigh
> To rare Beaumont; and learned Beaumont lie
> A little nearer Spenser, to make room
> For Shakespeare, in your threefold, fourfold tomb.

When Donne drew near his end he ordered a coffin to be made, in which was placed a board of the length of his body. He next caused himself to be wrapped in his winding-sheet as if he were dead. Being then placed upright in the coffin, he had enough of the winding-sheet unwound to show his thin, death-like face, and caused an artist thus to paint his portrait. This picture he kept in sight as long as he lived.

The day after Donne's burial some unknown person wrote with a coal on the wall above his grave:

> Reader, I am to let thee know,
> Donne's body only lies below:
> For could the grave his soul comprise,
> Earth would be richer than the skies.

Another satirist, contemporary with Donne, was Joseph Hall (1574–1656), Bishop of Norwich, who is also distinguished for his sermons and other religious writings. His prose-style is rich in imagery. The following extract will give an idea of his satires, and at the same time a vivid picture of life and manners in his time:

> A gentle squire would gladly entertaine
> Into his house some trencher-chapelaine,
> Some willing man that might instruct his sons,
> And that would stand to good conditions:
> First, that he lie upon the truckle-bed,
> Whiles his young master lieth o'er his head;
> Secondly, that he do, on no default,
> Ever presume to sit above the salt;
> Third, that he never change his trencher twice;
> Fourth, that he use all common courtesies,

> Sit bare at meals, and one halfe rise and wait:
> * * * * *
> All these observed, he would contented be
> To give five marks, and winter liverie.

Sir Henry Wotton (1568–1639), whose life, by Isaak Walton, makes him in his private character so interesting to us, must be classed among the poets, though he wrote but little verse.   Like Sackville, he was too much occupied with state affairs to give much time to authorship.   He was frequently sent on foreign missions, and was devoted with chivalrous affection to the daughter of James I., that unfortunate Electress Palatine who was for a single winter Queen of Bohemia.   To her are addressed the beautiful verses beginning:

> Ye meaner beauties of the night:

Still finer is the poem called "A Happy Life," which closes the description of an ideal Christian gentleman with the words:·

> This man is freed from servile bands
> Of hope to rise or fear to fall;
> Lord of himself though not of lands,
> And having nothing, yet hath all.

George Wither (1588–1667) was one of the few poets who belonged to the Puritan interest.   In his satire "Abuses Stript and Whipt," he declaims boldly against the vices of the age, which was that of James I.   For this he was thrown into prison, but he kept on with his writing and after a while was released.   When the Civil War broke out (1642), he raised a troop of horse and fought against the king. Being taken prisoner he was in danger of being hanged as a rebel; but Sir John Denham, a brother poet and a royalist, good-naturedly interceded for him, saying that he wanted to have the pleasure of knowing that there was one man in England who wrote worse verses than he did.   This joke probably saved Wither's life, and he lived on to a good old age. Whatever Denham might say, we can not deny the name of poet to the man who wrote the song containing the often quoted words:

> Shall I, wasting in despair,
> Die because a woman's fair?
> *   *   *   *   *   *
> If she be not so to me,
> What care I how fair she be?

The name of William Browne (1590–1645), author of "Britannia's Pastorals," must be included among the poets of this epoch. He is scarcely more than a name to us, and his "Pastorals" have made no great impression on the literature of his country. The descriptions of natural scenery are good, and Browne seems to have caught from Spenser such inspiration as he possesses.

Of poets, Giles and Phineas Fletcher come next in order of time. They were brothers, and cousins of John Fletcher, the dramatist who wrote with Beaumont. The first-named wrote religious allegories; the second is best known by a poem called "The Purple Island," which island is man's body.

A fine Scottish poet of the same time is William Drummond of Hawthornden (1585–1649). He had a delicate fancy and strong religious feeling, and his "Flowers of Zion" are still readable. He wrote also some good sonnets.

The greatest of the religious poets of the seventeenth century was George Herbert (1593–1633). He belonged to the noble family of Pembroke and was, therefore, connected with Sir Philip Sidney, the "mirror of knighthood." It is not difficult to trace in both cousins the characteristics which distinguished this illustrious family. Sincerity, consideration for others, uprightness, loyalty both to sovereign and to principle (not always easy to practise, in the days of Elizabeth and James I.), disinterestedness, generosity—all these were to be found equally in the gallant soldier and the meek divine. In the writing of each we see the delicacy, the refinement, the sentiment of a true poet, together with the quaint forms of expression which belonged rather to the age than to the individual. At Cambridge, Herbert did himself so much credit that King James declared that he took him to be "the jewel of that university." It is curious to remark that at this time the young man's heart was somewhat set upon worldly vanities. Even his admiring biographer, Isaak Walton, says: "His genteel humor for clothes seemed to prove that he set too much value on his parts and parentage, and if he showed any error it was that he kept himself too much retired and at too great a distance from all his inferiors." As may be supposed, this youthful characteristic entirely disappeared when he became the saintly man whose memory all delight to honor.

At thirty-three, Herbert resolved to devote himself to the church. After some years, he became rector of the little parish church at Bemerton (the next to the smallest in England), where the last three years of his life were passed. Here he wrote his "Temple," a collection of short poems connected with the religious life, in which there is the true poetic feeling, marred by the affectations which seem to have been inseparable from the verses written during the early years of the seventeenth century. We should be the poorer, however, without "The Temple," which is full of noble thoughts, and contains many fine images. Here are some detached verses:

> Sweet day, so cool, so calm, so bright,
>   The bridal of the earth and sky,
> The dews shall weep thy fall to-night,
>   For thou must die.

> Judge not the preacher, for he is thy judge.
>   *   *   *   *   *
> The worst speak something good; if all want sense,
> God takes a text and preacheth Patience.

Herbert's marriage reminds us of Hooker's—with a difference. A friend of his, named Danvers, told Herbert he should like to have him marry one of his nine daughters; whichever one he chose, but Mr. Danvers wished it might be Jane. A meeting was arranged between Herbert and this young lady; the rest of the story is best told in his own words:

At this time a mutual affection entered into both their hearts, as a conqueror enters into a surprised city, and made there such laws and resolutions as neither party was able to resist; insomuch that on the third day from this first interview Jane Danvers changed her name into Herbert.

She made an excellent wife, and Herbert, though marrying in haste, did not repent at leisure.

The end of so much goodness and sweet contentment came only too soon, the poet-preacher dying of consumption at the age of thirty-nine.

Lord Herbert of Cherbury (1581–1648), an older brother of George, was a statesman of distinction in the reigns of Elizabeth and James I. and a writer of philosophical and historical works. Among the latter there are a historic biography of Henry VIII. and an autobiography which throws much light on the history of his own time.

Next to Herbert, Francis Quarles (1592–1644) holds the highest place among the religious writers of the day, and his "Divine Emblems" are still found among the well-read books in old-fashioned libraries. Being on the royalist side he was ruined in the Civil War, and his death is thought to have been hastened by the destruction of his choice books and rare manuscripts, which became the prey of the Puritans.

Richard Crashaw (1613–50) who belongs to a somewhat later period, may be mentioned here as a religious poet, making a triad with Herbert and Quarles. He was brought up in the English Church, but afterward became a Roman Catholic.

His "Steps to the Temple" show great sweetness and a fine ear, although in richness and variety they are inferior to Herbert's "Temple." Crashaw wrote also secular poems, among the most graceful of which is the one addressed to an imaginary lady-love, beginning:

> Whoe'er she be,
> That not impossible she
> That shall command my heart and me:

He wishes her

> A face that's best
> By its own beauty drest.
> *   *   *   *   *
> Sidneian showers
> Of sweet discourse, whose powers
> Can crown old Winter's head with flowers.
>
> Days, that need borrow
> No part of their good morrow
> From a forespent night of sorrow.
> *   *   *   *   *
> Life that doth send
> A challenge to its end
> And when it comes, say "Welcome, friend."

Then if the reader knows

> Her, that dares be
> What these lines wish to see,
> I seek no further; it is she.

In the verses of Robert Herrick (1591–1674), we find a singular mixture of the secular and the religious spirit. Some in the former style are marvels of grace and airy fancy; others might better never have been written. He was a clergyman, and in later life repented of these latter and would gladly have blotted them out. His religious poems show deep feeling, but he could never shake off the habits of thought of his frivolous days. There is a story that he once threw his written sermon down among the congregation, abusing them for their inattention. *Per* *contra*, it is said that he was "much beloved by the gentry." Probably none of the gentry were present when he thus gave way to his temper. In 1648, the year of Cromwell's triumph and the beginning of the Commonwealth, being a royalist, he was turned out of his living, and went to London, where he had better company, but less to live on. Here he published a collection of short poems (many of them gems), which he named "Hesperides," because they were written in the west.* His religious poems he published under the title, "Noble Numbers."

As a lyrical poet, Herrick stands unrivalled by any of his contemporaries, and, as many critics think, by any English writer. His songs, "Gather ye roses while ye may," "To Blossoms," and "To Daffodils," find a place in every collection and will never grow out of date. Herrick lived to be eighty-three years old; a circumstance very remarkable when it is remembered that no other poet of note, born about the same time or within the thirty years following, lived much beyond middle life, except George Wither, who died at the good old age of seventy-nine.†

Thomas Carew (1589–1639) wrote many pretty lyrics, of which those best known are the two following:

> Ask me no more where Jove bestows
> When June is past, the fading rose, etc.

> He that loves a rosy cheek,
> Or a coral lip admires, etc.

Most of his poems, however, though graceful, do not rise above mediocrity. They were great favorites at the court of Charles I.

Sir John Suckling (1609–42), a younger poet, was also

---

* Hesperia was the old Greek name for any unknown land lying to the westward.

† Carew died at 50; Quarles at 52; Herbert at 39; Suckling at 32; Denham at 53; Crashaw at 37; Lovelace at 40.

read and quoted by the same gay set of pleasure-lovers. He had a lively fancy and some humor, the latter quality showing itself in his "Ballad on a Wedding," where he describes the impressions made on a rustic by the sight of London festivities; and in his lines beginning:

> Why so pale and wan, fond lover?
> Prythee, why so pale?
> Will, when looking well can't move her,
> Looking ill prevail?

Sir John, an exception to most of the poets of his time, was born to a fortune, but this did not save him from adversity when his hour came. Two accounts exist of his probable end; one says that he committed suicide on being driven from England in 1641 on account of his loyalty to the king, and the other that his death was owing to the malice of a servant who had robbed him, and, wishing to delay pursuit, left a penknife in Sir John's boot which inflicted a wound in the heel causing his death. Either way, it was a tragic end for one who had been the centre of a brilliant society and noted for his wit, gayety and liberality. A stanza from the "Ballad on a Wedding" will give an idea of its quality. The countryman is describing the bride:

> Her feet beneath her petticoat
> Like little mice stole in and out,
>   As if they feared the light:
> And oh! she dances such a way!
> No sun upon an Easter day
>   Is half so fine a sight.

The song quoted before is from one of Suckling's dramas.

We can not better close the list of "cavalier poets" than with the name of Richard Lovelace (1618–58), a type of the entire class. Of extraordinary personal beauty, with a university education, living a gay, thoughtless, social life until his loyalty to Charles I. brought him into trouble, we follow him through many vicissitudes until we see him dying, poor, neglected and dissipated, in an alley near Shoe Lane.

Lovelace, being an ardent royalist, was selected by the county of Kent to deliver a petition to the Long Parliament praying that the king might be restored to his rights. For this he was thrown into prison, where he wrote the beautiful song entitled "To Althea, from Prison," in which occur the lines:

> Stone walls do not a prison make
> Nor iron bars a cage.

He was released on heavy bail, and spent his fortune in vain efforts to help the royal cause. When this became hopeless he left his country and took service in the French army, being wounded in the battle of Dunkirk. It was before setting out on this enterprise that he wrote the exquisite lines "To Lucasta," (his lady-love), excusing himself for leaving her. We give the last verse:

> Yet this inconstancy is such
> As you, too, shall adore:
> I could not love thee, dear, so much,
> Loved I not honor more!

Alas! A false rumor that he had died of his wounds reached the ears of his Lucasta (Lucy Sacheverell), and she married another person. On his return to England he was again imprisoned. Released after the king's death, but disappointed in his love, shorn of his fortune, and broken in health and spirits, he sank miserably into the grave, a sad contrast to his brilliant early prime.

In considering these "minor poets," we must keep in mind, as a grim background to a variegated picture, the condition of the times they lived in; times of political upheaval, revolt against misgovernment, civil war, the beheading of a king, the establishment of parliamentary supremacy followed by a dictatorship, and the final restoration of monarchy in a modified and limited form. The wonder is, not that there was so little intellectual activity during those troublesome years, but that there was so much; especially as the triumphant party, the Puritans, were quite out of sympathy with such trivial matters as secular poetry. They chanted the Psalms as they marched to battle; but sentiment they looked upon as a snare of the devil.

Yet the bold, freedom-loving Englishmen kept on in their way, refusing to be carried away by bigoted enthusiasm or awed to silence by fear of the consequences of their utterances.

CHAPTER XIX.

SEVENTEENTH-CENTURY POETS, CONTINUED.

IN trying to preserve some order of time among writers of a century whose different parts were so widely separated in interest by the period of the Commonwealth and the years of struggle preceding it, the clearest method has seemed to be the grouping together of those most known and talked about at the same time.

William Davenant (1606–68) wrote a long, tedious poem called "Gondibert," but is better known by his efforts to revive the drama, which had languished under the Puritan Commonwealth. He is regarded as the connecting link between the Elizabethan dramatists and those of Charles II.'s time. He was imprisoned for being a royalist, but when he was released he returned to his old business as play-writer and theatre manager, and actually contrived to have plays acted even in the face of the strict Puritan laws, by blending music with them and calling them operas. Italian opera had lately been introduced into France, where it had become very popular; and Davenant's, although but a far-away imitation of it, passed muster as a musical entertainment.

After the Restoration, Davenant was again in favor. He had been made poet-laureate in 1637, on the death of Ben Jonson; this office was now restored to him, and he was appointed manager of a company called "The Duke of York's Players." In his patent a clause was inserted, stating that "Whereas the women's parts in plays have hitherto been acted by men in the habits of women, at which some have taken offence; we do permit and give leave for the time to come that all women's parts be acted by women on the stage."

It is said that Davenant's life was saved by the intercession of Milton under the Puritan rule, and also that the former returned the favor after the accession of Charles II. when the greater poet was a fugitive. The anecdotes may or may not be true; but it is pleasant to fancy these political opponents meeting on the common ground of interest in literature and treating one another as brothers.

Davenant seems to have regarded blank verse not as a rhythmic and splendid structure of words, having all the charm of poetry without the melodious fetters of rhyme, but as a mere dividing up of poor prose into wretched and formless lengths. Here is a specimen:

> How did the governors of the
> Severe house digest the employment my
> Request did lay upon their gravities?

Think of this awkward balderdash, as the work of a poet-laureate!

Edmund Waller (1605-87) wrote many pretty songs— "Go, lovely rose," "To a Girdle," and some others; but his character does not command our respect, and its shallowness shows itself in his writings. He could be equally flattering to King and Protector; and when Charles II. laughingly told him that his verses on the death of Cromwell were better than the address of congratulation to himself on his accession, the writer met him with the ready answer: "Poets succeed better with fiction than in truth, your Majesty." Waller's mother was a sister of John Hampden, and his sympathies would naturally have been given to the popular side; but although he espoused this cause at first, he was constant to none, and changed his allegiance as often as suited his convenience. He lived to be eighty-two years old, and shortly before his death wrote the poem in which these fine lines occur:

> Clouds of affection from our younger eyes
> Conceal that emptiness which age descries:
> The soul's dark cottage, battered and decayed,
> Lets in new light through chinks which time has made.
>
> Stronger by weakness, wiser men become,
> As they draw near to their eternal home;
> Leaving the old, both worlds at once they view,
> That stand upon the threshold of the new.

Of Waller's excellence as a critic, we may form some idea by his remarks about Milton. He says: "The blind old poet hath published a tedious poem on the fall of man. If its length be not considered as a merit, it hath no other."

Sir John Denham (1615–68), the good-natured poet whose joke saved the life of his political opponent, Wither, wrote a long descriptive poem about "Cooper's Hill" (a beautiful place near Windsor), which received high praise from Dryden. Posterity, however, has not borne out this good opinion, finding the verses cold and formal. One quatrain certainly deserves to be remembered. It occurs in an address to the river Thames:

> Oh, could I flow like thee, and make thy stream
> My great example, as it is my theme !
> Though deep, yet clear, though gentle, yet not dull ;
> Strong without rage, without o'erflowing, full.

Denham wrote a poor tragedy called "The Sophy," founded on a Turkish story.

Henry Vaughan (1621–95), a Welshman and one of the minor poets, wrote many devotional poems, collected under the title "Silex Scintillans," some of which are equal to Herbert's in purity of feeling and beauty of imagery. Here is a beautiful stanza on the departed:

> He that hath found some fledged bird's nest, may know
>   At first sight, if the bird be flown;
> But what fair dell or grove he sings in now,
>   That is to him unknown.

Abraham Cowley (1618–67), a precocious boy who published a volume of poems at the age of thirteen, was thought by many persons of his own day a better poet than Milton. Time has reversed this judgment, though Cowley's poems still read well in comparison with those of most of his contemporaries. He has no delicate little gems such as we find in the verses of Herrick, Waller or Lovelace; but his pieces have a sustained quality, and some of them are very pleasing. He is a votary of the "metaphysical" school which Donne made fashionable, and even his love-poems show no depth of feeling. His most ambitious work is the "Davideis," an unfinished poem intended for an epic on the life of David, king of Israel. It is written in heroic verse (ten-syllabled iambic metre), and shows a correct ear, but the execution is dreary and the treatment uninteresting. His fame as a poet must rest on his shorter pieces.

It is as an essayist, however, that Cowley takes his stand among the best writers of his day. Without the terseness of Bacon, and on the other hand without the prolixity and affectation of Browne, he gives us a foretaste of the grace and versatility of Addison. The essays are still interesting, and show the author to have been a man of learning, refined tastes and good sense.

Cowley was, like most of the poets of his day, a staunch royalist, and proved the sincerity of his attachment to

9

the cause by accompanying the royal family into exile in France. Upon the Restoration, he naturally expected some recompense for all this labor; but Charles II. preferred to spend his money on new favorites rather than to reward old services, and Cowley was suffered to end his life in poverty. When he died, the king paid him the compliment of saying that he had not left behind him a better man in England, and the poet was honored with a tomb and monument in Westminster Abbey, where he lies buried near Chaucer and Spenser. "He asked for bread and they gave him a stone."

Andrew Marvell (1620–78), at one time assistant-secretary to Milton while the latter was employed by Cromwell's government, was one of the few poets on the Puritan side. He is most famous as a satirist, not sparing, in his keen ridicule, either the king or the royal party, generally. If Charles II. had not been good-natured as well as profligate he would not have endured couplets like these:

> Ah Tudor! Ah Tudor! of Stuarts enough;
> None ever reigned like old Bess in the ruff.
> But canst thou devise when things will be mended?
> When the reign of the line of the Stuarts is ended.

The court-party would gladly have secured for their own side one who wielded so sharp a pen, and Lord Danby, the Lord Treasurer, was sent by the king with offers of money and position if Marvell would come over to his side. It was all useless; the old Puritan stood firm, and continued to satirize the government, in prose and verse, to the day of his death.

Marvell closes the short list of Puritan poets. Although his name and that of Wither pale beside the mighty one of Milton, all three did good service to their cause.

The most celebrated satirist on the royalist side, in fact, almost the only one, was Samuel Butler (1612–80), author of "Hudibras." He was the son of a farmer, and picked up a good education without going through a college course, though he studied for a short time at Cambridge. While still young he entered the service of Sir Samuel Luke, a Puritan justice-of-the-peace, whom he is supposed to ridicule in his verses. After the Restoration, Butler gave vent to his long suppressed feelings in the famous satire, which instantly became popular though it brought him no money. Charles II. carried about a copy of it in his pocket and often quoted from it, but he did nothing for the author, who died in poverty and obscurity a year or two after the publication of the last part of his poem.

"Hudibras" (which the writer rhymes with *ass*, thus settling the pronunciation of the name) is a pompous Presbyterian knight who starts out with his squire, Ralpho, to seek adventures and put down cavaliers. The idea is evidently suggested by the story of Don Quixote and Sancho Panza. They have many encounters with the Cavalier party, generally coming out worst; and the overflowing wit and bubbling humor prevented the nine cantos from becoming wearisome to the earliest readers. It is impossible to give an idea of the fun which appealed to the readers of that time; but a few couplets will show the keen wit of the author:

> What makes all doctrines plain and clear?
> About two hundred pounds a year.
> And that which was proved true before
> Prove false again? Two hundred more.

> Ah me! what perils do environ
> The man who meddles with cold iron!

> I am not now in fortune's power;
> He that is down can fall no lower.

> To swallow gudgeons ere they're catched,
> And count their chickens ere they're hatched.

> For those that fly may fight again,
> Which he can never do that's slain.

> He that complies against his will
> Is of his own opinion still.

CHAPTER XX.

JOHN MILTON.

IN a strictly chronological arrangement, the name of John Milton (1608–74) would have taken its place before several of the poets already mentioned; but Milton stands so emphatically alone in his generation, belonging to no group and to be compared with no other poet, that it has seemed best to consider him separately. Although not an aged man when he died, his life falls naturally into three parts, each marked by literary achievements which of themselves would have been enough to fill the record of an ordinary man and win for him enviable renown.

Milton is classed by all critics in all lands as one of the world's great poets. Macaulay ranked his and Bunyan's as the only two creative minds of the eighteenth century; and most authorities would consider this coupling of the names together as a greater compliment to the latter than the former, great as was the "inspired tinker." Both were "Non-comformists"; that is, in a certain sense Puritans; but Milton was so much a lover of liberty that he disclaimed absolute subjection even to Cromwell's government; as witness his refusal to apply for a license to publish his pamphlet on divorce, or his "Areopagitica" or plea for entire freedom of the press, which was, in fact an attack upon the Puritan parliament itself. He was an Independent to the uttermost.

It is one of the curious anomalies of the time that Milton's grandfather was a rigid Roman Catholic, and disinherited John, the Puritan poet's father, because he became an Episcopalian. The latter took up the business of scrivener, or writer of law-papers; but he must have had peculiar ability or some capital now unknown, for he was also a professional money-lender, and was able to educate his sons handsomely, to retire with a competence, and to make the poet an allowance sufficient to supply his moderate needs. Milton's life, up to thirty, was spent in leisure and tranquility; at school, at Cambridge University, at his father's pleasant country home in Horton, and in Continental travel. This is the time of the production of the lighter and more graceful of his poems; themselves of a quality fit to make his name immortal, even if he had not lived to write "Paradise Lost." The second period of his life includes the time of the Civil War and the Commonwealth; from the opening of the Long Parliament in 1640 to the restoration of monarchy in 1660. During this time he wrote chiefly political and theological works; he being a supporter of the Puritan cause. He lived fourteen years after the Restoration; and to this period of blindness, old age and comparative neglect we owe (beside some exquisite sonnets) "Paradise Lost," "Paradise Regained" and the grand drama of "Samson Agonistes," or the dying Samson.

He was born in Bread Street, London, and received the most careful training. As a boy he was an eager student, a leaning which his father never checked, even when it led him (at twelve years old) to pore over his books habitually till after midnight. This, considering the wretchedness of the candles and lamps of those days, seems to account for the failure of his eyesight, which led to total blindness thirty years later. At sixteen he entered Christ's College, Cambridge, where he passed eight studious years. His fellow-students nicknamed him "the lady," to which he retorted that he wished they could as readily doff their ass's ears as he could get rid of whatever of the woman there might be in him. There is a portrait of him at twelve years old which is only the first of many, all showing beauty and grace, and those of his late years, a majestic dignity.

He indicates in one of his sonnets, that though his eyes are sightless they are not disfigured.

Milton was among the writers called precocious; and in his case (as seems to be the universal rule) precocity showed itself in poetry. At twelve he wrote the admirable versification of the one hundred and thirty-sixth Psalm, beginning:

> Let us with a gladsome mind
> Praise the Lord, for he is kind:

and before he was twenty-one, his beautiful hymn on the Nativity. He spent six more years of study living at home with his father, who would have liked to see John take up some specific occupation; yet never let his not doing so interfere with their loving relations. The father was an accomplished musician, and from him the son took that taste for melody and harmony which was a delight and solace to the end of his life.

"The Masque of Comus," the best known of Milton's early poems, is one of the spectacular plays, popular in those days, which were played and sung at country-houses, out of doors or within, by hosts and guests dressed to assume allegorical characters. A sadder subject brought out a still more beautiful poem. "Lycidas," the most famous death-song in our language, was written on the occasion of the drowning of his friend Edward King while crossing the Irish sea.

Milton's younger brother had now married and was living with their father; which, greatly to his delight, left John free to travel abroad. At Florence, he visited old Galileo, still under ban for the heresy of saying that the earth moves.

The Civil War broke out while Milton was abroad; and patriotic duty turned his steps at once homeward, where he served the cause of freedom with a pen which was more effective than any sword or matchlock wielded at Edgehill. His father and brother had moved away from Horton, and their new home was too far from the centre of activity; therefore he hired humble lodgings in London, and took several pupils to teach; all children of his own friends. His school was of the most toilsome and painstaking kind, and one of the scholars has left a picture of the vast mass of knowledge which was forced upon them by their exacting master. "Hard study and spare diet" was the plan, and seven days' work each week the stint; for Sunday was given up to theology.

At the same time he was writing stoutly against prelacy and tyranny; and his powers of vituperation were great. Not long afterward he married a girl of seventeen (half his own age), whose maiden name was Mary Powell. She was the daughter of a staunch royalist; and as was the fashion among the Cavaliers, her home had been one of great gayety. Mistress Milton quickly tired of domestic duty and dullness, "plain living and high thinking," and almost as soon as the honey-moon was over she went off on a visit to her own people. Milton, absorbed in his work, did not miss her very much; but when the time set for her return passed, and his repeated letters asking her to come home brought no answers, he began to see that his wife wished to make the separation final. At this time he wrote certain pamphlets on divorce, advocating a change in the laws which should provide a remedy for such injuries as his.

In 1645, two years after the marriage, the battle of Naseby put the royalists at the bottom and the independents at the top of affairs; a state of things having among its consequences the return of Mistress Milton, and, after a short interval (the Powell mansion having been sold for debt) the arrival of the whole family, who were quartered on the long-suffering son-in-law. A letter, written by him to a friend in Rome, clearly shows the dreadful nature of the infliction. At his house (which stood in Barbican, a street in London), Mr. Powell died;

and a few months later Milton's own lovable and beloved father. Mrs. Powell saved what she could from the wreck of the family estate, and in course of time found another home, leaving Milton once more alone in his own house with his wife and his little girls. The school had probably been given up on the return of Mrs. Milton, if not before.

Milton's help had already been of great worth to the Commonwealth, and he now wrote continually in its support. Beside his political pamphlets he wrote a few sonnets; and for the first time a collection of his poems was made and published; including, among some less important, "Comus," "Lycidas," "L'Allegro," and "Il Penseroso." He also began to frame the scheme for "Paradise Lost," as is shown by some memoranda he has left suggesting

> Things unattempted yet in prose or rhyme.

After the beheading of the king, Cromwell's government became stable and recognized, and it was then that Milton was appointed to the office of Foreign Secretary and found use for his elegant accomplishments, the knowledge of Latin and several continental tongues. His controversial writings of the period show an acrimony, a coarse abusiveness, that seem inconsistent with his refined and gentlemanly nature; and we can only attribute it to the violence and bitterness of the time. One of these belligerent utterances was the proximate cause of his blindness. His sight had long been failing, and his physician told him that if he persisted in his task of writing a certain pamphlet (a reply to an attack by Salmasius of Holland) he would risk total blindness, but persist he did and the blindness followed. In one of his sonnets he glories that he lost his eyes in liberty's defence.

His better-known sonnet on his blindness is perhaps the grandest production of that form of verse in any language.

When I consider how my light is spent
Ere half my days, in this dark world and wide,
And that one talent, which is death to hide,
Lodged with me useless, though my soul more bent
To serve therewith my Maker, and present
My true account, lest He returning chide;
"Doth God exact day-labor, light denied?"
I fondly ask: But Patience, to prevent
That murmur, soon replies, "God doth not neea
Either man's work or His own gifts: Who best
Bear his mild yoke, they serve him best: His state
Is kingly; thousands at His bidding speed,
And post o'er land and ocean without rest;
They also serve who only stand and wait.

He still remained Latin-secretary to Cromwell; helped (among others) by his brother poet and warm friend Andrew Marvell. A year or two later his wife died, leaving him with three young daughters, the oldest only seven years old. He engaged a teacher for them, but refused to have them taught any other language than English, saying that one tongue was enough for a woman. The cruelty and wrong of this became apparent later; for when the girls were called upon to read aloud to their blind father, for hour after hour, page after page of Latin, not understanding a word of what they were reading, human nature could not bear it, and the love that should have bound father and daughters together was lost. It is a pity to have to give up the pleasant tradition that "Paradise Lost" was written by his daughters at the blind poet's dictation; but it is only a fiction. The records left of the daughters' conduct—especially that of the two elder—is shocking; and in his will their father speaks of them as his "unkind children," "they having been very undutiful to me." (He was then living with his third wife, and the will was in her favor.) After some years of unhappiness the daughters went away to learn embroidery, whereby they maintained themselves. They never married, and therefore (as seems usual with poets) the line came to an untimely end.

At the restoration of Charles II., Milton's name is known to have been on the proscribed list, and it is supposed that his life was only saved by the intervention of some one having influence at court (whether Davenant or another) who had love for Milton or poetry. It would be hard, one would think, to lead a helpless blind poet to the block; yet Milton's words against the Stuarts had been so many, so bitter and so powerful, that the poet himself must have been surprised at finding his life spared. In fact, only a few were beheaded except those personally concerned in the condemnation and death of Charles I.

His third wife was a very capable woman, who made the last eleven years of his life quite comfortable; in spite of an extreme narrowness of means, caused by a heavy fine exacted at the Restoration, and the loss of his house in the great fire of London in 1666. We can not but fancy that there was a knot of the old Puritan worthies, bound together by a community of memories, of principles and of misfortunes, who stood manfully together in adversity as they had in battle and triumph; and that in such a society, John Milton could never be forlorn though sightless, in misery though poor. Indeed, we learn that he had several devoted friends, both old and young, who came and sat with him, read to him, wrote for him, so that he complained no more of loneliness.

His older works may have given him some income at this time; but for "Paradise Lost"—one of the world's greatest sun-bursts of poetry—he received just £5 in hand and £5 more for each additional 1500 copies; payments which reached £20 in all!

It would be impossible to describe "Paradise Lost" and superfluous to praise it. It simply may be said that no English education, no cultivation attained by any English-speaking person, can be held to approach completeness which does not include the knowledge of that greatest of English poems.

CHAPTER XXI.

BUNYAN. THE DIARISTS.

JOHN BUNYAN (1628–88) holds a dual place in the world's regard; first as a martyr—almost an apostle—of religion and morals; second, as a genius in literature. He was born at Elston in Bedford-shire. His father was a tinker, which in those days was nearly synonymous with vagrant, for tinkers in general were disreputable wanderers like the gypsies, if not like them beggars and pilferers. But Bunyan's father seems to have had a home of his own, and to have sent his son to the village-school—at the serious outlay of fourpence a month, for in those days education was a rare luxury to the poor.

Bunyan early felt a strong religious bent; as was shown by fits of morbid remorse for trivial faults, and strenuous, though often ineffectual, attempts to cure them; yet the chief sins from which sprang this remorse were dancing, ringing the church-bells, playing "tip-cat" (a harmless boyish diversion) and reading the "profane" romance of Sir Bevis of Southampton; a fabulous knight whose exploits were like those of the better known myth Guy of Warwick. The last-named sin we are prone to pardon—if not praise —for two reasons: In the first place the world in general has long since ceased to condemn the reading of fiction as such, provided it contain nothing debasing to morals or destructive to piety; and, second, it must have been the power gained in this way that enabled Bunyan to construct, in later years, the immortal allegory of the "Pilgrim's Progress."

As to the "ringing," there is something significant and almost pathetic in that. It was not any unlawful or outrageous practice. It was merely a joyful peal on the church-bells given out on holidays and Sunday evenings, as a kind of serenade to the retiring people. But to the Puritans (of whom Bunyan was one) all amusements were sinful, undevout, worldly, and therefore unworthy of God's people. So poor Bunyan, torn between natural gayety and imposed restraint, says:

Before this I had taken much delight in ringing, but my conscience beginning to be tender, I thought such practice vain, and therefore forced myself to leave it; yet my mind hankered; wherefore I would go to the steeple-house and look on, though I durst not ring.

At about seventeen he enlisted as a soldier in the parliamentary army that was fighting against Charles I., the Roundheads against the Cavaliers. This experience was another help to his pen in later years. His pages abound in camps and fortresses, and drums and trumpets calling Christians to arms; as well as giants, dragons, lions and enchanted caves and castles. In his "Holy War" (which it is said would be the best allegory in literature if he had not also written the "Pilgrim's Progress"), his description of the losing and retaking of the city of Mansoul shows the thoughts, knowledge and experience of a soldier in Cromwell's army.

After the end of his military career he married, at about nineteen, the woman who became the good genius of his life. Whatever was best in him she fostered, and from all that was evil she weaned him by the charm of her gentleness and purity. We lose our regret at his giving up the dancing, tip-cat and bell-ringing when we learn that he was not so much driven from them by his own bigotry as drawn from them by her gentle influence. At about this time he experienced such a spasm of pious fervor as amounted nearly to what is known as "religious mania," and almost unsettled his reason, although this did not show itself in regard to the common affairs of life; in them his conduct was uniformly discreet. He felt as certain of the physical presence of the devil as did Luther in his prison on the Wartburg. He thought himself another Judas; and, as he tells us in his autobiography, expected to burst asunder in the midst like his prototype. Spiritual peace followed the storm, but it was years before his mind recovered its tone.

His pastor in the Bedford chapel (Baptist) dying, Bunyan, who had shown himself powerful in prayer and exhortation, unwillingly became a preacher; and his intense fervor made him a power in the work. Illiterate he was—but so were his hearers, and zeal more than atoned for all deficiencies.

The law forbade any man to preach who had not been regularly ordained, and the poor tinker, the self-taught, self-made exhorter, though during the Commonwealth he had been unmolested, fell under the royal ban in the first year of the restoration. The king forbade him to speak, but his conscience forbade him to keep silence; brute force prevailed over mere conscious rectitude and Bunyan spent nearly twelve years in Bedford jail. His prison stood upon a bridge, and his cell was said to be damp enough "to make the moss grow upon the prisoner's eyebrows." It was so dark that it was only by long habit he could work. Yet work he must to support his wife and children. As the tinker's trade was impossible in confinement, the kind jailor helped him to an expedient through which a pittance might be earned; it was the putting tags on stay-laces; and the poor prisoner furnished yearly many thousands of these to the hawkers or peddlers. What made his case the harder was that one of his children was blind; a thought that added the last pang of anguish to his imprisonment. Said he: "Poor child! I can not bear that even the wind should blow on thee; and now thou must suffer cold and hunger, thou must beg, thou must be beaten—and yet," he added, "I *must* do it." This is pathetic, tear-compelling, even after the lapse of centuries.

Bunyan could not be idle. He drew his fellow-prisoners together in a religious society in which he was pastor, and labored to do them good. He had for his only reading a Bible, Fox's "Book of Martyrs," and one or two other religious books; these he read over and over until he knew them almost by heart. His one relaxation was indulged in by stealth; a recreation which proved also an immortal creation; the writing of the first part of the "Pilgrim's Progress."

His own account of the way in which his book grew is most interesting. He says:

> When at first I took my pen in hand
> Thus for to write, I did not understand
> That I at all should make a little book
> In such a mode. Nay, I had undertook
> To make another, which, when almost done,
> Before I was aware, I this begun.
> And thus it was. I writing of the way
> And race of saints in this our gospel-day,
> Fell suddenly into an allegory
> About their journey and the way to glory
> In more than twenty things which I set down;
> This done, I twenty more had in my crown
> And they again began to multiply
> Like sparks that from the coals of fire do fly.

Looked at from any point of view, the "Pilgrim's Progress" is one of the most remarkable works of imagination ever produced. That a man who had read so little should show such varied invention was strange; but that he should be capable of a sustained flight of creative fancy, where nothing is forced or out of place, and where each illustration has the aptness usually found only in a practised writer, is wonderful indeed.

When his book was finished he showed it to several of his pious friends. Some liked it, perceiving at once its unique merit; while others were shocked at it. The Lord's people, they thought, ought not to wish truth offered to them in so frivolous a form, nor enjoy it when it did not come in the shape of sermons, psalms and pious dissertations. But the work was done; the lamp was lighted and burns on, now and forever.

In 1672, a law was passed by which the restrictions on irregular preaching were removed or modified, and he stepped out of the dismal jail to light and life; even in a few years to ease and renown. Yet nothing disturbed the even tenor of his way. He kept on preaching, talking and working for good. He published in all sixty books, large and small. He went constantly from place to place, stirring up the people to well-doing; and showed himself especially strong in the ending of quarrels. It was while engaged on one of these errands of righteousness that he brought on the illness that caused his death. He rode a long distance to plead with an angry father the cause of a disinherited son; he prevailed; then he rode back home in a pouring rain which drenched him to the skin. A fever followed, of which he died in a few days.

So passed away one of the most striking, large-hearted, admirable, lovable figures in literary history. The picture of that humble, unlettered worker, soldier, preacher, prisoner; "The Shakespeare of Theology," as some enthusiast has called him, toiling and preaching in his jail, tagging the staylaces for the few pence it would earn for the dear ones at home, thinking now of the blind darling out of his sight as he was out of hers, now of the haps and mishaps of Christian and Hopeful, and always of his duties to God and his fellow-men—the picture once impressed upon the soul can never be effaced; and one feels a glow of thankfulness that his life ended in peace and honor, instead of what is, alas, more usual, martyrdom.

About 1650 some new kinds of writing became popular; for instance the "diary," a personal record of current events. This gave rise to a class of writers known as "the diarists," of whom John Evelyn (1620–1706) and Samuel Pepys* (1633–1703) were the chief exemplars. Each of them was a man of good social standing, each wrote several books of which all but one are now forgotten, and each wrote one (quite worthless when written) which will endure for ages, growing in value as the years pass. Then, too, of each it may be said "a better man might be better spared"; several greater writers would have caused less of a blank in literature if they had left their works unwritten.

The reason of this seeming paradox is to be found in the diarists' choice of a subject, accidental as that choice was in each case. Neither of their diaries was written with any idea of publication. The choice happened to fall upon the common things about them, the actual occurrences of every-day life—things too trivial for the attention of poet, essayist, dramatist, historian or scientific writer. In our day this photographic view of life and manners is embalmed in the realistic novel; but that is the invention of a later time than the age of "the diarists," and if they had not (unconsciously) caught and transcribed the scenes they lived in, those scenes would have perished from the world with the actors in them. Of such writers as Evelyn, Pepys and Boswell it may again be said, "They builded better than they knew."

Evelyn's life extended over eighty-six years, and included the greater part of the space filled in history by James I.,

---

* This name is now pronounced "Peps" though the fact that somebody in that day wrote it "Peeps," would tend to show that the latter gives more nearly the colloquial sound.

JOHN MILTON.

Charles I., the Commonwealth, Charles II., James II. and Queen Anne. He was an active man and a great traveler, spending at one stretch twelve years abroad. The larger part of the first volume of his diary is taken up with a description of his journey on the continent. In Holland he saw, for the first time, an elephant, and his naïve wonder and quaint description are amusing. His portrayal of continental life and manners is interesting, particularly that of the wretched galley-slaves, chained to their seats and their oars. At home he gives a glimpse of what was called "sport"—a horse baited to death with dogs, cock-fighting, dog-fighting, etc., and adds; "I was heartily weary of the rude and dirty pastime."

Near Tunbridge Wells he was set upon by foot-pads, robbed, and left bound to a tree, from which after long efforts he worked loose his swollen hands. One of the robbers was afterward captured, but he would not appear against him, being unwilling, as he says, to hang the fellow. He stayed manfully in London through the great plague of 1665, but unfortunately leaves little note of it save dreary statistics; deaths 2,000, 4,000, 5,000, and 10,000, weekly. Of the great fire of 1666 he gives a vivid description. Being like most other literary men of his time, a staunch royalist, he called Cromwell always "The Usurper," and said of his burial; "It was the joyfullest funeral I ever saw. No one cried but the dogs!"

Samuel Pepys, the second "diarist" (whom by the way Evelyn speaks of as an "extraordinary ingenious and knowing person"), was a less respectable character and far more amusing and valuable chronicler than was the other. How astonished would both have been could they have known that their names would go down to posterity linked together!

Pepys was a strange conglomeration of quite discordant elements, but on the whole, the most disreputable personage who ever betrayed himself by posthumous confessions. He was the son of a tailor, and though in that day a trade was recognized as a bar to possible reception in high society, yet he, through his tact and cleverness, found himself among almost the highest. He was a marvel of vanity, simplicity, gluttony, self-control, affectionateness, brutality, faithlessness to domestic ties, faithfulness to every other trust and duty he assumed, extravagance and economy, ignorance and scholarly tastes, generosity and meanness, piety and utter immorality, and withal of power to gain and keep public respect. He kept his journal largely in cipher; changed the cipher from time to time and wrote much of it in Spanish, to complete the disguise in which he had wrapped up his record. It was not deciphered until within the present century.

We first make his acquaintance when he is very poor, just married to a beautiful young girl and having nothing wherewith to support her. He had, however, a "patron," Lord Sandwich (a connection of Mrs. Pepys), who, early in their married life gave the young couple a little room in his house, wherein, Pepys says, his wife washed his soiled linen. In the midst of this uncertainty as to daily bread, he was offered the position of secretary to some naval officer, which he accepted with joy and filled with ability. The very next day he received a letter addressed "Samuel Pepys, Esquire" (he had before been only "Mr.") of which he says "God knows I was not a little proud." Upon taking this office he employed a ship's mate to teach him "mathematics," and one of his journal entries reads: "Up at 4 o'clock and at my multiplication-table hard, which is all the trouble I meet with in my mathematique." His advance was now steady—even rapid— and great. He became not in name, but in effectiveness, the chief power in English naval affairs; and brought the navy from a corrupt ruin to a comparatively respectable institution.   At the same time he enriched himself by peculation; and even in his diary there exists a significant entry which records a new arrangement for the victualing of Tangier, which will save the king £1,000 and gain Pepys £300 a year.   Again; he would not be "bribed to be unjust," though he was "not so squeamish as to refuse a present after."

The contents of Pepys's diary, the picture it presents of morals and manners in the last days of the Stuart dynasty, belong rather to a history of England than to a history of English literature.   In style the work has the charm—also the imperfections—of absolute, unstudied, artless frankness.   Looking toward no reader, he made a confidant of himself.   The growth of the language in its colloquial form is well illustrated; as all his talk is of clothes, food, drink, visiting and other common matters.   At a tavern where a party had ordered supper he says "we found a sallat and two or three bones of mutton for ten of us, which was very strange."   At another time he remarks "I did send for a cup of tee, a China drink which I never had drank before."   Again: "This morning observing some things not to be laid up as they should be by my girl, I took a broom and basted her till she cried extremely, which vexed me; but before I went out I left her appeased."   Being unexpectedly invited to a large dinner he says: "I not being neat in clothes, which I find a great fault in me, could not be so merry as otherwise, and this makes me remember my father's rule for a gentleman, which was to spare in all things rather than that."   (A very natural principle for a tailor!) At his cousin's house they had "a little breakfast and a very poor one, such as I could not feed on because of my she-cozen's gouty hands."   Another entry reads: "Went to the burial of my Aunt Kit, where beside us and my Uncle Fenner's family there was none of any quality, but only poor and rascally people."

Pepys had a salary attached to his office, but, as his biographer remarks: "Public men must have starved if they had not taken fees, for the king had no idea of wasting his money paying salaries." At the time of his death there was owing to him £28,000, not a penny of which was ever paid; and the original vouchers or acknowledgments of indebtedness remain in the family to this day. So we know that Samuel maintained his family, and accumulated a fortune beside, by "fees" extracted from the public by a salaried (?) officer.

Before we set the old fellow down as an unmitigated snob and fraud, we must consider the corrupt and shameless age in which he lived; and remember that he, this tailor's son, uneducated except by his own efforts, collected a curious and valuable library, and left it to Magdalen* College, Oxford, where it exists to this day as "The Pepysian Collection."

CHAPTER XXII.

MISCELLANEOUS WRITERS.   SEVENTEENTH CENTURY.

THE one contemporary historian of the Commonwealth is Edward Hyde (1608–74), afterward Earl of Clarendon, a most notable figure in the history of the time. Born of an ancient though not noble family, he belonged of right to the highest social circle, and enjoyed the society of the best minds of his time. He was bred to the law, and had already attained some distinction in his profession, when, in April, 1640, he took his seat in the Short Parliament, and during its session of three

---

* Pronounced "Maudlin," a word which has been added to our language through the fact that the Magdalen was always represented weeping.

weeks distinguished himself as an advocate of reform. In the Long Parliament, which met in September of the same year, he was equally zealous for the popular cause, and strong in his condemnation of ship-money; but when Episcopacy was threatened with downfall, he changed to the royalist side and was from that time forth one of the king's firm supporters.

After the king's cause was hopelessly lost, Clarendon occupied himself in writing his "History of the Rebellion," of which only four books were finished when he was called upon to join Prince Charles (afterward Charles II.) in his exile in France. During the years that passed before the Restoration, Hyde was constant in his efforts to provide for Charles's support, often a difficult task, and he shared in the home-coming in 1660.

He was now both Lord Chancellor and Chancellor of the Exchequer, and was soon created Earl of Clarendon. His daughter Anne married the king's brother James, Duke of York. Hyde, as minister of Charles II., sold Dunkirk to France, that the ever-grasping king might have more money at command. This was a political mistake, for it touched the national pride, and the earl was impeached by the Commons and only saved himself by voluntary exile. He spent the rest of his life in France, completing both his history and his autobiography, which together form a valuable contribution to the records of his time.

As a historian he is not impartial, but there is no doubt of his honest desire to tell the truth, though his predilections naturally cause some bias in favor of the royal partisans.

Of the Noncomformist preachers of England during the seventeenth century, none is so widely known as Richard Baxter (1615-91), author of "The Saints' Everlasting Rest," and "A Call to the Unconverted," both of which hold their place on the shelves of our religious libraries. Baxter began life as a clergyman of the Established Church; he was a friend of monarchy, and incurred the displeasure of Cromwell by his assertion of the king's rights; but he could not conscientiously take the oaths required of all clergymen after the Restoration, and felt it his duty to cast in his lot with the Dissenters. When he was seventy years old, a passage in one of his books complaining of the severities practised toward Dissenters was held to be seditious, and he was brought to trial before the infamous Judge Jeffreys, the perpetrator of "The Bloody Assizes." At the trial, Baxter and his lawyers vainly endeavored to speak in his defence. The Judge would not listen, but silenced their attempts at an answer by roaring out, "Richard, thou art an old knave! Thou hast written books enough to fill a cart, and every book is as full of sedition as an egg is full of meat. Dost thou think we will let thee poison the court?" Before such a judge it was useless to try to plead. Jeffreys imposed an enormous fine which it was impossible for Baxter to pay, and he was thrown into jail, where he lay for a year and a half, being finally released at the intercession of a friend. He lived to see the downfall of the vile magistrate, and died full of years and honors, having the satisfaction of seeing his brother Dissenters again in the enjoyment of that freedom for which he had contended so valiantly.

William Penn (1644–1718), the well-known Quaker or Friend whose name is so pleasantly connected with the settlement of our own country, wrote several religious books, the most popular being one written in prison—"No Cross, No Crown." He also published "A Brief Account of the People called Quakers," for the information of the public, who were strongly prejudiced against the Friends on account of the intemperate conduct of some of their number. This body suffered much persecution, very severe penal laws being directed against them, both in old and New England.

Robert Barclay, of Ury in Scotland, whose name is made familiar to us by Whittier's fine poem, was another Friend who "bore witness to the truth." At one time he was shut up, with others, in a prison so dark that unless the keeper left the door open they could not see to eat the food brought to them. Barclay wrote several books, the most important one being an "Apology [Vindication] for the people called in scorn, Quakers," and a spirited setting forth of their doctrine.

Of the sermon-writers who form so brilliant a galaxy during the reigns of Charles II. and William III. we can do no more than mention the names. Isaac Barrow, Robert South, Edward Stillingfleet, William Sherlock, Thomas Ken (Bishop of Bath and Wells), and John Tillotson (Archbishop of Canterbury), were all eloquent preachers. Bishop Ken wrote some beautiful hymns. Their sermons collected and published, have passed into literature.

Sir William Temple (1628–99), like Clarendon, was both a statesman and a man of letters. He negotiated, on the part of England, the celebrated Triple Alliance, and arranged the marriage, productive of such benefit to his country, of the Princess Mary and William of Orange, afterward the "William and Mary" of English history. In the intervals of a most active life, he still found time for writing his graceful "Essays," and for practising with great success his favorite recreation of gardening. He lived at Moor Park, in Surrey, where we shall hear of him again as the patron of Jonathan Swift. His "Memoirs," or recollections of the public events in which he had taken part, are instructive and interesting.

Thomas Hobbes (1588–1679), scholar, philosopher and man of science, is one of the most remarkable figures of the seventeenth century. Born in the year of the Spanish Armada, he lived for ninety-one years a busy intellectual life, continuing to write until within a very few years of his death. His writings are chiefly political, and are founded on a singular conception of the nature of government. He sets out with the idea that the groundwork of all human actions is selfishness, and argues that to keep the ferocious and selfish horde in order, a strong government is necessary; if strong, then the stronger the better, a despotic monarchy being the best of all. The work in which these theories are propounded is called the "Leviathan."

His first work was a translation of Thucydides, intended to show his countrymen the evils of a government by the people. At eighty he wrote the "Behemoth," a history of the Civil War, of course from the royalist point of view. His works were most displeasing to religious people, and to those inclining toward republicanism, but were applauded by those of the monarchical party.

The age was, naturally, rich in political writers. Sir Robert Filmer upheld the cause of monarchy to an extent that to us seems absurd. According to his theory, the king alone should make laws, the business of the parliament being only to carry out his decisions and to give advice and assistance when asked to do so.

James Harrington (1612–77), in a political work called "Oceana," claimed that all government was based on property. This pleased neither royalists nor republicans, and Cromwell ordered the publication of it to be stopped. Mrs. Claypole, the Protector's daughter, interceded for Harrington and the book was published, Cromwell at the same time remarking that what he had won by the sword he should not allow himself to be scribbled out of.

Another writer on the Republican side was Algernon Sidney (1622–83), a connection of Sir Philip's family. Though belonging to the aristocracy, he had always been a hater of tyranny. On the false testimony of a worthless politician, he was convicted of a share in the Rye-House plot (for dethroning Charles II.) and sentenced to the block, where he suffered at the same time with Lord Russell, who was beheaded with as little reason. In connection with the latter we have the name of Lady Rachel Russell, his heroic wife, whose "Letters" give her a niche in English literature, as her character and conduct place her in the rank of England's noblest women.

We may mention here the other two women whose names figure among the writers of the seventeenth century. Mrs. Catherine Phillips, known among her contemporaries as "The Matchless Orinda," and highly praised for her lovely character and domestic virtues, wrote verses that were published after her death.

Mrs. Aphra Behn (died 1689), the first woman novelist of England, was taken when very young to Surinam, in Dutch Guiana, and there witnessed some of the horrors of negro slavery, which she represented in her novel of "Oroonoko," a sort of forerunner of "Uncle Tom's Cabin." Mrs. Behn was also a dramatist. Strange to say, her dramas are extremely coarse; a fault doubly surprising in a woman, and possibly springing from an ambition to vie in forcibleness with the stronger sex.

Anthony à Wood (1632–95) is one of the most frequently quoted writers of the period. He was an enthusiast about antiquities; a collector of all sorts of scraps of information, especially about Oxford. Now that all the manuscripts and other sources of knowledge of the earlier centuries may be supposed to have been explored, we can scarcely estimate our debt to the men who made it their business to hunt up what but for them would have passed out of sight and remembrance.

Sir Roger L'Estrange (1616–1704) was a writer of some repute in his day, and one of the first persons to publish a newspaper. He began with "The Public Intelligencer" (1663), stating in his first editorial that he disapproved of newspapers. "I think it makes the multitude too familiar with the actions and counsels of their superiors, too pragmatical and censorious, and gives them a kind of colorable right and license to be meddling with the government." Still he is willing to do what he can "to redeem the vulgar from their mistakes and illusions." In 1666 he established the "London Gazette," which still exists.

The very first so-called "newspaper" or "news-letter" printed in English was the "Weekly News," begun by Samuel Butters, May 23, 1622. Butters had been in the employ of the nobility and gentry for many years as a gatherer of news which he dispatched in written sheets from London to the country. We hear of him in 1611 as printing occasionally a news-slip, and in 1621 he published one or two numbers of "The Courant or Weekly Newes from Forein Parts." This seems to have died untimely, but to have been followed by the sheet first mentioned. The first daily was the "Daily Courant," published in 1703, and the first penny-daily, the "Orange Postman," in 1709. On the continent there had been efforts in the way of periodical news-distribution for a long time; tradition telling of a printed sheet in Nuremburg in 1457.

Gilbert Burnet, Bishop of Salisbury (1643–1715), was born in Scotland. He wrote a "History of the Reformation of the Church of England" which received the thanks of Parliament. He was not in favor with the English Stuart-kings because his tendencies were too Republican; but he was on intimate terms with William and Mary in Holland, and accompanied them to England at the Revolution.

At his death, he left in manuscript the valuable "History of His own Time," which was not published until many years after.

CHAPTER XXIII.

SEVENTEENTH-CENTURY SCIENTIFIC WRITERS.

IN the departments of mental and physical science, the seventeenth century possessed two great minds which alone would have made the age famous—John Locke and Isaac Newton; the former by his treatise on the mind of man, and the latter by his "Principia" and other works.

John Locke (1632-1704) belonged to a family which, in the great civil strife of 1640-60, took sides with the Parliament, so that a belief in freedom of thought was a part of his inheritance. He studied first at Westminster School and then at Oxford; and it was in those venerable halls that he learned, as Bacon had done at Cambridge, to dislike the method of Aristotle, and desire to substitute for it in the intellectual world, as Bacon had done in the physical, experiment for hypothesis.

He made choice of medicine as a profession, but, fortunately for the world, his health proved too delicate for the hard work of a physician's life, and he devoted himself to more purely intellectual pursuits. After some diplomatic employment, he entered the family of Lord Ashley (afterward the first famous Shaftesbury) as tutor to his son, and there met habitually the greatest men of the day. When Lord Shaftesbury "fell from power" (the expression in England for being dismissed from the king's council), Locke accompanied him in his exile, living for several years in Holland, where he met the first scholars of the day, and devoted himself to work on the "Essay" that was to make his name famous. The idea of writing this suggested itself to him when he was talking after dinner with some friends in London. They were discussing some topics connected with morality and religion, and found themselves hampered by difficulties in getting at a clear idea of the subject. Locke remarked that it would be well to examine their own capabilities, and see what objects their understandings were, or were not, fitted to deal with. He thought when he began that the solution of these difficulties might be contained on one sheet of paper. But the more he thought about it, the longer it grew, and twenty years of toil resulted in the work entitled "An Essay on Human Understanding." In this he contends that man, though gifted with reason, has no ideas which are born with him; that he must receive into his mind impressions from without, in other words sensations, and by reflection and observation form his ideas concerning them. He follows the Baconian method so far as to insist that men should gain their knowledge from a study of nature, or of things themselves, before attempting to state the laws which govern them, or to form theories about them. This system makes observation the test of correctness. His dictum on the true means of becoming well-informed ought to be learned by heart by every student. "Reading furnishes the mind only with materials of knowledge; it is thinking which makes what we read our own."

Locke's noble "Letters on Toleration" are in advance of his age; for men were yet only slowly learning that the suppression of others' opinions is insulting to humanity, which is entitled to freedom of thought. He also wrote two treatises on government, wherein he urged the right of all men to liberty, political as well as religious; thus enforcing the principles of "The Glorious Revolution of 1688"; principles that have since become the acknowledged foundation of all government in England.

In Locke's "Thoughts concerning Education" may be traced many of the ideas now universally accepted among educators, but which were then new to the English people. Locke was engaged with Lord Shaftesbury on the preparation of a plan of government for the province of Carolina in America, which was found impracticable from the fact that although abundant provision was made for an aristocracy, the common people who were to support its dignity were not forthcoming. His last days were spent in a delightful retreat, the country-house of Sir Francis and Lady Masham, where, true to his independent spirit, he declined to go except upon condition that he should render a *quid pro quo* for his living. Here he enjoyed the society of congenial minds, and faded gently away, reaching the age of seventy-two, notwithstanding the delicacy of his constitution.*

Isaac Newton (1642–1727), called the greatest of natural philosophers, was born of a good though not a wealthy family in Lincolnshire, and from his childhood showed a strong bent for study of all sorts, especially for that of mathematics. At twenty-three he wrote his first mathematical work, "The Theory of Fluxions," which proved an important help in calculating the movements of the heavenly bodies. His next branch of study was optics, where again he made valuable observations in regard to light. His discovery of the law of gravitation was made long before it was published to the world in the "Principia." Researches in science only deepened Newton's religious feelings, and he spent much time in the study of the Bible. To some one who was lost in wonder at his vast and constantly increasing stores of knowledge, he said, "To myself I seem to have been like a child picking up pebbles on the sea-shore, while the great ocean of truth lay unexplored before me."

He lived thirty years after writing his "Principia," being

* On one occasion he sends for a pound of tea from Holland (probably as a medicine). He must have it, he says, and commissions his friend to give forty florins a pound for it if necessary— equal to at least $50 of our money.

occupied during a large part of this time in government service, in control of the mint. He was knighted in 1705, and died at a great age in the same year with King George I., namely 1727. He was never married.

Like many men of genius, Newton is reported to have had no great fondness for school-study. He cared quite as little, however, for boys' sports; and amused himself with mechanical inventions, like windmills, clocks, sun-dials, etc., and is said to have made a wheeled carriage to be moved by the person riding in it, a precursor of the modern bicycle. When he first looked into Euclid, he found the propositions so self-evident that he threw it aside and looked about for something more difficult to study. Having once found out what was the bent of his mind, he became an intensely hard student, and let no subject go until he had mastered it thoroughly. At one time, for some reason not under-stood, his mind became slightly affected, and for a year or two he was not himself.*

Anecdotes abound illustrative of Newton's simple-heart-edness and utter absence of self-consciousness. His relative, Humphrey Newton, who served him five years (1683–89) writes about him as follows:

His carriage was very meek, sedate, humble, never seemingly angry, of profound thought, his countenance mild, pleasant and comely. I can not say I ever saw him laugh but once, which was at that passage which Dr. Stukely mentioned in his letter to your honour. The passage was as follows: 'Twas upon occasion of asking a friend to whom he had lent Euclid to read, what progress he made with that author and how he liked him; he answered by desiring to know what use and.

---

* We must give up, though with regret, the pretty story of Newton and his dog, Diamond, which runs thus: While Newton was absent from his study, the little dog overturned a lighted candle among his papers, destroying in a few moments the work of years. Mr. Newton (not then Sir Isaac) only gave vent to his feelings in the mournful remark, "Oh, Diamond! Diamond! thou little knowest the mischief thou hast done!" Later authorities deny the whole story.

benefit in life that study would be to him.   Upon which Sir Isaac was very merry.

One of the men of science whose works give them a place in the history of literature was Robert Boyle (1627–91), a celebrated chemist and natural philosopher, who lived a little earlier than Locke. He wrote many works on philosophy and some on religion; the latter subject seeming to have interested the minds of the philosophers of that age and to have been inseparably connected with their researches in science. Locke, Newton and Boyle were all profoundly religious men.

CHAPTER XXIV.

LATER DRAMATISTS.   SEVENTEENTH CENTURY.

AMONG the most characteristic of the writers of the seventeenth century were the later dramatists, who have been purposely left until now that they might be spoken of together. James Shirley, who died in 1666, has been mentioned as the last of the Elizabethan dramatists. Dryden, who died in 1700, was the central figure of a new set of play-writers, who, to great power and versatility, added a love of what was immoral and unworthy in fiction, and who reflected only too faithfully the tastes of Charles II.'s court, and furnished such plays as pleased its members. Dryden, the greatest poet and the most original thinker of the century after the death of Milton, deserves his full share of the blame attaching to these perverters of public morality; but his great gifts were also used in other ways, and we have to consider him not only as a dramatist, but as poet, satirist, essayist, translator and critic.

John Dryden (1631–1700) had the usual education of

a gentleman's son, going first to Westminster School* and then to Cambridge. He seems not to have written anything for print until he was twenty-seven years old, when he published "Stanzas on the Death of Cromwell," as laudatory as were all poems written in that time on that subject. Eighteen months afterward he welcomed the return of Charles II. in a long poem called "Astræa Redux." After producing several pieces of no great merit, he tried his hand at play-writing. His first play, strange to say, was a failure. Then, in conjunction with Sir Robert Howard, he wrote another, called "The Indian Queen," and this being better received he went on by himself, and for the next thirty years plays continued to come from his industrious pen. These abound in passages of great beauty and power, though Dryden had no creative imagination, and his dramas have not kept the stage as have Shakespeare's. They are poorly fitted for acting, from their licentiousness, which offends the taste of an age of greater refinement. Another reason may be found in the fact that Dryden had the idea that rhyme was essential to poetry, and wrote many of his plays in rhyme. This to the ears of modern critics, weakens their effect, though his verse is always rhythmical and polished. He did more than any other man of his time to form a taste for what is called the artificial school in poetry; that in which the desire for following exact rules, especially as to rhythm, overtops the necessity for grand thoughts. His first long poem, after those in praise of rulers, spoken of above, was called "Annus Mirabilis," or the "Year of Wonders," being a description in verse of the great events which came

---

* Here he studied under the famous Dr. Busby, who might have been called the Knight of the Birch from his fondness for using that instrument, and who refused to take off his hat in the king's presence for fear the boys should think there was a greater man in the world than himself.

almost literally within a year—the Great Plague (1665), the Great Fire (1666) and the Dutch War. The last of his noted poems, written thirty years later, was "Alexander's Feast," or "Ode on Saint Cecilia's Day," which he himself pronounced to be "the best ode ever written in English." Those who admire Milton's "Ode on the Nativity" may not agree with him; but Dryden's has stood the test of nearly two hundred years' reading.

As a translator, Dryden is open to criticism. He allowed his own individuality to predominate over his author's, and one can not help feeling that it is Dryden, and not Chaucer or Ovid, Homer or Virgil, who is before us. Dryden's first great satire, "Absalom and Achitophel," appeared in 1681, and was directed against the Earl of Shaftesbury (Achitophel), who was supposed to have incited Charles II.'s son, the Duke of Monmouth (Absalom), to rebel against the king, his father. The finest piece of character-painting in this is directed against the Duke of Buckingham:

> A man so various, that he seemed to be
> Not one, but all mankind's epitome;
> Stiff in opinions, always in the wrong,
> Was everything by turns, and nothing long.

The next year appeared "Mac Flecknoe," a satire against several of the minor poets, some of whom had offended Dryden in their writings, and especially against Shadwell. The spirit of this may be discerned in the lines:

> The rest to some faint meaning make pretence,
> But Shadwell never deviates into sense.

Dryden had been appointed poet-laureate on the death of Sir William Davenant, and as literature was beginning to be paid, though poorly, he received enough from the sale of his dramas and from his pension as "Historiographer Royal" to live comfortably. His marriage with Lady Elizabeth Howard, daughter of the Earl of Berkshire proved un-

11

happy. He did not find her congenial, and she, desiring more of his attention and companionship, wished she were a book, because then he would care for her.

Soon after the accession of James II., Dryden changed his religion and went over to the Roman Catholic faith. This has of course been severely commented upon as showing a desire for worldly profit. Biographers in dealing with the subject take opposite sides according to their political bias, and after much discussion the question is still unsettled as to whether it was or was not a matter of conscience. His satire on "The Hind and the Panther," the two animals representing the Roman and Anglican Churches, is an able defence of his position, though not equal in force and conciseness to "Absalom and Achitophel." In these years came the Revolution, and on the accession of the Protestants, William and Mary, Dryden was dismissed not only from the post of Historiographer Royal which he had held for nearly thirty years, but also from the laureateship, and had the mortification of seeing the despised Shadwell appointed to the latter in his place. This made the last twelve years of his life a time of comparative poverty, but his days were tranquil and dignified to the end.

Dryden's prose, while small in quantity compared with his poetry, is noted for its vigorous, idiomatic English, its good sense and its manly statement of the writer's ideas. These prose-writings are numerous, though short, and consist mainly in essays or prefaces to his various poetic works.

Among Dryden's best-known plays are "All for Love," "The Conquest of Granada," "The Indian Queen," "Don Sebastian," and "Aurungzebe."

The last glimpses we have of Dryden are very picturesque. They represent him as a ruddy-faced old man, going every day to Will's Coffee-House, then the resort of wits and men of letters, where he had his special easy-chair, in the most comfortable corner by the fireside in winter and in front of the open window in summer. There he sipped his port and uttered his opinions, sure of being listened to with respect and admiration. The poet Pope was once taken to see the old king of letters, and through life retained a pleasant memory of the incident, though he could have been only a young lad, as Dryden died when Pope was twelve years old. He lies buried in Westminster Abbey.

It was shortly before the end of Dryden's life that Jeremy Collier, a clergyman of the Church of England, published a severe attack on "The Immorality aud Profaneness of the English Stage," which created great excitement among the play-writers, and was the occasion of much ill-feeling. There is no question but that the scolding was well deserved, and Dryden acknowledged its justness, though he added that Collier himself had offended against good manners in his language. Collier had, in fact, used very intemperate expressions in his zeal for good morals; but he had stirred up the poisonous flood of licentious play-writing and a general purification of its waters was the result. All Englishmen of the better class acquiesced in the necessity for a change; and no such undisguised or half-concealed immoral suggestion has ever since appeared on the English stage as disgraced it during the latter half of the seventeenth century.

It is not necessary in a book like this to give a detailed account of each of the dramatic writers who make up the great company of Dryden's time. A few words on each must suffice, and readers who wish to know more about them must go to Professor Tyler's valuable "Manual of English Literature," or to special biographies and essays.

The list is headed, in time though not in importance, by George Villiers, Duke of Buckingham (1627–88), the witty favorite of Charles II., whose burlesque, "The Rehearsal," is a wonderfully clever take-off on the kind of dramatic writing then in vogue. It is full of fun from beginning to end, and is still good reading, as is shown by the many quotations from it to be found in modern authors. It has the further merit of being more free from indelicacy of dialogue than any other play of its time.

Sir George Etherege (*c.* 1636–89)* wrote dramas of a light, gay order, and was himself a wit about the court of Charles II. He was possessed of a handsome fortune. This he gambled away and then married a rich widow to replenish his purse. His best plays are "Love in a Tub," and "Sir Fopling Flutter." He was sent as minister to Germany, and, according to tradition, broke his neck falling down stairs while drunk.

William Wycherley (1640–1715) is said to have introduced the "Prose-Comedy of Manners"—in other words, to have been the first to represent real modern life on the stage. The life of his own day was probably represented only too truly in his ingenious and lively but highly immoral plays, of which the "Country Wife" is usually considered the best.

Mrs. Aphra Behn (1642–89), who has already been mentioned as the writer of "Oroonoko," also wrote several plays, of which "The Rover, or the Banished Cavalier," was the most popular.

Thomas Otway† (1652–85) is almost exclusively a writer of tragedy, and occupies a much higher plane than most of his contemporaries. His tragedies of "The Orphan" and "Venice Preserved" show an unusual power of depicting distress and suffering, and the latter is still occasionally acted. Like many of the dramatists of his day, he tried

---

* *c.* stands for *circa*—about.

† His name is connected with Dryden's in an amusing way: They lived on different sides of the same street; and on one occasion Otway wrote on Dryden's door:

Here lives Dryden, a poet and a wit.

When Dryden saw it he let it stand; but added directly underneath:

There lives Otway, opposite.

his hand at acting, but he soon abandoned it. He led a dissipated life, became miserably poor, and died in a tavern where he had taken refuge to avoid a debtor's prison.

Nathaniel Lee (*c.* 1657–92) was the son of a clergyman. He wished to be an actor, but meeting with no success in this art, he tried writing plays, the most popular of which was "The Rival Queens." At one time he became insane, and was an inmate of Bedlam for several years. Some one said to him there, "It is easy to write like a madman." "No," said Lee, "but it is easy to write like a fool." He recovered and was again able to write; but died poor, like most of his tribe.

In Thomas Southern (1660–1746) we have an agreeable variation from the story of misery and poverty. His plays were not great, but they were of purer morals than most others then written, and two of them "The Fatal Marriage," and "Oroonoko" are much commended. The latter, founded on Mrs. Behn's novel, added strength to her protest against slavery.

Sir John Vanbrugh (1666–1726) was famous both as an architect and a dramatist. "The Provoked Wife" is called his best play, while Blenheim House, (the palace built by the English people for the Duke of Marlborough) and Castle Howard are his most ambitious buildings. He built many other country residences for the aristocracy, in a somewhat ponderous style, which caused some wit to propose as his epitaph:

> Lie heavy on him, earth, for he
> Laid many a heavy load on thee.

William Congreve (1670–1729) was one of the most successful dramatists of the age. His comedy of " Love for Love," and his tragedy "The Mourning Bride" (the only one he wrote), had equal success. He was also a devotee of society in the time of Queen Anne and George I.; was courted and caressed by the gay world and preferred to be known as a man of fashion rather than as a writer. He died rich, bequeathing his fortune to the young Duchess of Marlborough, who did not need it, rather than to his own kindred who did; and was buried in Westminster Abbey. It seems incredible, but is related on good authority, that the volatile duchess had an ivory image of Congreve made after his death, which was always placed at table with her, and a wax one in a bed-chamber, with gouty feet which she had regularly blistered and rubbed by her doctors, as had been done to the poet's in his lifetime. He was blind for several years before his death.

Colley Cibber (1671–1757), the son of a sculptor of considerable repute, was one of the most successful actors of his day, and wrote several plays, besides altering and adapting some of those he acted. It was he who inserted into Shakespeare's "Richard III." various lines which many suppose to have belonged to the original; for instance:

> Now, by Saint Paul, the work goes bravely on!
>
> The aspiring youth that fired the Ephesian dome
> Outlives in fame the pious fool that raised it.
>
> Off with his head! So much for Buckingham!
>
> Richard's himself again!
>
> A weak invention of the enemy.

In 1730, he succeeded the Rev. Laurence Eusdon as poet-laureate, and retired from the stage, except for an occasional appearance.

Pope, being angry with Cibber for some remarks about the Roman Catholics, dethroned Theobald from his seat on the throne of Dulness in the "Dunciad", and put Cibber in his place; an absurd change, for Cibber was anything but dull. The latter took it very good-humoredly, and his only revenge was to publish "A Letter to Mr. Pope, Inquiring into the Motives that might Induce him in his Satirical Works to be so Frequently Fond of Mr. Cibber's Name."

Of the two, we are inclined to think that the lesser man appeared to the greater advantage.

Nicholas Rowe (1673-1718) was the first editor of the works of Shakespeare. (They had been printed several times.) What Rowe did was the ordinary task of an editor, namely to revise and correct the original work by the light of the best information to be obtained on the subject, and to give, in addition, an account of the author's life. Rowe's "Life of Shakespeare" is interesting as giving the traditions current in his time; beyond this it has no especial value.

Rowe was himself a dramatist, and produced, among others, two tragedies which continued for a long time favorites with the public—"The Fair Penitent;" and "Jane Shore." He was created poet-laureate after Nahum Tate, a composer and collector of hymns, who had occupied the position since the death of Shadwell. In connection with Nicholas Brady, Tate made a metrical version of the Psalms of David which superseded that of Sternhold and Hopkins, written some two hundred years earlier.

George Farquhar (1678-1707), the third of a brilliant group of painters of the manners of society (the other two being Vanbrugh and Congreve), was the son of a clergyman. Smitten by the desire to become an actor, he tried his fortune on the stage for a short time in Dublin, then obtained a lieutenancy in the army, and before he was twenty produced his first comedy, "Love and a Bottle." His last comedies were the best—"The Recruiting Officer," and "The Beaux' Strategem,"—the latter written at the age of twenty-nine, while he was slowly dying of want and dissipation. His was a sad story. A woman who was in love with him entrapped him into marrying her by pretending to have a fortune—a bait at which he, being in need, eagerly caught. She had nothing, and he toiled to support a family without ever reproaching her for the deceit.

CHAPTER XXV.

JONATHAN SWIFT.

HAVING now finished the list of Dryden's contemporary dramatists and immediate successors, which has taken us far into the eighteenth century, we will go back to a name belonging almost equally to both centuries.

Jonathan Swift (1667–1745), better known to us by the title of Dean, was a genius, a wit, a great writer and a most unhappy man. He was born in Dublin, though his parents and ancestors were English and he never showed, as most Irishmen do, any pride in the country of his birth. His father died before Jonathan could know him, leaving Mrs. Swift so poor that she was compelled to accept the aid of charity for the expenses of the funeral. The boy himself was of a proud and haughty spirit, and poverty touched him in his tenderest point by making him dependent on others. He was sent to school and to college by the generosity of an uncle, who, however, as Swift imagined, gave his assistance grudgingly, and instead of gratitude the young man always cherished bitter feelings toward him. Bitterness, indeed, continued to be the predominating characteristic of his life, and though capable of strong affections, he went through the world with his heart full of hatred. He did himself little credit at college and obtained his degree "by special grace," which meant that he did not deserve it. In the year of the Great Revolution (1688) when he was twenty-one years old, his uncle became incapable of supporting him further, and he went, by his mother's advice, to ask employment of Sir William Temple, whose wife was a distant connection of Mrs. Swift's. Here again the young man was forced to eat what he called "the bitter bread of dependence," for although Sir William took him as his secretary, the great man's manner toward him was supercilious, and he occupied a position but little above that of a servant, while feeling himself entitled to rank as a gentleman. During his college-life he had been an assiduous reader, though not prominent in the studies required for a degree, and he brought to the service of Temple a mind well stored with information of a fragmentary kind, and a zeal for study which induced him to spend in reading all the time that could be spared from his duties. He was not admitted to his patron's table, and the accounts of his rough and often insolent behavior in later life make us readily believe that to the courtly and fastidious Sir William his manners must have been highly displeasing.

After a while Swift quarrelled with Temple, and following most mistaken advice, became a clergyman; he with his heart full of contempt and loathing for all mankind, took the solemn vows which bound him to teach the religion of "Peace on earth; good-will to men." He received the "gift" as it is called in England, of a small country parish in Ireland; but finding the dulness intolerable he returned to Moor Park and remained in Temple's service until the death of the latter (1699). During this period, the baronet and the secretary got on better together, and Swift seems to have been received into the family on the footing of a friend. Temple desired him to be his literary executor, and Swift edited the works of his patron with a dedication to King William.

As no advancement of any kind followed this act of courtesy, Swift set about devoting himself seriously to literature, at the same time holding two livings (parishes) in Ireland. The first work which drew public attention to him was his ingenious "Battle of the Books," in which he attempts to prove the superiority of Greek and Roman

classics to the works of modern writers. Then came the
"Tale of a Tub," a work partly political and partly religious,
in which he represents the three warring Churches under the
names of Peter (the Roman Catholic), Jack (Calvin the
Presbyterian), and Martin (Luther, who stood for the Church
of England). It has been said that but for the "Tale of a
Tub," Swift would have died a bishop. The book is not
immoral in its tendency, but contains so much coarse wit at
the expense of all three of the Churches it discusses, that
Swift never obtained higher promotion than to be Dean of
St. Patrick's Cathedral in Dublin; a stately edifice in which
he is buried.

Of Swift's two loves,—the "Stella" and "Vanessa" of his
writings,—the former appeals more to our interest, the latter
to our sympathy.

He married "Stella" secretly (she was a lowly-born
beauty), and always refused her entreaties that the marriage
should be made public. The other, "Vanessa" (a Miss
Vanhomrigh), fell deeply in love with him, and they visited
and corresponded for years, until the lady heard of his intimacy with "Stella" and wrote the latter about it. "Stella"
disclosed the marriage and put Swift in a furious rage
with "Vanessa," whom he visited once more, only to
throw down her letter before her and depart without a
word. Poor "Vanessa's" heart was broken and she died
within a few weeks. Stella lived five years after this; and
left him a hopeless mourner at her death. His letters to
her, under the form of a journal, are full of interest, and
show that the savage Dean could be as playful as a kitten
where his affections were engaged. He had but one soft
spot in his heart, and when the object of his tenderness
was removed a hardness came upon him which continued
to the end of his life.

. The number of political pamphlets that came from Swift
is almost incredible. He began by being first a fierce whig,

and became a tory when the measures of the other party no longer pleased him; in each case writing against his opponents with a pen steeped in gall. He won the hearts of the Irish people by bitter attacks on England, especially in "Drapier's Letters"—a series of articles against "Wood's half-pence," * which raised his popularity almost to idolatry. These were followed in about two years (1726) by "Gulliver's Travels," perhaps the most famous satire ever published. To us who know it chiefly in its abridged form as a fairy-story, it seems harmless enough; but to the people of the time, who understood its allusions and its hidden meanings, it was the acme of bitterness.

This was Swift's last great work. He grew more and more morose, became very deaf, and was subject to fits of giddiness which were the precursors of a disease of the brain that ended in imbecility. For three years before his death he did not speak, but would walk up and down his library for ten hours a day, looking at the backs of the books he could no longer read or understand, never even sitting down to take his meals, but snatching a few mouthfuls in passing, from the plate left for him by his attendant. Before the madness came on, he had a dreadful premonition of his fate, and left by will the greater part of his fortune to found a hospital for idiots and insane persons, which remains a monument to his memory.

Addison describes Swift as "the most agreeable companion, the truest friend, and the greatest genius of the age." There must have been something very lovable about the man to secure for him the devotion of two superior women, and the good words of many of his own sex, who would have characterized him as warmly as did Addison.

Some good sayings of Swift's, possibly not generally known to be his, are worth quoting:

---

* See "A Short History of England," p. 324.

The two noblest things, which are sweetness and light.—*Battle of the Books.*

The reason why so few marriages are happy is because young ladies spend their time in making nets, not in making cages.

He gave it for his opinion that whoever could make two ears of corn, or two blades of grass, grow where one grew before, would deserve better of mankind and do more service to his country than the whole race of politicians put together.—*Gulliver's Travels.*

Bread is the staff of life.—*Tale of a Tub.*

CHAPTER XXVI.

POPE AND OTHER POETS.

RESERVING the highest rank for the English poets whose domain was among the sublimities rather than the humanities of literature; and assigning to the second place those whose verses were inspired by wit and ingenuity rather than by originality, grandeur and majesty of thought; we have no hesitation in placing Pope at the head of the latter class. Perhaps no writer who ever lived has given more quotations to the world; some of them having passed into the rank of proverbs; "the wisdom of many expressed in the wit of one."

Alexander Pope (1688-1744) was born in London, of Catholic parents. His father was a respectable linen-draper (dry-goods merchant), a fact of which Pope had the weakness to be ashamed, under the aristocratic traditions which make any useful and profitable industry a badge not of honor but of degradation. His mother, was, however, of "good family," an accident the son made the most of. He was very small, very weak, somewhat crooked, and extremely infirm in health; circumstances that furnished gall to his pen and wormwood to his life. He himself says:

> The muse just served   *   *   *
> To help me through this long disease, my life.

The sadly misshapen back he inherited from his father; though both his parents seem to have been healthy and both lived to old age. The boy had so sweet a voice that they nicknamed him "the nightingale"; and he is said to have been gentle and winning. Dr. Johnson says of him, "the weakness of his body continued through life, but the mildness of his mind ended with his childhood." To his honor be it said that he was devoted to his parents through their whole lives.

The anti-Catholic laws during his forming years (in the reign of Queen Anne) prevented the children of Romanists from getting the same education as other boys got, and Pope's teaching was of the most desultory kind. An aunt taught him his letters and he picked up most of the rest of his knowledge by himself. This he afterward held as an advantage, seeing that he read for the sense whereas others gained only the words. He taught himself to write by copying the printed letters, and was always proud of his ability at writing in this fashion; but his usual handwriting was cramped and ungraceful. He learned a little Latin from the parish priest and probably a little Greek from a Catholic school he attended at Twyford. There he wrote a lampoon or satirical poem on his master; for which the punishment was a whipping, and this brought about his removal from the school by his father. His next school was in London, where he made a sort of drama which was acted by his school-fellows; assisted by the gardener, who took the part of Ajax. So early did Pope give proof of fondness for Homer; with whom his name was later famously connected by his translation of the classic author's works.

When Pope was about twelve, his father retired from business with a comfortable fortune, and bought a country-place to which he removed, and where his brilliant son lived at home, carrying on his cultivation by an enormous quantity of desultory reading. Among the rest he knew Dryden's poetry well, and he one day got a friend to take him to Will's Coffee-House where he met the old poet; for the only time in his life probably, as Dryden died not long afterward.

His home seems to have been happy and congenial; himself the bright particular star and ruling spirit. While living with his father he always carried to him his verses; and when the elder was not satisfied with them he returned them as "not good rhymes," an ordeal very favorable to the high standard of accuracy and verbal perfection which marks all his work. At this time he says that poetry was his only business and idleness his only pleasure. He confesses that he then thought himself, at sixteen, "the greatest genius that ever was."

He started on his poetic career with the advantage of a clear perception of what should be his aim. He once remarked to a friend: "It seems not so much the perfection of sense to say things that have never been said before as to express those best which have been said oftenest."

At seventeen, he claimed and secured the standing of a man of letters. He frequented Will's Coffee-House, and his "Pastorals" were published by the well-known printer Jacob Tonson. These are graceful poems on the four seasons; old-fashioned and sometimes fantastic, yet full of promise. But before he was twenty-one, he published the "Essay on Criticism," which took London by storm and which to this day we read with pleasure. There is nothing very profound about it. Profound, Pope could never be; but it says indisputable things in so clever a way that they seize our fancy and fascinate us in spite of our stricter judgment. Here is an extract from the poem; wherein the author laughs at the rhymesters called poets who grind out their verses as if by machinery:

> Then they ring round the same unvaried chimes
> With sure returns of still-expected rhymes:

> Where'er you find "the cooling western breeze,"
> In the next line it "whispers through the trees."
> If crystal streams "with pleasing murmurs creep,"
> The reader's threatened (not in vain) with "sleep".
> Then at the last and only couplet fraught
> With some unmeaning thing they call a thought,
> A needless Alexandrine ends the song,
> That like a wounded snake, drags its slow length along.

His next achievement was the mock-heroic poem called "The Rape of the Lock," a work which most critics place highest among his writings. Like Cowper's "Task" and Milton's "Comus," it had an incident in real life for its basis, and upon that slight foundation the poet went on to build a charming superstructure of fun, wit, beauty, and romance. Mistress Arabella Fermor, from whom the lock of hair had been stolen, and Lord Petre who had stolen it, were reconciled by the verses. Everybody was thrown into good humor except one Sir George Brown, who had used his powers, fruitlessly, to settle the quarrel, and who was offended by the following unflattering portraiture of himself; a sketch which illustrates both the poem and the manners prevalent in the high life of the day:

> Sir Plume, of amber snuff-box justly vain,
> And the nice conduct of a clouded cane.
> With earnest eyes and round, unthinking face,
> He first the snuff-box opened, then the case.

Pope had now, at twenty-six, nearly reached the height of his success. He was in the society of the best minds of the age; Swift, Addison, Steele, Gay, Bolingbroke, Mary Wortley Montagu and a host of others who made illustrious the reigns of William and Mary, Anne, and George I. A quaint little figure he must have been; scarcely four feet high, his misshapen body encased in stiff stays without which he could not stand; and, over these, several garments of different sorts which swelled out his meagre form to something like the normal breadth of man. He had to be dressed and undressed like a child, and his three pairs of stockings, worn one over the other, were patiently drawn on by the maid-servant. We do not read that he was especially brilliant in his talk; the place he held in society must have been due partly to his far-famed power with the pen, and partly to his standing as a man of fashion and fortune; for on his father's death he inherited a large estate, to which he added considerable earnings in literature. (For his translation of the Iliad and Odyssey he received nearly £8000.) He was twenty-nine when, with his widowed mother, he moved to Twickenham (on the Thames, opposite Richmond) where he lived through the rest of his life; making that place famous as the home of wit and genius.

With pen in hand, Pope could be a strong friend or a bitter enemy. By his misfortune or his fault—or, as is usual, a combination of both—the last thirty years of his life were full of strife with those who had been his friends. It was the era of personal vituperation, and Pope was a champion in the dealing of foul blows. Many persons know "The Dunciad" by name; none need wish to know more of it than the name. It is a scurrilous satire at the expense of Pope's contemporaries; not only the eminent, but also the insignificant; persons who would never be heard of by posterity if they were not pilloried in these verses. There are a few bright conceits in "The Dunciad"; for instance:

> Gentle dullness ever loves a joke.
>
> *   *   *
>
> While pensive poets painful vigil keep,
> Sleepless themselves, to give their readers sleep.
>
> *   *   *
>
> Poetic justice, with the lifted scale,
> Where, in nice balance, truth with gold she weighs,
> And solid pudding against empty praise.
>
> *   *   *
>
> The right divine of kings to govern wrong.

Pope himself thought the "Essay on Man" his best

ALEXANDER POPE.

work. He put much labor on it, polishing each couplet until it suited his fastidious ear, and published it anonymously, curious to know what people would say about it; and then took the rude plan of asking his friends for their opinion before announcing his authorship. Doubtless he was, on the whole, satisfied with its reputation; but later writers do not set it, as a whole, high in the scale of philosophy. One critic described it by travestying a line it contained which speaks of Creation as: "A mighty maze, and not without a plan," which he applied to the poem —substituting "quite" for "not."

The essay consists of four "Epistles" to Lord Bolingbroke; the first lines reading:

> Awake my St. John!* leave all meaner things
> To low ambition and the pride of kings.

Its best aspect is as a string of gem-like couplets rather than as a solid fabric. Wherever the eye lights, some glittering generality fastens the attention. Here are a few instances:

> Hope springs eternal in the human breast:
> Man never is, but always to be, blest.
>
> * * *
>
> Lo, the poor Indian! whose untutored mind
> Sees God in clouds, or hears him in the wind.
>
> * * *
>
> All are but parts of one stupendous whole,
> Whose body Nature is, and God the soul.
>
> * * *
>
> All nature is but art, unknown to thee;
> All chance, direction which thou canst not see;
> All discord, harmony not understood;
> All partial evil, universal good;
> And, spite of pride, in erring reason's spite,
> One truth is clear: Whatever is, is right.
>
> * * *
>
> Know then thyself, presume not God to scan;
> The proper study of mankind is man.

---

* Pronounced "Sinjen."

12

> The young disease that must subdue at length,
> Grows with his growth and strengthens with his strength.
>
> * * *
>
> Vice is a monster of so frightful mien,
> As, to be hated, needs but to be seen;
> Yet seen too oft, familiar with her face,
> We first endure, then pity, then embrace.
>
> * * *
>
> A little learning is a dangerous thing;
> Drink deep, or taste not the Pierian spring.
>
> * * *
>
> Order is heaven's first law.
>
> * * *
>
> Honor and shame from no condition rise;
> Act well your part, there all the honor lies.
>
> * * *
>
> What can ennoble sots, or slaves, or cowards?
> Alas! not all the blood of all the Howards.
>
> * * *
>
> A wit's a feather, and a chief a rod;
> An honest man's the noblest work of God.
>
> * * *
>
> If parts allure thee, think how Bacon shin'd,
> The wisest, brightest, meanest of mankind!
>
> * * *
>
> Slave to no sect, who takes no private road,
> But looks through Nature up to Nature's God.
>
> * * *
>
> Formed by thy converse, happily to steer
> From grave to gay, from lively to severe.

The books which earned Pope his highest meed of instant praise and profit were his translations from Homer—the very work which time has retired because better translations of Homer have followed it. In this he was helped by Fenton and Broome, who, however, received but a small share of the profits. It had the advantage of the already eminent fame of its translator, and also of having been looked forward to with interest through all the six years during which Pope had been working on it. Its beauty was in the exquisite diction, phraseology and versification of which Pope was master; its fault was in the fact that Homer was disguised and lost sight of. Most later translations have had the advantage of freedom from the shackle of rhyme —witness Bryant's majestic rendering into blank verse; and still later, Lang's and Butcher's, which is mere strong-sounding prose; all versification being sacrificed to literalness of interpretation; almost word for word.

Pope's life came to a gently quarrelsome close at Twickenham. His friends were always near by and his enemies a little farther away. To some one who had complimented him on retaining the poetical spirit he answered, "I am fast sinking into prose!" A few weeks before his death he sent copies of his "Epistles" to certain intimates, saying, "I am like Socrates, dispensing morality to my friends on my death-bed." When his doctors remarked on his better appetite, or stronger pulse, or some such favorable aspect of the case he answered: "Here I am, dying of a hundred good symptoms." The end came at last so quietly that the friends at his bedside did not know when he ceased to breathe. The poor misfitted sheath had carried its sharp, bright blade for fifty-six years.

———

The age of Queen Anne (1702–14) was not a propitious one for poets. Beside Pope, only two rose above mediocrity—Prior and Gay. Of the host of their verse-writing contemporaries, but little more than the names is now remembered.

Matthew Prior (1664–1721) was first brought into notice by the Earl of Dorset, himself a poet of whom Macaulay says that his few songs and satires sparkle with wit as splendid as that of Butler. Dorset found young Prior reading Horace for amusement in the "Rummer Tavern," kept by the boy's uncle; and becoming interested in him, sent him to Cambridge, where he graduated with honor. Not long afterward he wrote, in connection with Montague (another titled poet, who afterward became Earl of Halifax), a satire on Dryden's "Hind and Panther," called "The City Mouse and Country Mouse." His gay verses and ready wit soon brought him into favor at court, and he was appointed by King William III. ambassador to The Hague. On his way thither he visited Versailles and was shown room after room filled with paintings representing the victories of Louis XIV. (It must be remembered that this was during the life-time of that monarch.) Some Frenchman asked him whether King William's palace had any such decorations. "The monuments of my master's actions," said Prior, "are to be seen everywhere except in his own house." The year before William's death he "ratted," as the English call it, to the tories, and so was quiet for some years, being sent as ambassador to France when they again came into power. We give below a few of his stanzas:

> Nobles and heralds, by your leave,
> Here lies what once was Matthew Prior,
> The son of Adam and of Eve;
> Can Bourbon or Nassau claim higher?—*Epitaph on himself*

> Be to her faults a little blind,
> Be to her virtues very kind;
> Let all her ways be unconfined,
> And clap your padlock—on her mind.—*Advice to a Husband.*

> That air and harmony of shape express,
> Fine by degrees, and beautifully less.—*Henry and Emma.*

John Gay (1688–1732), whom Pope has described as being "In wit a man, simplicity a child," was another poet who lived a comfortable, easy life through the kindness and generosity of friends. His serious poems have long since been forgotten; but his sparkling ballads and his "Beggar's Opera" still afford delight to readers. Gay was a good-humored satirist, and gave such offence to the court-party that his "Polly," a sequel to the "Beggar's Opera," was not allowed to be put on the stage; but on this very account the sale of it was immense, and the author was handsomely paid by his publishers. Of his ballads, "Black-eyed Susan" is the most picturesque and well sustained. His "Fables"—mostly versifications of Æsop's, adapted to modern conditions—are pleasing and rhythmical.

Gay's friends included almost every one who knew him. Pope was strongly attached to him, and the list contains many other well-known names; but since Thackeray delivered his lectures on "The English Humorists," it has been impossible to dissociate from the name of Gay his sentence describing the latter's position under the roof of the Duke and Duchess of Queensberry, who took care of him for several years before his death. "With these kind, lordly folks Gay lived, and was lapped in cotton, and had his plate of chicken, and his saucer of cream, and frisked, and barked, and wheezed, and grew fat, and so ended."

In the poem of "Trivia, or the Art of Walking the Streets of London," Gay gives a description of the London of his day, as valuable as that of Lydgate's "London Lykepenny."

Of the lesser poets of Anne's time, "The Augustan Age of English Literature," Thomas Parnell is remembered chiefly for his poem of "The Hermit." He was an Irishman by birth, entered the Church, lived mostly in London (disliking Ireland as his countryman Swift had done), and was known as a man of learning and agreeable qualities. "The Hermit" is written in heroic couplets, smoothly versified, and is an excellent specimen of the serious poetry of the age. A few lines will show its character:

> The pair arrive; the liveried servants wait;
> Their lord receives them at the pompous gate;
> The table groans with costly piles of food,
> And all is more than hospitably good.
> Then, led to rest, the day's long toil they drown,
> Deep sunk in sleep, and silk, and heaps of down.

A poem called "The Splendid Shilling," by John Phillips, gained its author much reputation. Ambrose Phillips, a friend of Addison, wrote pastorals. Thomas Tickell helped Pope with his translation of Homer, and also wrote poems of his own. Addison wrote some beautiful hymns; also a poem called "The Campaign," in honor of Marlborough's victories; but his fame as essayist eclipses that which he enjoys as poet. Of the poem just mentioned, two lines have become historical. They refer to the Duke:

> And pleased the Almighty's order to perform,
> Rides in the whirlwind and directs the storm.

Of his hymns, that beginning,

> The spacious firmament on high,

is grandest in its imagery.

CHAPTER XXVII.

ADDISON AND STEELE.

THE early part of the eighteenth century was not rich in poets, but it produced two essayists such as the world up to that time had never seen— Addison and Steele. These two wrote together, in a literary partnership which was the more remarkable because they were of such different temperaments. Addison was calm, stately, somewhat cold in disposition, gracious and courteous in manner; a man to be admired rather than loved. Steele, on the other hand was warm-hearted, impulsive, reckless, regularly sinning and repenting by turns, loved and pitied, helped and still not despicable; a strange "bundle of contradictions," yet always faithful to Addison. Addison himself was described by Bernard Mandeville (a moralist and essayist of the time), as "a parson in a tie-wig"; * thus giving the idea that he had the gravity and decorum of a clergyman while leading a secular life.

The literary circle of the wits of Queen Anne's reign and the ten years following it, has probably never been surpassed. Fancy a company composed of the writers of that age; what an assembly it must have been! The dark, strong, overmastering Swift; the keen, sharp-witted little Pope; the courtly, gracious Addison; the irrepressible Dick Steele; the stately Bolingbroke; the witty Congreve, and the gentle Gay. All these made up a company such as the world does not often see; one whose strongly marked individualities have become almost impossible since the general smoothing off of manners to a recognized type. We can but glance at a few of the most noted among the brilliant group.

Joseph Addison (1672–1718) was the son of a clergyman. He was sent to the famous Charter-house school as a private pupil, and there met Steele, who entered it on the charitable foundation, at the nomination of a friend.

A poem by Addison in praise of King William and the peace of Ryswick, drew attention to the young man and obtained for him a pension of £300 a year—fully equal to $3000 now. Addison made good use of it while he had it. It ceased to be paid at King Willlam's death. He traveled abroad, charming every one he met (and he took care that his acquaintances should be of the best) by his polished manners and elegant scholarship. He never stopped studying, being as earnest in cultivating that rich field, his mind, as if he had still been at college preparing for a degree.

When his pension stopped Addison returned to England, with old college debts still unpaid and without a

---

* Tie-wigs were at this time used only by men of fashion; whereas "parsons"—*i.e.* clergymen—wore the more dignified full-bottomed wig.

profession; for in that day literature alone had scarcely begun to be considered in the sense of something by which to make one's living. A pension, a government office, or some paying occupation, was necessary to eke out an author's income if he had no private resources.

In a previous generation Dryden had written, bitterly, in asking for the payment of arrears of his own pension, "It is enough for one age to have neglected Mr. Cowley, and starved Mr. Butler" (author of "Hudibras"). And Otway, who at length died for want of sufficient food, wrote:

> Tell 'em how Spenser died, how Cowley mourned,
> How Butler's faith and service were returned.

It was considered then the duty of the public in general to take care of all authors; and as "what is everybody's business is nobody's business," the duty was often left unperformed.

A man so brilliantly gifted as Addison was not long in finding something profitable to do. He wrote "The Campaign," already mentioned, and was rewarded with an office which the next year was exchanged for that of Under Secretary of State, after which there was no more trouble about money matters.

It was not Addison, but Steele, to whom came the idea of the first purely literary periodical; an idea which, later, resulted in the "Spectator." Defoe had already tried the experiment of mingling light reading with the heavy political articles which formed the staple of his "Review"; but Steele's "Tatler" (begun 1709) was, from the first, mainly devoted to social topics, though giving the news in a gossiping way. It was a penny-paper, issued three times a week, and soon became popular, Addison joining in it. In less than two years the Tatler came to an end, giving way to its more celebrated successor, The Spectator. The latter journal came out daily, and was read by thousands at the breakfast-table with the eagerness that is now reserved for the morning newspaper. Addison had found his strong point; wit, humor, grace, the finest shades of criticism, the most delicate satire, flowed from his pen; while, strange to say, it was Steele, the rollicking, dissipated, always needy co-laborer, whose papers show the deepest tenderness and reverence for woman, and the truest testimony to the beauty and sanctity of home.

Addison's aim, in his contributions to the delightful periodical, may be best learned from his own words:

It was said of Socrates that he brought philosophy down from heaven to inhabit among men; I shall be ambitious to have it said of me that I brought philosophy out of closets and libraries to dwell in clubs and assemblies, at tea-tables and in coffee-houses.

As we can not read everything, and so many great and charming writers are constantly demanding our attention, the names of a few of Addison's essays in the Spectator are given,* which it may be well to read first, to get an idea of his style and to encourage a taste for going farther.

In reading the Spectator, note that Addison's papers are distinguished from Steele's by being signed with one of the four letters, C. L. I. O., these denoting either the name of the muse of history, or one of the four places, Chelsea, London, Islington and the Office where the articles were written.

The numbers of the Spectator telling the story of Sir Roger de Coverley, a delightful imaginary character invented by Steele but continued most gracefully by Addison, have of late years been published as a separate book. Doctor Johnson says:

---

* Number CLIX., "Vision of Mirza;" LXXXIII., "Visit to a Picture Gallery;" CII., "On the Management of the Fan;" CLXV., "Against the Use of Foreign Words;" XVIII., "On Italian Opera;" III., "Vision of Public Credit;" also the papers on "Milton," beginning with CCLXVII. and continuing for eighteen successive Saturdays.

Whoever wishes to attain an English style, familiar but not coarse, and elegant but not ostentatious, must give his days and nights to the volumes of Addison.

Addison, who to us is known best by his essays, was to his contemporaries more celebrated as a successful drama-tist. After the "Spectator" had died down, he wrote the tragedy of "Cato," a somewhat formal though polished drama founded upon the old Roman story. The play came out at a time of great political excitement, and was raptur-ously applauded by the whigs, who professed to discover in it attacks on the tories, their enemies. We find it rather dull reading now, though it has some fine and even grand passages. Cato's soliloquy on immortality, uttered the night before his suicide, beginning:

> It must be so! Plato, thou reasonest well;

is worthy of being committed to memory; and the lines:

> 'T is not in mortals to command success,
> But we'll do more, Sempronius, we'll deserve it;

contain within themselves the whole philosophy of life.

Addison's conduct toward Steele, his playmate at the Charter-house, his college-friend, the companion and liter-ary associate of his prosperous years, has been severely censured; but we think without reason. Poor Steele, a borrower by profession, always in debt, always in trouble, had borrowed of the frugal and careful Addison a thousand pounds, giving him as security a mortgage on his house at Hampton. Steele lived as if he had the purse of For-tunatus; gave splendid dinners when, as a biographer says, he had not money to buy bread and cheese; set up a carriage and pair for his wife and a riding-horse for himself; took and furnished a handsome house in London while he was still in debt for one at Hampton; and plunged deeper and deeper into extravagance until finally Addison, whose patience was fairly worn out, sold the house and furniture, paid himself, and handed the rest of the purchase-money to Steele. Even a friend is justified in refusing to pour money into a leaky receptacle like Dick Steele's pocket.

At forty-four years of age Addison married the Countess Dowager of Warwick, to whose son he had been tutor. The marriage did not prove a happy one; the lady was haughty and condescending, apparently thinking she had done the man of letters great honor in marrying him, and treated him as if he were beneath her; and Addison's pleasantest hours were spent away from home. He frequented Button's Coffee-house, which seems to have been a successor to Will's, where Dryden used to sit; and there he met agreeable companions, and drank more wine than was good for him. Drinking was the vice of the age, and it can not be denied that it was Addison's weakness. He died three years after his marriage, leaving a daughter, who died unmarried. Holland House in London, the town-residence of the Earls of Warwick, where Addison spent his married life, still stands in its shady park, and has been the resort of many pilgrims and the dwelling-place of much elegance and cultivation.

When Addison found his end drawing near, he sent for his step-son, the Earl of Warwick, who was a worthless young man and an evil liver, saying to him, "I wish you to see in what peace a Christian can die." The Earl did not long survive him.

Richard Steele (1672–1729) was born (in Dublin) in the same year with Addison, and was the son of an Irish attorney. A part of his story has already been given. He left Oxford without a degree, contrary to the wishes of his friends, in order to enter the army, which he did as a private soldier. His whole life is shadowed forth in a remark of his own: He said that when he mounted a war-horse and planted himself behind King William III., against Louis XIV., he lost the succession to a good estate, from the same humor which he had preserved ever since, of preferring the state of his mind to that of his fortune.

Steele, according to the fashion of the day, tried his hand at writing comedies. His first, "The Funeral," ridiculing the hollow parade which takes the place of grief, was well received; one or two others had indifferent success, and the last, "The Conscious Lovers," in which he takes strong ground against duelling, was immensely applauded. Steele's comedies were all comparatively pure in morals, being in singular and noble contrast to those by authors of the school of Dryden who were still writing for the stage. Public taste was undergoing a change for the better, and such periodicals as the "Tatler" and the "Spectator" did much toward cultivating a higher literary standard in keeping with the rebound of morals and manners which marked the close of the Stuart dynasty in England.

Steele was twice married, each wife bringing him money, which makes his improvidence the less excusable. His second wife, the "Dear Prue" of his four hundred notes and letters, seems to have been a thrifty person, and, notwithstanding his real affection for her, often to have been in want of the guineas which he was spending all too freely on wine and company. These notes are written from all sorts of places, mostly from taverns and coffee-houses, and now and then from the inside of a debtor's prison. Sometimes he encloses a guinea or two for his wife, or a little present of some tea or a few walnuts, while she, poor woman, is constantly dunned by the baker and the shoemaker, and is dining frugally at home with her children. Many of the notes are excuses for not coming home, sometimes real ones, and then again, as we can not but suspect, made up for the occasion; and once he says, after excusing himself on the score of dining with a friend, "Dear Prue, do not send after me, for I shall be ridiculous." He probably had his small trials, as she had her great ones.

Steele was, as might be expected, a zealous whig politician, and as the condition of parties was changeable, he found himself sometimes on the top, sometimes at the bottom of Fortune's wheel. He rushed frequently into print, and on one of these occasions was expelled from the House of Commons for libel. In speaking of the many journals begun by him after "The Tatler," "The Spectator" and "The Guardian" (for each of which Addison wrote), one of his biographers says, "So ready was Steele at this kind of enterprise, that apparently whenever he felt strongly on any subject he at once started a journal to give vent to his feelings." The same writer gives a list of eight of these periodicals, beside the three mentioned above. When the whigs came into power with the accession of George I., Steele's fortunes improved; he was knighted and received a profitable appointment, but the more he had the more he spent. To avoid his creditors he was at last obliged to retire into Wales and live on an estate his wife had owned there.* She had then been dead for some years, but his daughters were with him. Friends who visited him describe him as keeping his sweet cheerfulness to the end, in spite of paralysis, and one of our latest pictures of him is of his being wheeled out on the lawn to see the village sports, and pencilling an order to the mercer for a new gown to the best dancer.

---

*One anecdote about Steele's palmy days has been told many times. He had built himself a private theatre, and to try whether the hall was well adapted for hearing he placed himself in the most remote part of the gallery, and begged the carpenter who had built the house to speak up from the stage. After a moment the carpenter began in a voice perfectly audible: "Sir Richard Steele! For three months past me and my men have been a-working in this theatre, and we've never seen the color of your honor's money; we will be very much obliged if you'll pay it directly, for until you do, we won't drive in another nail!"

Steele was the author of the felicitious 'phrase, used in speaking of an admirable woman: "To love her was a liberal education."

CHAPTER XXVIII.

AGE OF ANNE.   LESSER ESSAYISTS.

WHEN Addison and Steele have been named, and Swift, having been discussed, is set aside, it seems as if there could not be much more to say of the essayists of the Augustan Age, as the first part of the eighteenth century has been called. And yet there were others who exercised a powerful influence. Dr. Arbuthnot (1675–1735), a friend of Pope, wrote a powerful political satire called "The History of John Bull," intended to bring into ridicule the interference of England in the War of the Spanish Succession, and directed especially against Marlborough. Later he became a member of the Scriblerus Club, which included most of the wits of the day, and began, in connection with Pope, the "Memoirs of Martinus Scriblerus." It was of him that Swift said, "If the world had a dozen Arbuthnots, I would burn my [Gulliver's] Travels!"

Sir Samuel Garth (died 1710) was also a distinguished physician, and wrote a mock-heroic poem called "The Dispensary," which ran through many editions.

John Dennis (1657–1734), called in his own day "The Critic," wrote many short essays on various subjects, and some poor poetry. He used one expression which has passed into a proverb. He had invented a new kind of stage-thunder (the same as is still used in theatres), and once, after the failure of one of his plays, he was attending a representation of "Macbeth," and heard his own thunder used in the scenes. In a rage he exclaimed, "See how the rascals use me! They will not let my play run, and yet they steal my thunder!"

Louis Theobald (1691–1744) was a writer of unsuccessful plays, a translator, and an editor of Shakespeare.   In the last capacity he did best, and thereby excited the anger of Pope (who had also tried his hand at the same work), to such a degree that he was made the first hero of the "Dunciad;" Colley Cibber's name being substituted for Theobald's at a later period.

Matthew Henry (1662–1714) was the author of an excellent commentary on the Scriptures.

William Warburton (1698–1779), Bishop of Gloucester, a man of immense learning and a noted theological writer, was one of the many editors of Shakespeare.   The great dramatist, after being comparatively neglected for a hundred years, was brought into notice, as it were, by a continuous line of editors and commentators, lasting down to the edition of Dr. Johnson (published 1765), after which the subject was allowed to rest until a new interest was awakened in it during the nineteenth century.

The most learned man of the eighteenth century, and one who has been called the finest classical scholar England ever produced, was Richard Bentley (1662–1742.)   His editions of the Greek and Latin poets attested his prodigious learning, but the crowning proof of his superiority was given in the discussion on the so-called "Epistles of Phalaris."*

George Berkeley (1685–1753), Bishop of Cloyne in Ireland, was a man of varied talents and of a rare charm of character.   Even the unsparing satirist, Pope, ascribes

> To Berkeley, every virtue under heaven.

---

* This was a book attributed to a Sicilian tyrant living in the sixth century B.C., the same Phalaris who caused a brazen bull to be made in which he roasted his unfortunate victims alive. The letters, really a production of a thousand years later, or thereabouts, gave rise to the

As a man of science he wrote "The New Theory of Vision"; as a metaphysician, "The Principles of Knowledge"; as a theologian, "Alciphron."   In opposition to the materialistic tendencies of the time, he maintained what is called the "idealistic theory," namely, that the qualities which we attribute to matter exist only in our own minds. The materialists said that the existence of mind could not be proved; he tried, without much success, to show the same as to the existence of matter.   His life is to us now more interesting than his works. Always eager to benefit his fellow-creatures, he formed a plan for establishing "A College for Savage Indians in America," for which he collected large subscriptions, and obtained the promise of £20,000 from government. He then set sail for Newport, Rhode Island, to wait there for the promised grant. The money never came, and Berkeley after spending two years in vain expectations, returned to England. During his residence in Newport he was constantly occupied in doing good, and made himself beloved by all classes of people.

It was in view of his proposed undertaking in America that he wrote the famous poem of which the last verse runs:

> Westward the course of empire takes its way;
> The first four acts already past,
> A fifth shall close the drama with the day;
> Time's noblest offspring is his last.

One of the most remarkable religious works ever written

---

fiercest literary quarrel of modern times. They were accepted as genuine by many well-known writers, Sir William Temple and Dean Swift among others. Dr. Bentley's doubts concerning them being attacked by Bishop Atterbury and Charles Boyle (nephew of the great chemist), Bentley utterly used up his assailants in a scathing reply in which he proved them to be both ignorant and arrogant. They could not retort, but the angry feelings excited ceased only with the lives of the combatants.

belongs to the eighteenth century. This is the "Analogy of Religion, both Natural and Revealed, to the Constitution and Course of Nature," by Joseph Butler (1692–1751), Bishop of Durham. Of this work, Sir James Mackintosh says, "It is the most original and profound work extant, in any language, on the philosophy of religion." Butler's was not a speculative mind; he brought every subject to the test of the strictest reasoning, and produced a train of argument of wonderful coherence and exactness. He left, besides, a volume of admirable sermons.

Isaac Watts (1674–1748), author of hundreds of hymns and "Divine Songs," was a dissenting clergyman. He wrote, beside hymns and sermons, various treatises on education and other subjects. His gentle and kindly disposition made him many friends; and on going to make a short visit to Sir Thomas and Lady Abney, the intercourse proved so mutually agreeable that he remained with them until his death, a period of thirty-six years. Some of Watts's hymns are still to be found in every collection.

Dr. Philip Doddridge (1702–51) also wrote some beautiful hymns, and many sermons. He composed what Dr. Johnson called one of the finest epigrams in the English language. It is a paraphrase of Doddridge's family motto, "*Dum vivimus vivamus*":

> Live while you live, the epicure would say,
> And seize the pleasures of the present day.
> Live while you live, the sacred preacher cries,
> And give to God each moment as it flies.
> Lord, in my views let both united be;
> I live in pleasure when I live to Thee.

The brothers John and Charles Wesley, the founders of Methodism, have a place in literature from their fine hymns. John Wesley (1703–91), wrote also "A Plain Account of the People called Methodists," and some religious works. With them was associated George White-field, famous for his impassioned pulpit oratory. All these came to America and labored for some time in Georgia, then a comparatively new colony. Whitefield's sermons were published after his death. With money collected by himself he founded in Savannah, an orphanage for boys which is still (1892) prosperous and useful, after more than a hundred and fifty years of existence.

It has been customary in framing lists of the eighteenth-century novelists, to include among them the name of Daniel Defoe (1661–1731). As a writer of fiction, this author undoubtedly did much to foster the taste for stories of imaginary persons, places and occurrences; but the word novel in its modern sense as a picture of real human life and death, joy and sorrow, love and hate, is in no wise applicable to the stories of Defoe.

This remarkable man was the son of James Foe, a prosperous London butcher, and himself prefixed the "de" to his name after he had reached middle life. He got a good elementary education from Charles Morton, a dissenting preacher who, being driven from England by persecution, came to America and was afterward made vice-president of Harvard College. It is mentioned of this teacher that he "included English among school-studies"—an indication that such an addition to the course was not a common one. Possibly Defoe's strong, clear, idiomatic English style may be owing to his father's fortunate selection of a master for him.

In politics, he was generally on the losing side. He took part in Monmouth's rebellion (1685), but escaped the clutches of Kirke and Jeffreys, and later wrote several political tracts against James II. After wandering abroad for some years, he went into business in London, failed for a very large sum, made a compromise with his creditors, and afterward most honorably paid them in full.

In his first published book, "Essay on Projects," Defoe took the part of a social reformer, advocating savings-banks for the poor, the founding of insurance companies, improvement in public highways (then in a disgraceful condition), abolition of the press-gang, and a college for the higher education of women. This last it was reserved for the nineteenth century to carry into effect. In urging it, Defoe says, "A woman well bred and well taught, furnished with the additional accomplishments of knowledge and behavior, is a creature without comparison. . . . . She is all softness and sweetness, love, art and delight." A staunch whig, he was strongly in favor of William III., and his satire called "The True-born Englishman" (1698) was read, even by the king's enemies, with delight, on account of its broad humor and manly sentiments. Defore says that eighty thousand copies of it were sold in the streets. Of monarchs false to their great trust he says:

> When kings the sword of justice first lay down,
> They are no kings, though they possess the crown.
> Titles are shadows, crowns are empty things;
> The good of subjects is the end of kings.

During the latter part of the reign of William III., Defoe was at the height of his prosperity. With the reign of Queen Anne his fortunes changed. Indignant at a bill in Parliament aimed against the Dissenters, he wrote a pamphlet called "The Shortest Way with the Dissenters," advising that their ministers should be hung or burned, and the congregations banished. This satire was considered by the government a libel, and the author was sentenced to fine, imprisonment and the pillory.*

---

* When the officers were looking for him, he was advertised as "a middle-sized spare man, about forty years old, of a brown complexion, and dark-brown hair, though he wears a wig, having a hook nose, sharp chin, gray eyes, and a mole near his mouth."

Pope, a political opponent, has a fling at him in regard to the latter punishment:

Earless on high stood unabashed Defoe—

but there was no question of cropping of ears, and the satirist had little reason to be abashed. He was surrounded by an admiring crowd, who drank foaming tankards of ale in his honor, and threw bouquets at him instead of the customary stones and rotten eggs. He even found means after the first day's exhibition to write and have published some bold verses called a "Hymn to the Pillory," which the government apparently did not dare to suppress. After standing three times in the pillory and paying his fine, he was taken to Newgate prison, where he remained for more than a year (1703–4).* While there he edited and published his "Review" (already spoken of as the prototype of the Tatler and Spectator). Much of his work is rough and unpolished, but some of his ideas anticipate those of modern philanthropy. Such are the essays entitled "Giving Alms no Charity," and another against national workshops.

Defoe's first work of pure fiction is a pretended "Apparition of Mrs. Veal," a ghost-story told with such wonderful naturalness that it imposed on nearly everyone who read it.† Such writing Defoe excelled in. His simple, colloquial English, coupled with his ability to throw himself into the character he was portraying, gave a verisimilitude to his narratives such as had never before been attained by any writer.

In spite of the success of this book, Defoe seems to

---

* During this time his wife and six children were supported by charity.

† The story goes that this was written for the purpose of selling a dull work called "Drelincourt on Death," to which it was prefixed, with the result of selling off the whole edition. Some discredit has been thrown on this statement, but there seems no reason to doubt it.

have dropped fiction entirely until after the accession of George I. (1715). Three years later, when the author was fifty-seven years old, appeared the matchless "Robinson Crusoe," founded on the adventures of a real sailor, Alexander Selkirk. The name Crusoe was borrowed, being that of an old schoolmate of Defoe. From this time he poured out tales in rapid succession: "Memoirs of a Cavalier," "Moll Flanders," "Journal of the Plague-Year," "History of Captain Jack," etc. The cavalier story imposed upon Lord Chatham, and the history of the plague upon everybody. It is hard to this day to read the latter book without the impression that the author is telling his personal experience, but we know that he was only five years old in 1666.

Defoe stands singularly apart from the great writers of his time. Of all others we say, "he was a friend of so-and-so," but Defoe, from the peculiarites of his character, seems to have had no friend. There is a mystery about the closing years of his life, but it is pretty well ascertained that he died in hiding, trying to escape from his creditors.

CHAPTER XXIX.

THE FIRST NOVELISTS.

OF the novelists, properly so called, whose writings belong to the beginnning of the eighteenth century, Samuel Richardson (1689–1761) comes first. He was the son of a joiner and was bred a printer in the old-fashioned way; served an apprenticeship of seven years, learning his trade thoroughly; married his master's daughter, and set up for himself in the same business. He had from boyhood had a special aptitude for letter-writing, and when thirteen years old was employed by some young women of his acquaintance to write their love-letters for them. When he was near the age of fifty, a bookseller proposed to him to prepare a sort of "Complete Letter-Writer," by means of which unlearned people would be able to compose that difficult thing, a letter to a friend. Richardson, improving upon the idea, thought he might throw these letters into the form of a connected story; and the result was the famous novel "Pamela."*

In this story, the heroine is a young servant girl from the country, who takes a place in the household of Squire Booby, and relates, in letters to her friends, her varied experiences. The friends answer her, giving advice, and thus the story is told. This is the first English novel having love for its main interest. "Pamela" had such success that the author was encouraged to try another novel, also in the form of letters, and wrote "Clarissa Harlowe," which is considered by many persons his finest work. Here the heroine is in good society, though not the highest. When Richardson complained that the ladies were too much interested in Lovelace, the villain of his second novel, they answered that he had given them nothing else to like. Upon this hint he wrote his last work, "Sir Charles Grandison," the hero of which has become a synonym for courtliness, propriety, dignity, and if we must say it, insufferable tediousness. Sir Charles is Richardson's ideal gentleman; and as the author himself was not "to the manner born," it was natural that he should overdo the matter in describing those who were. "Sir Charles Grandison," however, has had its admirers even in more recent years; and when one falls in with a volume of it in some old-fashioned library, it is well to spend an hour over its pages, so as to understand what kind of reading delighted the readers of the last century.

Richardson himself is described as being "a stout, rosy,

---

* Pronounced Pam'ela.

vain, precise little man, carrying himself with sensitive dignity," and considerably elated by the prominence into which his newly-found talent raised him. Ladies made a pet of him, and constantly urged him to write more stories for their entertainment; but he kept on quietly in his own path, and having written his three novels of low, middle, and high life, withdrew into the country and passed his remaining years in the enjoyment of a prosperity earned by many years of steady industry.

One trial, however, Richardson had. A gay, dissipated young man of the town, not liking the virtuous conduct of the older man's heroines and the sobriety and correctness of his "Sir Charles," wrote a novel expressly to ridicule all that had been held up to respect and veneration in Richardson's work.

The young man was Henry Fielding (1707-54), whose "Joseph Andrews" was begun with the aim of caricaturing, particularly, "Pamela," though the work grew under his hand to a degree of excellence which cast its original purpose into the shade. This was his first novel, though not his first work, by many; and its success turned the bent of his genius toward romance - writing, wherein he gained the high place he holds as the originator of the novel of real life in English literature.

Fielding's was a younger branch of the family of the Earls of Denbigh. His father was General Fielding, a man of much distinction of the convivial sort, who, when his son had finished his law-studies, made him an allowance of £200 a year "which anybody might pay," as Fielding expressed it, to indicate that his father did *not* pay it. Poverty drove him to depend on his pen and his wits, and he employed them in writing for the stage. He wrote some twenty-four comedies, farces, and extravaganzas in the years between 1732 and 1743, some of them translations or adaptations from the French, and others original satires on the people and things about him.   None of them "held the stage" beyond his own day (though succeeding writers used them largely), yet they gave him occupation and support and paved the way for his subsequent eminence.

He married (1735) Miss Cradock, a belle of Salisbury, who had £1500 of her own; and on his succeeding, at the death of his mother, to a small estate in Dorsetshire, they went to live there.   Fielding took up the character of a country squire, with servants, horses, dogs, etc., in playing which part his slender means were soon used up.   Then he returned to London, where he passed the rest of his days in much activity, some solid distinction and not a little extravagance and dissipation.   He was called to the bar and had a fair practice; but never ceased the industrious use of his pen; writing one valuable law-book and contributing to journals, political and literary.   Eight years after marriage his lovely and loving wife died; a blow which is said to have threatened to deprive him of reason.   He was appointed justice of the peace, an office which he filled with credit and success, using the position to put an end to certain gross abuses that had prevailed in that office.   Later, he became Chairman of the Sessions, which necessitated his attendance at the bench.   These experiences brought from his pen "An inquiry into the increase of thieves and robbers," and other valuable tracts on serious subjects.   They also gave him the particular knowledge requisite for depicting to perfection, as he did in his novels, the ruffianly element then rampant in English low-life.

Although possessed of these solid qualities, his inherited tendency to dissipation, and the prevailing fashion of high living, brought about their inevitable results, debility and fatal disease.   (Lady Mary Wortley Montagu described him as one who forgot every evil when he was before a venison pasty and a flask of champagne).

The warfare he waged on the gangs of desperate ruffians

then infesting London was too much for his wasted forces and he was compelled to retire from his official duties. In 1754 he sailed for Lisbon in search of health, arriving after a stormy passage of which he (a worker to the end) left an account, published after his death. He died there at the comparatively early age of forty-eight; dropsy, jaundice and asthma being the dreadful immediate means of his taking off.

Passing by the theatrical experience already mentioned (wherein, by the way, he became at one time manager of a company) we come to the work through which he achieved his great renown. His first novel was "Joseph Andrews," as we have seen. Its success was immediate. It introduced the real into the domain before possessed by the ideal. The world recognized it as the greatest work of fiction yet produced in England. The age of Arcadian romance seemed to be at an end, and the more difficult achievement of interesting readers with the common life about them was at last shown to be possible. The humor is akin to that of Cervantes, and "Parson Adams" is the Quixote of the book. His "History of Jonathan Wild the Great," is able and valuable, but repulsive; being a description of low profligacy with only a foil of moral excellence. "The History of Tom Jones, a Foundling," is his greatest work, and often called the greatest of English novels. It has a long, complicated and ingenious plot wherein virtue is rewarded and vice punished — yet the sympathy of the reader is left, often, with the offender. Therefore its influence is not in the direction of virtue; for as has often been said (and should always be remembered), the tendency is bad of any novel which leaves the heart of the reader on the side of the wrong-doer; even though the latter may be punished and the unloved exemplary person carry off all the rewards at the author's disposal.

"Tom Jones" is quite unfit for general reading in our more decent day; as indeed are all Fielding's works.

In his third and last novel, "Amelia," the heroine is said to be drawn from the character of his lovely first wife. This was also a very great novel, judged by the standard of his times.

Of late years it has become almost a fashion to rank Fielding as the greatest of English novelists. If this be true, it is with vast allowances for the time in which he wrote. He was perhaps the most original and courageous, inasmuch as he discovered the new realm of fiction; was the Columbus of a new Indies of wealth, grandeur and magnificence not even yet fully explored. As to his being the greatest novelist in the sense of having written the greatest novels, that can scarcely be maintained. There are hundreds of tales written since his day, by scores of novelists, each of which, judged by its intrinsic merit, must be placed above any one of Fielding's. Scott, Dickens, George Eliot and many others have given us works each in some respects and some in all respects greater than "Tom Jones," or any other novel of a past century.

Thackeray wrote, in his generous, whole-souled way:

What a genius! What a vigor! What a bright-eyed intelligence and observation! What a wholesome hatred for meanness and knavery! What a vast sympathy! What a cheerfulness! What a manly relish of life! What a love of human kind! What a *poet* is here! . . . . It is wonderful to think of the pains and misery that man suffered; the pressure of want, illness, remorse which he endured, and that the writer was neither malignant nor melancholy, his view of truth never warped and his generous human kindness never surrendered.—*Lectures on the English Humorists.*

We read with a quiet smile this enthusiasm on the part of one, himself the writer of novels more noble than those he is praising. "Hatred for meanness and knavery"! "Love of human kind"! "View of truth never warped"! "Generous human kindness"! All these things do not describe fun which is found in the discomfiture of the helpless by the hand of insolent roystering strength. Nor does it comport with rational ideas of "hatred of meanness and knavery" to glorify the giving away to friends of money that should be paid to creditors. These are Fielding's notions of "sympathy," and the best that can be said in their defence is that they have prevailed in England even to this day. It is not uncommon in English fiction (and perhaps in fact) to regard the creditor, the "dun," as an enemy. He who has trusted you with his money or goods, which you have used and not returned as promised, is sacrificed to a "friend" in need, and the act is admired! You have been generous with the money of somebody else, and yet are not marked as a thief but as a hero! Happily this absurdity is almost unknown in the literature of the more logical, working, debt-paying portion of the race. But it is characteristic of Fielding and his heroes.

Tobias Smollett (1721–71) was, like Fielding, of a good family (Scottish) and, also like him, was early in life obliged to depend on himself. After travelling about the world as surgeon's-mate on board a vessel in the royal navy, he, too, found wherein his forte lay, and began to write novels. Among these are "Roderick Random," "Peregrine Pickle," and "Humphrey Clinker," the latter written many years after the others, and generally thought to be his best. He also wrote a "History of England," which has not kept its ground against the standard work of Hume, written at about the same time; though the latter part, from the period where the greater historian broke off (1688) to 1765, is occasionally to be found in libraries as a supplement to Hume's.

Among the progenitors of the modern novel, Smollett is third in time and in estimation; Richardson being first in date and in decency, and Fielding first in power. Smollett's pen was both bitter and foul. He was of an unhappy temper, and found, as such persons do, an unfriendly world to live in; for as has been well said, mankind is like a mirror, in that it gives back smile for smile and frown for frown.

His coarseness seemed to be an inherent part of his being, a thing loved by the writer for its own sake rather than forced upon him by his devotion to truth to nature and the times of which he was telling.

The best work he did was in describing life in the navy; and the race of British sailors of the old day found in his writings a passport to immortality. They have already passed away, but their memory is embalmed forever in Smollett's romances.

The last of the group of novelists we have mentioned (although he is scarcely entitled to that name) is Laurence Sterne (1713–68) who was born in Ireland, son of an army officer, and grandson of an Archbishop of York. He was a clergyman, though one would not guess it from his writings. His "Tristram Shandy" depicts, with great humor, characters whose individuality gives them an imperishable place in our literature. "Uncle Toby" and "Corporal Trim" are no more to be forgotten than are Cromwell and Barebones. The airy creations of fiction will live as long as the solid characters of history. In "The Sentimental Journey," satire is exchanged for sentiment and, although coarseness is not far to seek, it is subordinated to a vein of tender philanthropy, benevolence, and pity for all suffering which palliates if it does not excuse the other. True, Thackeray maintains that the sentiment is forced and affected, and much of it merely a cunning mask for indelicate suggestion; but that has not been the conclusion of readers in general.

His story of the imprisoned starling has drawn many tears, and has become an English classic:

"I can't get out!" said the starling, and to every person who came through the passage it ran fluttering to the side toward which he approached it with the same lamentation of its captivity, "I can't get out!" said the starling. "God help thee!" said I, "but I'll let thee out, cost what it will;" so I turned about the cage to get the door. It was twisted and double-twisted so fast with wire there was no getting it open. . . . . The bird flew to the place where I was attempting his deliverance, and thrusting his head through the trellis, pressed his breast against it as if impatient. "I fear, poor creature, I can not set thee at liberty." "I can't get out, I can't get out!" said the starling.

Perhaps it is characteristic of Sterne's superficial and ineffectual sentiment that, the wire being so obstinate, the poor starling remains a prisoner through all the ages during which the story shall remain a part of literature.

The well-known and often-quoted phrase "God tempers the wind to the shorn lamb," is not taken from the Bible, but from Sterne; a fact about which there is a very general and very natural mistake.

CHAPTER XXX.

EARLY EIGHTEENTH - CENTURY POETS.

IN grouping together the poets who followed Pope, we do not give them in order of merit, but of date of birth. The earliest, Edward Young, (1681–1765) was a clergyman and wrote, beside much other verse, "Night Thoughts," a long religious poem in nine books, of which the main subject is the immortality of the soul. Dr. Young had much to sadden his life in the loss of friends, and his principal poem is tinged with a melancholy which does not necessarily belong to the subject. The didactic style of Young is now out of fashion; but his poem contains many fine lines, which are worth some little search to find. We subjoin a few of these:

Tired Nature's sweet restorer, balmy sleep!
    *   *   *
The bell strikes one. We take no note of time
But from its loss.
    *   *   *
Poor pensioner on the bounties of an hour.
    *   *   *
Be wise to-day; 't is madness to defer.
    *   *   *
Procrastination is the thief of time.
    *   *   *
All men think all men mortal but themselves.
    *   *   *
He mourns the dead who lives as they desire.
    *   *   *
Who does the best his circumstance allows,
Does well, acts nobly; angels could no more.
    *   *   *
How blessings brighten as they take their flight!
    *   *   *
Wishing, of all employments, is the worst.
    *   *   *
Man wants but little, nor that little long.
    *   *   *
Early, bright, transient, chaste as morning dew,
She sparkled, was exhaled, and went to heaven.
    *   *   *
                           Like our shadows,
Our wishes brighten as our sun declines.
    *   *   *
Death loves a shining mark.
    *   *   *
Pigmies are pigmies still, though perched on Alps;
And pyramids are pyramids in vales.

Allan Ramsay (1686–1758), son of a Scottish peasant
in Lanarkshire, rose from an apprenticeship at wig-making
to be a bookseller in Edinburgh, and reached middle
life before he published his first volume of collected verse.
Later, his pastoral play of "The Gentle Shepherd," written
partly in dialect, gave him at once a recognized place
among poets, and drew the best society of the town to
his humble shop. The scene-painting of the "Shepherd"
is of homely life, enlivened by homely sentiment and overflowing humor. The play is interspersed throughout with
graceful songs, among which "Lochaber no more," and
"The Yellow-haired Laddie" are deservedly popular. The

"Gentle Shepherd" is said to be the only Scotch pastoral poem ever written.

Ramsay had various ups and downs of fortune, preserving through them all the sunny cheerfulness which appears in his writings, pleased with his success and the appreciation of cultivated people, and very happy in his home-life.

Of Richard Savage (1698–1743) we should probably have heard but little had it not been for Dr. Johnson's generous and friendly "Life." His biographer sums up his history by saying that he was "doomed to poverty and obscurity, and launched upon the ocean of life only that he might be swallowed by its quicksands or dashed upon its rocks." If Savage had been a great poet we might relate his misfortunes in detail; but as he did not rise above mediocrity it is enough to say that his life was a wretched and unhappy one, whose vicissitudes were embittered by his own ill-regulated passions and vicious excesses. One of the interesting facts connected with it is that he and Dr. Johnson used sometimes to walk the London streets at night together, when neither one had the means to pay for a lodging and the supper which should have preceded it. One couplet of Savage's will live:

> He lives to build, not boast, a generous race;
> No tenth transmitter of a foolish face.

A curious instance of the ideas prevailing at that time is afforded by Savage's expectations from Queen Caroline (wife of George II.). When he had killed a man in a tavern brawl and was under sentence of death, she procured his pardon, and he afterward wrote a birthday ode addressed to her, calling himself her "Volunteer Laureate," for which he received a present of fifty pounds. Colley Cibber, the actual laureate, remonstrated against having his laurels thus borrowed or stolen; but Savage paid no attention, and once a year sent the queen a poem in return for which he received the same gift. The drollest part of it all is that

Savage was indignant because the queen did not give him a handsome pension, sufficient for his support; arguing that since she had saved his life, it was her duty to preserve it.

James Thomson (1700–48), the son of a Scotch Presbyterian minister, went, at the age of twenty-five, to seek his fortune in London. He was handicapped from the start by the failure of remittances which he expected from home, and by losing all his letters of introduction, which were stolen from his pocket as he was carrying them along the street carefully tied up in a corner of his handkerchief. His first paying occupation seems to have been teaching a child to read. His poem of "Winter" was sold to a bookseller for three guineas; and Thomson, having had the worldly wisdom to dedicate it to Sir Spencer Compton (one of George I.'s ministers), received a present of twenty guineas more. The reading world at once perceived the merit of "Winter," and in the course of two or three years the poem received the addition of Summer, Spring, and Autumn, and became the fine completed poem called "The Seasons." He was the first poet in whom love of nature overshadowed interest in man, and many of his descriptions of natural scenery are exquisite. The "Hymn to the Seasons," appended to the longer poem, is an epitome of the whole. The line to Spring:

> Come, gentle Spring, ethereal mildness come,

is very often quoted; sometimes in serious delight at the season's beauties; oftener in sarcastic allusion to its trying and afflicting vagaries. In one canto occur the famous lines:

> Delightful task! to rear the tender thought,
> To teach the young idea how to shoot.

Thomson, of course, tried his hand at dramatic writing. Almost everybody did so in those days. His tragedy of "Sophonisba," founded on the old Numidian-Roman story, was marred by one unlucky line:

> O Sophonisba! Sophonisba O!

Upon hearing which, some wag in the gallery called out:

O Jemmy Thomson! Jemmy Thomson, O!

and roars of laughter turned the tragedy into a farce. The objectionable line was afterward altered to:

O Sophonisba! I am wholly thine.

but the play was voted better for reading than for acting, and for burlesquing than either.

Thomson was incurably lazy, but his poetic gifts stood him in good stead, and he obtained from time to time such employment as was well paid and at the same time left him leisure for literary work. At one time he lost a sinecure office which yielded him a comfortable income, because his indolence prevented him from making the necessary application for its renewal. Poets, however, were scarce in those days, and he soon obtained another office, that of Surveyor General of the Leeward Islands, for the duties of which he employed a deputy, pocketing £300 per annum—at least $3,000 of our present money— in addition to what he paid the deputy.

His "Castle of Indolence" is his finest and most artistic poem. This, however, has never attained the popularity of the "Seasons." The former has an admirable moral, well worked out in Spenserian verse. Here is one stanza:

> I care not, Fortune, what you me deny;
> You can not rob me of free nature's grace;
> You can not shut the windows of the sky,
> Through which Aurora shows her brightening face;
> You can not bar my constant feet to trace
> The woods and lawns, by living stream, at eve;
> Let health my nerves and finer fibres brace,
> And I their toys to the great children leave;
> Of fancy, reason, virtue, naught can me bereave.*

---

* It is worth while to observe, here, the extra metrical foot which lengthens the final line from a pentameter to a hexameter. This, which is the kind of line called "Alexandrine," gives a much admired variation to the stanzas where it occurs.

14

John Dyer (1700–59), a Welshman, wrote a pretty descriptive poem called "Grongar Hill," in the octosyllabic metre made afterward so popular by Scott. A longer poem, "The Fleece," about sheep and their products, is, from the prosaic nature of the subject, unattractive.

Robert Blair (1700–46), a Scottish clergyman, was the author of "The Grave," which has been called, by high critical authority, an imitation of Young's "Night Thoughts." Of this charge it is a sufficient refutation to say that "The Grave" was written before "Night Thoughts," and has no other resemblance to that poem than being long, written on a serious subject, and in the form of blank verse. It is well sustained, and has some noble passages; for instance:

> Sure, the last end
> Of the good man is peace! How calm his exit!
> Night - dews fall not more gently to the ground,
> Nor weary, worn - out winds expire so soft.
> Behold him! In the evening tide of life,
> A life well spent, whose early care it was
> His riper years should not upbraid his green:
> By unperceived degrees he wears away,
> Yet, like the sun, seems larger at his setting.

Robert Blair must not be confounded with Dr. Hugh Blair (1718–1800), a well - known critic and writer on Rhetoric.

William Shenstone (1714–63) was the author of "The Schoolmistress," a really bright and readable sketch of the old - time "dame" school - teacher, but disfigured by an affectation of archaisms. His "Pastoral Ballad" is much more agreeable reading:

> My banks they are furnished with bees,
> Whose murmur invites one to sleep;
> My grottos are shaded with trees,
> And my hills are white over with sheep.

And so one is rocked, as it were, by the soft swaying of the verse, and almost ready to weep with the shepherd when his Phyllis turns out to be faithless.

CHAPTER XXXI.

EIGHTEENTH-CENTURY POETS — CONTINUED.

ITH the name of Thomas Gray (1716–71), a host of tender associations press upon us. We find ourselves, in fancy, in the "Country Church-yard," looking on the scene of the "Elegy." The glimmering landscape fades upon our sight; we hear the drowsy tinkling of the sheep-bells; the heaving turf reminds us of the generations gone before whom no cheerful sound shall ever more rouse from their lowly bed. Then we think of Wolfe, on his last night, as the boat dropped softly, with muffled oars, down the St. Lawrence, and hear him repeat to a brother-officer,

> The boast of heraldry, the pomp of power,
> And all that beauty, all that wealth e'er gave,
> Await alike the inevitable hour;
> The paths of glory lead but to the grave:

and say that he would rather be the author of that poem than to take Quebec—he at the moment on a path of glory that led him on the morrow to the grave.

We are surprised to read that the father of young Gray was of a harsh and violent disposition, and made his wife's life so wretched that she was obliged to separate from him and support herself and her son by keeping a shop in Cornhill, London. By his mother's efforts Thomas received a university education at Cambridge, though he left college without a degree. While there he formed a friendship with Horace Walpole, and the two set out for a tour on the continent, Walpole paying all expenses. They turned out to be uncongenial companions, and after a quarrel in Italy, for which Walpole at a later day took all the blame upon himself, Gray returned to England. Soon after this his father died, leaving some property, but not enough to enable the son to enter the law, as he had proposed doing. He therefore settled down for life at Cambridge, where he would have the best opportunities for study. It was while he was here that most of his poems were written, though the first one of importance, the "Ode on a Distant Prospect of Eton College," (where Gray was prepared for Cambridge), he kept by him five years before he gave it to the public. He became a proficient in every branch of learning he undertook (he did not study mathematics), was a fine Latin and Greek scholar, was familiar with the literature of several modern languages, and was profoundly versed in the natural sciences, as well as in architecture, archæology and music. And from all this, the only benefit we of the nineteenth century have is a half-dozen exquisite poems, a dozen or so of others of less merit, though all carefully finished, and a volume of delightful letters; for, like others of that leisurely time, Gray was an admirable letter-writer. It is pleasant to think that his devoted mother lived to read the Elegy and to enjoy the appreciation which the public gave it. It instantly became popular and has stood the test of time, being felt to this day, by perhaps a majority of readers, to be the most perfect poem in the language.

Three years before Gray's death, the professorship of modern history at Cambridge was bestowed upon him; a tardy recognition of his great claims. This made him easy as to money matters (he had always before been poor), but his health was beginning to fail and he had not much enjoyment of the new distinction. He died of gout, the same disease which had carried off both his father and mother; and was buried at Stoke Pogis, the churchyard of the "Elegy," in the same tomb with his mother. His epitaph on her is touching in its simplicity. It runs thus:

Beside her friend and sister here sleep the remains of Dorothy Gray, widow, the careful mother of many children, one of whom alone had the misfortune to survive her.

Gray was refined and delicate in his tastes, even to fastidiousness. He possessed the art and industry to give that last touch to labored composition, the touch which removes all trace of labor. In the "Elegy," there is not a fault of thought, of diction, of rhyme or of rhythm; and yet it reads as if the lines had flowed spontaneously from the Castalian spring, the words falling gently to their places without the intervention of a mortal hand.

Of Gray's other poems, the favorites are the "Ode on a Distant Prospect of Eton College," "The Bard," "Ode to Adversity," and "The Progress of Poesy." In the latter are the grand lines describing Milton:

> Nor second he, that rode sublime
> Upon the seraph - wings of ecstasy,
> The secrets of the abyss to spy.
> He passed the flowing bounds of space and time;
> The living throne, the sapphire blaze,
> Where angels tremble while they gaze,
> He saw; but blasted with excess of light,
> Closed his eyes in endless night.

Gray was offered the laureateship on the death of Colley Cibber (1757), but declined it. It was then bestowed on William Whitehead, a poet and dramatist of no great merit.

When Dr. Burney visited Voltaire at Ferney, the great Frenchman inquired what poets were then living in England. Dr. Burney replied, "We have Mason and Gray." Posterity has decided that one of these should be known in later centuries as far as the English language is spoken, and the other utterly forgotten except as a name in the list. William Mason (1725–97), in his day called "one of the most eminent of living poets," is now remembered chiefly as having been the friend of Gray.

A sad interest hangs about the name of William Collins (1721–59), whose poems, few but most exquisite, bear the stamp of true genius. His ode beginning:

> How sleep the brave, who sink to rest
> By all their country's wishes blest!

and the lofty and sustained "Ode to the Passions," are among the finest examples of such poetry in our language. Strange to say, these beautiful poems, published with other odes, "fell flat" on the public taste of his own day; and the author, who lacked steadiness of purpose and noble aims, became dissipated and despondent. He had gone to London, full of high hopes and strong in the confident possession of genius, ·and the neglect of his work took away his spirit and his hope and he plunged into the deepest excesses. Once only after this melancholy deteri-oration had begun, did he light up for awhile, and he then wrote the beautiful ode on the death of Thomson:

In yonder grave a Druid lies;

but soon sank again into mental inaction. After years of struggling with poverty an uncle died and left him what to the poor author was a fortune; but too late for him to enjoy it. He paid to the bookseller all the money the latter had lost in publishing the "Odes," and then, collecting all the copies he could find, threw them into the fire. He lived for ten miserable years longer, in a state of mental incapacity—sometimes of violent mania—almost forgotten by the world; and when at last death released him, no notice was taken of the event.

Of Mark Akenside (1721–70) it is not necessary to say much. He was the son of a butcher in Newcastle. Being desirous of entering the Presbyterian ministry he received assistance from a fund established for use in such cases; but, changing his intentions, he resolved to study physic, and at once repaid the sum which had been contributed.* He became a physician, and at twenty-three wrote the one poem with which his name is connected, "The Pleasures of

---

*A couplet from a poem written at this time exhibits his aim in life:
Still true to reason be my plan,
Still let my actions speak the man.

Imagination." This work, smooth in rhythm and correct in imagery, was favorably received by the reading public of his day, but has fallen into neglect in ours, when we have so much that is grand and noble to read that we do not feel disposed to spend much time on the utterances of mediocrity.

CHAPTER XXXII.

SAMUEL JOHNSON.

THE great Dr. Johnson! Such was the name commonly given to Samuel Johnson (1709–84) by his contemporaries. Those who knew him late in life have described his rolling gait, his untidy wig, his seamed and scarred face, his peering, near-sighted eyes, until we feel as if we had seen him in the flesh, so strongly is his image impressed upon our minds. We watch him twitching and tossing his large ungainly body from side to side as he walks the streets, carefully touching every post along the road, going back to complete the ceremony if by chance he had missed one: we see him sawing violently backward and forward as he sits reading a book on the open common, and we wonder what there is about this strange being to render him an object of veneration and of profound interest.

Johnson was born in the old cathedral city of Lichfield, and was the son of Michael Johnson, a learned bookseller. Being scrofulous, his parents took him to London to be "touched" by Queen Anne for the "King's Evil"; and among his earliest recollections was one of being taken before a tall lady in a long black hood and a stomacher covered with diamonds. The royal touch, however, produced no effect, and the miserable inheritance of disease threw a cloud over his whole life. It made him inert and melancholy; though when roused in any intellectual dispute, he easily overtopped his companions. His father, who was poor and always growing poorer, managed to send him to college, but could not equip him properly, so that while the professors were amazed at his wonderful powers and great attainments, the students made themselves merry over his ragged clothes and dirty linen. He used to shuffle along in by-paths to avoid showing the holes in his shoes; but when some kind person left a new pair at his door he pitched them out of the window, enraged at being considered an object of charity.

When Johnson had been three years at Oxford, his father died, leaving barely enough to provide for his widow the necessaries of life, while the son struggled onward, trying all sorts of things, school-teaching among the rest. But few would wish to send their boys to a person of whom it could be written, "He has such a way of distorting his face (w^h though he can't help), ye gent. think it may affect some young ladds." This want of control over his muscles was one of the many fearful results of scrofula, and one of the symptoms of a mental disease, verging on insanity, against which he strove all his life.

Two of Johnson's three pupils were the sons of his old friend Captain Peter Garrick, and one of them, a rosy-cheeked lad, was destined to a fame comparable to that of his great teacher. When in a few months the school failed, master and pupil went up to London together to seek, each, his fortune. The younger became the greatest actor of the century; the elder the literary despot to whom all the world of letters looked up with unquestioning submission.

At twenty-five years old, while still in Lichfield, Samuel Johnson married a widow of nearly double his age, in whom his friends saw only an ill-looking, ignorant and affected person, with children as old as Johnson himself;

but whom he really loved, retaining his affection for her as long. as she lived.

In London, Johnson picked up such literary work as he could find to do. He made translations, wrote prefaces, furnished short articles for the "Gentleman's Magazine," and offered his one dramatic effort, the tragedy of "Irene," to the booksellers. "You might better buy a porter's knot and go to shouldering trunks," said one of them to him, looking at his broad shoulders and big, awkward, figure. He often went hungry in these days, and once signed himself, in writing to a publisher, *impransus* — without a breakfast, or fasting. He used to boast that he got a better dinner for eightpence than his friends did for a shilling. "I give sixpence for meat and a penny for bread, and a penny to the waiter," said he; "while they drink wine and give the waiter nothing." During these years of miserable privation we hear little of his wife, who lived sometimes in London and sometimes at or near Lichfield, according to their circumstances. At one time Johnson was occupied in writing out, in his own language, the debates in parliament. (These debates it was then illegal to publish). A listener reported the speeches to him and they were published under feigned names, the whole being styled, "Debates in the Senate of Lilliput." About this time Johnson had a gleam of success in the acceptance by a bookseller of his poem of "London," for which he received ten pounds. This was an imitation of a satire of Juvenal, a Latin poet, but Johnson made it his own by such lines as these:

> This mournful truth is everywhere confessed:
> Slow rises worth by poverty depressed.

In a poem written ten years later on the "Vanity of Human Wishes," he bids us

> Mark what ills the scholar's life assail:
> Toil, envy, want, the patron and the gaol.

In this last poem occur the well-known lines:

> He left the name at which the world grew pale,
> To point a moral, or adorn a tale.

"London" had an immediate success, and brought the author into notice; but many weary years were to pass before he would earn a comfortable living. In 1750, he began "The Rambler," a periodical modeled somewhat on Addison's "Spectator." It was not very popular, though it added something to his income. It died down after awhile, and at a later time he started a similar periodical under the name of "The Idler," which had a history quite like that of the "Rambler". He also contributed to like ventures undertaken by other men.

Meanwhile he had begun and was busy upon the great work of his life; namely, the first complete Dictionary of the English Language, a book which occupied him for seven years, and is a monument of labor. During its progress his wife died, sincerely mourned by him; and some years afterward he lost his old mother, who lived to the age of ninety. Being without money to pay the expenses of his mother's funeral, he wrote, in the evenings of a single week, the tale of "Rasselas, Prince of Abyssinia," in a kind of diction that Macaulay styles "Johnsonese"—a stately use of dignified Latinized language, which suggested Goldsmith's good-humored remark that if Dr. Johnson should undertake to write a fable about little fishes, he would make them talk like whales. Toward the end of Johnson's life, however, his style became simpler, though always having a certain quality about it which may be called grandiose.

Dr. Johnson wrote good letters, and one of his to Lord Chesterfield is so celebrated that a sketch of his life is incomplete without some mention of it. The Earl, rich, fashionable and courted, was known as a friend of letters, and Johnson, in his early struggling days, sacrificed his pride so far as to ask him to become a patron of his dictionary, that laborious work to which so many years of his life were given. Chesterfield apparently took no notice of the appeal, but, when the work was finished, signified in some way to Dr. Johnson that he should like to have the work dedicated to himself. In reply the great lexicographer addressed him one of the most scathing letters on record. The following extracts show its style and tenor:

February 17th, 1775. My Lord: I have been lately informed, by the proprietor of *The World*, that two papers, in which my Dictionary is recommended to the public, were written by your Lordship. . . . Seven years, my Lord, have now passed since I waited in your outward rooms, or was repulsed from your door; during which time I have been pushing on my work through difficulties, of which it is useless to complain, and have brought it at last to the verge of publication, without one act of assistance, one word of encouragement, or one smile of favour. Such treatment I did not expect, for I never had a patron before. . . . . The notice you have been pleased to take of my labors, had it been early, had been kind; but it has been delayed till I am indifferent, and can not enjoy it; till I am solitary and can not impar it; till I am known and do not want it. I hope it is no very cynical asperity not to confess obligations where no benefit has been received; or to be unwilling that the public should consider me as owing that to a patron, which Providence has enabled me to do for myself. . . . . I have long wakened from that dream of hope in which I once boasted myself with so much exultation, My Lord, your Lordship's most humble, most obedient servant, SAM. JOHNSON.

Chesterfield did not reply to Johnson's bitter words, but always kept the letter open on his table where all might read it; and it was Johnson who afterward published it. Chesterfield at the time was deaf and went little into society; he said he would have turned off the best servant he ever had if he had known that he denied him to a man who would have been always more than welcome. Therefore it seems that the neglect complained of by the "great bear"*

---

* One of Johnson's nicknames was "Ursus Major," but Boswell says (referring to his kindness of heart) that he had nothing of the bear but the skin.

was more accidental than intentional, if not more apparent than real.

Turning for a moment to the Dictionary itself, we easily perceive its many excellencies and its few defects. Among the latter is the fact that the range of authors whom Johnson quotes as authority is extremely limited, and that he leaned toward the classic rather than the Saxon element of the tongue.* Another thing which would be a fault if it were not rather a bit of brightness, lightening up the dull sameness of lexicography, is to be found in the Johnsonian personality which occasionally puts itself in evidence. The best known instances are in the following definitions:

The first is introspective: "Lexicographer: A writer of dictionaries; a harmless drudge that busies himself in tracing the original and detailing the signification of words."

The second is suggestive of his irrepressible dislike of the Scotch: "Oats: A grain which in England is generally given to horses, but in Scotland supports the people."

The third is an expression of contempt for those who live on public bounty. "Pension: An allowance to any one without an equivalent. In England it is generally understood to mean pay given to a state hireling for treason to his country."

---

* Mrs. Richardson says: The Johnsonian style is in pompous and long-syllabled words, many of them words of Latin origin. He underrated the value of strong, homely English, and when he had expressed himself in plain, direct words, he was apt to translate himself into a more verbose style. Boswell gives some good instances: Speaking of one of the comedies of the time of Charles II. he said, "It has not wit enough to keep itself sweet," and immediately changed this to "it had not enough vitality to preserve it from putrefaction." Macaulay finds a still better instance: When he was travelling in the Hebrides he writes: "When we were taken up stairs, a dirty fellow bounced out of the bed in which we were to lie." Afterward, when he printed the journal of these travels, he gives the account thus: "Out of one of the beds in which we were to repose, started up at our entrance, a man black as a Cyclops from the forge."

The latter definition is of course utterly indefensible; for the idea of pensions (whether always the ruling motive or not) is that they are given as late pay for foregone public service. It becomes doubly absurd in the light of the fact that Johnson himself, when old and poor, received from the government a pension of £300 a year.

From the year (1762) in which Dr. Johnson began to receive his yearly allowance we have no more dismal narratives of battling with poverty. That sum in addition to his earnings meant to him luxury and comfort. He did not feast the rich and entertain the great; his table was shared with several poor dependents, none of them particularly agreeable, whose only claim on him was that they were in want of kindness. A poor blind woman, a helpless, worn-out surgeon, two or three destitute ladies whom no one else befriended — such were the people with whom he surrounded himself as sub-pensioners, while he had the rare tact to make them forget that they were such, and to treat them on a perfect equality as friends.

The most brilliant men of the day were his familiar companions, and they met, as was fitting, at the Literary Club, which was founded by Sir Joshua Reynolds. There met together such men as Burke, Goldsmith, Sir Joshua, Garrick, Sheridan, Gibbon, Adam Smith—but the list grows much too long. In the midst of this circle sat Dr. Johnson, rolling, puffing about in his chair, contradicting, laying down the law, and yet none the less eagerly welcomed in the splendid assembly. There must have been some magic about the conversation of such a person to make his peculiarities tolerated by the class of men who surrounded him.

It was also after the king's pension was granted him that Johnson first saw James Boswell (1740–95), a Scotchman, who was to play so important a part in his life and bring that life before us almost as vividly as if we had been observers of it. Boswell was a hero-worshiper; knowing

Johnson by reputation, he never rested until he was presented to him; and from that time forth was his shadow
whenever he could leave his own home and his business in
Edinburgh.   To Boswell we owe one of the most complete
biographies ever written.   He is so bent on shedding lustre
upon his idol that he does not at all shrink from throwing
the same strong light on his own weaknesses and failings,
but gives us the full benefit of the photographic pen-and-
ink picture.   One would not wish to have a Boswell of one's
own, but it is a gain to the world that there should have
been one to record the sayings of Samuel Johnson.   Boswell's life of Johnson stands side by side with Pepys's
autobiography; both are marvels of frank and faithful personal portraiture.

Among Johnson's warmest friends was Mrs. Thrale
(1741–1821).   She was the wife of a rich brewer at Streat-
ham, near London, of a literary turn herself, and very fond
of brilliant company,   At her house Dr. Johnson always
found a warm welcome, delightful company, and an unlimited number of cups of tea, which he swallowed to the
amazement of all beholders.   It is said that he was known
to drink nineteen at a sitting.

After Mr. Thrale's death his widow married an Italian
gentleman named Piozzi, and as Dr. Johnson chose to be
displeased at the match he quarrelled with her, and an
estrangement was the end of a friendship of many happy
years.   Mrs. Thrale wrote a pretty fable called "The Three
Warnings," and late in life published an autobiography.
Her book, "Anecdotes of Dr. Johnson," gives many amusing glimpses of him as he lived.   After receiving his pension Johnson wrote but little, and when he did write it was
mostly by fits and starts.

His edition of Shakespeare, prefaced by a memoir, did
not add to his reputation as a critic.   Criticism, in fact, was
not his forte, which lay rather in observation and reflection.

Of his political pamphlets, the one entitled "Taxation no Tyranny," is very amusing to us Americans, as it defends the policy of George III. in the war of the Revolution. His "Journey to the Western Islands" (the Hebrides), taken in company with Boswell, is an interesting description of a country then little known. His last work, "Lives of the Poets," was finished three years before his death. This book is not a safe guide for young people's information, for Dr. Johnson was a man too prejudiced to see always fairly, and, as has been said, his strength lay elsewhere than in criticism.

After a long period of ill-health, having outlived most of those who had been his house-mates, and many of his intimate friends, Johnson died. His mind remained unclouded to the last, and he left behind him group of sincere mourners, not the least of whom were the poor whom he had befriended.

CHAPTER XXXIII.

OLIVER GOLDSMITH.

SIDE by side with the burly figure of Dr. Johnson, in the mind's eye, appears a short gentleman whose plain, good-natured face is much pitted with small-pox, and whom the great Doctor addresses by the familiar name of "Goldy." This is Oliver Goldsmith (1728–74), a man of abilities so varied that we scarcely know whether to class him among essayists, poets, dramatists, novelists or satirists, for he appeared in all these characters and played each with credit. His life was a strange medley of brilliant successes and wretched failures; his character a strange compound of gentle and noble traits with faults so pitiable that one always thinks of him as "Poor Goldsmith!"

His father was an Irish protestant clergyman, whom he describes as being "passing rich with forty pounds a year." The boy was sent to Trinity College, Dublin, as a "sizar" — a student who was boarded and taught gratuitously, but who (at that time) was expected to perform many duties in return which are usually done by servants. He gained little credit in college either for scholarship or conduct, and barely secured a degree. In the meantime his father had died, leaving a mere pittance to support his widow; and Oliver was obliged to look out for himself. Now begins the sad tale of his throwing away his opportunities, his utter lack of self-control, and his incurable wastefulness. He tried nearly all the professions in turn and succeeded at none; then determining to emigrate to America, his friends made up a purse for him, and had the mortification to see him return in six weeks, having squandered his money, sold the horse they had provided for him, and allowed the ship to sail without him. Next, his uncle having given him money with which to pursue his studies on the continent, he lost it all one night in a gambling - house before starting. A purse was again made up for him, with the contents of which he stayed awhile at Edinburgh, professing to study medicine but really idling away his time. From there, after a year or two, he went to Leyden and did the same thing again. Being unable, because of his lack of application, to obtain a doctor's degree, he decided to travel on the continent; but before setting out, he was tempted by the sight of some rare Dutch tulips, and spent the money on which he was to travel in buying them as a present for his uncle. So he started, according to his own account, with a guinea in his pocket, a single shirt in his wallet and a flute in his hand, to make the tour of Europe. He played for the peasants (who gladly gave him a bed or a supper), and was often entertained

OLIVER GOLDSMITH.

at the gates of convents. Having thus seen France and Italy, and having, as he asserted, obtained a doctor's degree from the University of Padua, he returned to England (penniless, of course), and after trying a half-dozen ways of getting along, settled down at his true vocation—that of a writer. At first it was all drudgery; he was not known, and had to do such odds and ends of work as the publishers would give him. Even then his great talent would have earned him a competence, but for his absolute incapacity to keep a shilling. He could not meet a beggar in the street, without emptying his own pockets. His owing the money he thus lavishly flung away made no difference to him; it gave him pleasure to give, and while he was gratifying himself, the claims of those who had trusted him were as nothing. When he went to be examined for a position as surgeon's mate, a friend lent him a suit of clothes, that he might make a respectable appearance. Meeting on his return some one who told him a tale of distress, he pawned the clothes. His whole biography bristles with such irritating anecdotes.

Goldsmith wrote several "Histories"—slight compendiums of the annals of Greece, Rome, and England, in which he did little more than translate into his own flowing language facts picked up in various quarters without much pretension to accuracy and none to research. These books were what would now be called "pot-boilers"— productions put out merely to supply his daily needs. Yet the books are most readable, and did more to popularize the study of history and make it attractive to young people than any others written in his own age or for some generations afterward. An attempt to interest the young in science was not so commendable. In his "Animated Nature," a book on natural history, his mistakes are so glaringly absurd as to excite laughter; and putting them forth seriously, as he did, and sending them into the

15

world as statements of fact was little better than literary swindling.*

Beside the two principal poems we have mentioned — "The Traveller" and "The Deserted Village"— Goldsmith wrote some shorter pieces, the best of which is "Retaliation."

Here are some beautiful lines from "The Deserted Village." The poet is speaking of the village pastor (believed to represent his father):

> As some tall cliff that lifts its awful form,
> Swells from the vale, and midway leaves the storm,
> Though round its breast the rolling clouds are spread,
> Eternal sunshine settles on its head.

Goldsmith's "Citizen of the World" consists of a series of essays professing to be written by a learned and well-bred Chinaman who finds himself in London and writes home to his friends, in a strain of gentle satire, his impressions of English society. His novel, "The Vicar of Wakefield" was shown to Dr. Johnson while Goldsmith was locked up in his room arrested for debt by his landlady. The kindly Doctor took it out to a bookseller, and returned with sixty pounds, with which Goldsmith paid his rent, scolding his landlady heartily for having used him so ill. To such persons, a demand for the payment of a debt is either a good joke, or an insult. His comedy of "The Good-natured Man" had a fair success; while the more brilliant "She Stoops to Conquer," is a favorite to this day.

Goldsmith's chief hold on the attention of posterity lies in his one novel, "The Vicar of Wakefield." It is a simple,

---

* Macaulay says of him (*Encyc. Brit.*): "He relates, with faith and perfect gravity, all the most absurd lies which he could find about gigantic Patagonians, monkeys that preach sermons, nightingales that repeat long conversations. 'If he can tell a horse from a cow,' said Johnson, 'that is the extent of his knowledge of zoölogy.' . . . In defiance of the evidence of his own senses, he maintained obstinately, and even angrily, that he chewed his dinner by moving his upper jaw."

pastoral story, told (in the first person) by an English country vicar, and presenting the most perfect picture ever drawn of the manners and customs of rural life in those days; and at the same time it teaches an immortal lesson of piety, charity, nobility of character, purity in life, and courage under misfortune. All this is lighted up with a wealth of wit, humor, pathos and sentiment which combine with its other qualities to make the book a classic of the English tongue for all times.

His receipts, though they had been large, did not justify the extravagance of his living, and his debts pressed heavily upon him. He died of a kind of low fever, after a short illness, and was mourned alike by rich and poor.

Dr. Johnson wrote the Latin epitaph for his tomb in Westminster Abbey, a part of which has been thus translated:

He left scarcely any kind of writing untouched, and touched nothing that he did not adorn. * * * His memory is cherished by the love of Companions, the faithfulness of Friends, the reverence of Readers.

CHAPTER XXXIV.

EIGHTEENTH-CENTURY MISCELLANEOUS WRITERS.

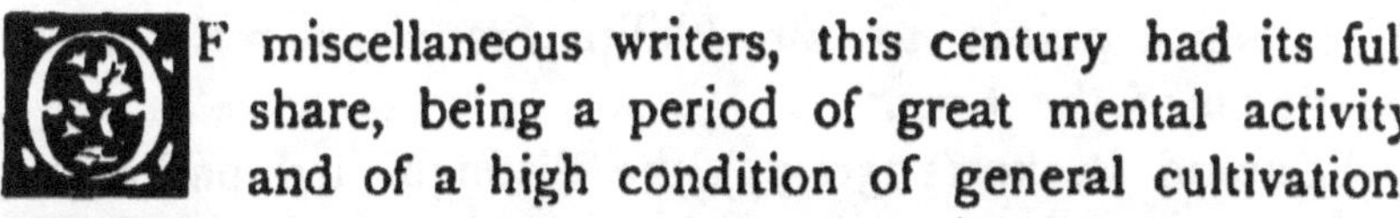

F miscellaneous writers, this century had its full share, being a period of great mental activity and of a high condition of general cultivation. Henry Home, Lord Kames (1696–1782), a Scottish judge, wrote a work on "Elements of Criticism," which was, until the middle of this century, used as a text-book in schools. Dr. George Campbell (1719–96), a Scottish divine, wrote, beside books on theological and other subjects, a "Philosophy of Rhetoric," which is still considered a standard work. The two brothers Warton were both poets and literary critics. Joseph Warton (1722–1800), published an essay on the "Genius and Writings of Pope," taking a view of his position as a poet which is now accepted as the correct one.   Thomas Warton (1728-90) wrote an admirable "History of English Poetry," on which he was engaged for many years, and which shows scholarship, fine judgment and enormous research.   In 1785, he succeeded William Whitehead as poet-laureate.   Sir Joshua Reynolds (1723-92), the most famous artist of his day, has a place in literature as the author of "Discourses on Painting."   Gilbert White (1720-93), a clergyman, wrote "The Natural History of Selborne"— a delightful description of the plant and animal life he found in his own parish; doing for the observation of nature what Isaac Walton had done for angling.   Every object which engaged his attention he touched with a loving hand.   Sir William Blackstone (1723-80), an eminent jurist, wrote "Commentaries on the Laws of England," which have the merit of being written in such clear, simple English that even those unlearned in the law can read and profit by them.   An unknown writer published (1769-72) a series of sarcastic articles, reflecting severely on the government and attacking many prominent officials by name.   These letters were signed "Junius," and though every effort was made to discover the offending author, his name remains a secret to this day.   The preponderance of evidence points to Sir Philip Francis, a well-known politician of the time.

Edmund Burke (1730-97), the distinguished parliamentary orator and statesman, was born in Dublin, and was the son of a thriving Irish attorney.   In respect to the extent and versatility of his powers, he has been compared to Francis Bacon.   As a man of letters he takes a very high rank; as a patriot not even the breath of envy has ever sullied his fame.   His "Reflections on the French Revolution" is a masterpiece of political wisdom.   His speeches on our war of the Revolution are fervent, eloquent appeals to reason and justice, which, unfortunately for the British government, were uttered in vain. In the domain of pure literature, the "Essay on the Sublime and Beautiful" is the best known of his works.

Thomas Reid (1710–96), a Scottish philosopher, instituted a reactionary movement directed equally against the idealism of Berkeley and the materialism of Hume, which has been called "The Philosophy of Common Sense." He was followed by his countryman Dugald Stewart (1753–1828), who had as a student attended his lectures, and who improved upon his methods, while following out the same general lines of thought. The third member of this distinguished trio was Thomas Brown (1778–1820), who had been a student under Professor Stewart, and is best known by his essay on "Cause and Effect." He succeeded Stewart as professor of moral philosophy at the University of Edinburgh.

William Cobbett (1762–1835) was a political writer of great vigor, and acquired immense popularity with the working classes by the rough energy with which he abused the government. He edited a periodical called "The Register." He spent some years in this country, where he was repeatedly tried for libel, and in one of the cases was fined $5000 for saying that the celebrated Dr. Rush of Philadelphia killed nearly all the patients he attended. Returning to England, he was repeatedly fined and imprisoned, but he never ceased publishing his paper, even while he was in America, which he again visited; this time to avoid being arrested for debt. While here he wrote an "English Grammar;" a work apparently so much needed that ten thousand copies were sold in a month.

Adam Smith (1723–90), also a Scotchman by birth, claims a place among the philosophers by reason of his "Theory of Moral Sentiments," but is better known as the founder of the science of political economy, as discussed in his book, "The Wealth of Nations;" still a standard treatise and the best known work on its theme.

Jeremy Bentham (1748-1832) was the apostle of utilitarianism. He began life as a lawyer, but his intense disapproval of English law, as it then existed, made it impossible for him to identify himself with it, and for forty years he was the fierce and active opponent of the whole system. Among his many works the best known is the "Theory of Legislation." His ideas may be summed up in the expression that what is to be sought for in all law-making is "the greatest good of the greatest number." Thomas Paine (1737-1809) passed much of his life in America, was a warm advocate of its separation from Great Britain, which he supported in his pamphlet entitled "Common Sense," and later wrote a popular book, called "The Rights of Man," in defence of the French Revolution. William Godwin (1756-1836) wrote a work on "Political Justice," which did much toward shaping the thought of the time, and awakening attention to the rights of the people, as distinguished from the demands of the privileged classes. In his novel of "Caleb Williams" he urges the same ideas, and has succeeded in making a most interesting story, not only without love, but almost without a female character. His wife, Mary Wollstonecraft Godwin (1759-97), a woman of great ability, wrote (before her marriage to him), "Thoughts on the Education of Daughters," and "A Vindication of the Rights of Women." Many of her ideas on these subjects, though considered revolutionary at the time, are now commonly accepted.

Among theologians the most noted (after Bishop Butler) is William Paley (1743-1805), an acute thinker and powerful writer. "The Principles of Moral and Political Philosophy," "A View of the Evidences of Christianity," and "Natural Theology" are his principal works.

Joseph Priestley (1733-1804), an eminent Unitarian minister, was also an explorer in the domain of physics, and is especially known as the discoverer of oxygen, a revelation which opened the way for an immense advance of knowledge in the direction of natural science. He was a man of great learning, and a fearless seeker after truth. Espousing the side of the French Revolution, he incurred the enmity of an ignorant mob in Birmingham, who burned his house and chapel, and with them all his most valuable possessions. He and his family escaped, and afterward came to Pennsylvania, where he spent the last ten years of his life.

The eighteenth century was rich in good letter-writers. There was a leisurely tone about life, for all who were not obliged to work for their daily bread, which encouraged this graceful accomplishment.

Of these famous letter-writers, the earliest was Lady Mary Wortley Montagu (1690–1762), daughter of the Duke of Kingston. She began her social life almost in her babyhood, her father sending to bring her from the nursery at the close of his dinner-parties, when he would make her stand on the table and recite or chatter for the amusement of his guests. She married Edward Wortley Montagu, and spent some years in Turkey, where he was ambassador, bringing with her from that country into England the system of inoculation for small-pox. Her letters, both when abroad and at home, are full of gayety, wit and good sense, and are written with that ease and naturalness which are essentials to good letter-writing. She was for some time the friend of Pope, but when he injudiciously made love to her, she laughed at him and so made him her bitter enemy.

The poet Gray, of whom we have already spoken, wrote beautiful letters, as did Cowper, of whom we shall speak later. The most illustrious of the group was Horace Walpole (1717–97), son of Sir Robert Walpole, so long Prime Minister of England. Though not born to fortune, he lived "on the fat of the land," having a large income from government posts given him by his father.   Being fond of literature, his taste and knowledge were cultivated in every possible way; by travel, study, and intercourse with the best minds of his time, at home and abroad.   He built at Twickenham a Gothic villa called Strawberry Hill, on which he lavished money and taste until it became one of the curiosities of England, and it was shown as such until late in the present century.   His "Letters," which fill nine large volumes, touch upon almost every point of interest in the political and social life of the time, and are written in racy, sparkling English which puts him in the front rank among the authors of his century.   He tried his hand at only one fiction, "The Castle of Otranto," a wild Gothic romance which is interesting mainly because he wrote it.   His "Anecdotes of Painting in England," with sketches of the lives of artists, is a standard work on the subject.

The letters written by Lord Chesterfield (1694–1773) to his son, may be included among the achievements of this letter-writing century.   They are intensely worldly, and might have been the work of a Pagan in the time of Cicero, but they are witty, brilliant and polished, showing great knowledge of the world and remarkable powers of observation.   Lord Chesterfield was also a statesman of ability.

CHAPTER XXXV.

THREE GREAT HISTORIANS.

THE principal historians of this period form a group by themselves.   Hume, Robertson and Gibbon (the first two Scotchmen) were a triad not often to be found in contemporary history, though more than equalled in our own century.   Writing in different styles and on widely different topics, they were still all historians;

and each succeeded in giving to the time of which he wrote an interest until then unknown on any similar subject.

David Hume (1711–76), born at Edinburgh of an old Scottish family (who before him spelt the name Home), was a philosopher as well as a historian. He began his literary career with a "Treatise on Human Nature," and wrote essays on political, moral, and literary subjects. His principal work, the "History of England," was written in a curiously irregular way. He began with the first two Stuart kings (1603–49), writing from a strongly royalist point of view. This did not agree with the prevailing ideas of the time, and so few copies were sold during the first year that the author thought seriously of abandoning his country and exiling himself to France, under a feigned name, to conceal his mortification. After a while, however, the tide turned, and when he published the next instalment of his book, continuing the history to the Revolution (1688), it was better received. Next he wrote the story of the Tudors, and last of all he began with the time of Julius Cæsar and completed the whole. It was the first philosophical history of England that had ever been written, and made its author famous. The style is beautifully simple and clear, graceful and yet vivacious; but Hume is no longer regarded as an authority as to facts. He took statements as he found them with too little discrimination, and later and more painstaking historians have noted innumerable inaccuracies in his work. Still, there is no one history that will take its place. Many admirable books deal with different portions of the history of England, but no one continuous account of equal value exists covering that period of seventeen hundred years, so that Hume's history will for the present hold its place. Smollett's history is usually printed as a continuation of Hume's and brings the narrative down to 1765, the year of the American Stamp-Act.

In religion, Hume was a skeptic; in philosophy a materialist. He was a subtle thinker and reasoner, and was bold and original in his ideas. In private life he thus describes himself in his posthumous book, "My Own Life":

A man of mild dispositions, of command of temper, of an open, social and cheerful humor, capable of attachment, but little susceptible of enmity, and of great moderation in all my passions.

Hume's friends bear out this favorable self-portraiture, and add that he was a charming companion, full of gayety and of a delicate humor which never transgressed the bounds of good taste. He spent most of his life in Edinburgh.

William Robertson (1721–93) was also a Scotchman but of a very different type of mind. He was the son of a clergyman and himself took orders; and his writings are pervaded by a religious spirit. His "History of Scotland" brings down events in that country to the beginning of the reign of James I. in England (1603), and is a carefully written work, though without the marks of genius which makes Hume's "England" so attractive. Robertson's greatest work is "The History of the Emperor Charles V.," which involves almost every country in Europe, and gives opportunity for much picturesque detail. It is written with conscientious care, and is as accurate as the means at the writer's disposal would allow. The history has since been edited by Prescott, and much new material added which was inaccessible to Robertson. The fault of the latter was that he glorified his subject too much. The emperor seemed to be, so to speak, always on his throne, wearing his crown and sceptre; whereas the real man had at least his share of human weakness, and was by no means an ideal hero. Robertson's last work of importance was a "History of America." written with the same painstaking earnestness which distinguishes his other books.

Edward Gibbon (1737–94), the last and greatest of the three writers we have been considering, was born near London, and studied at Oxford. Of his attainments, he tells us that he possessed "a stock of erudition that would have puzzled a doctor, and a degree of ignorance of which a school-boy would have been ashamed." This means that on account of ill-health he had studied irregularly, while his reading had been omniverous and enormous. Becoming a Roman Catholic, he was obliged to leave college, and was sent by his father to a protestant clergyman at Lausanne, Switzerland, with whom he remained five years, becoming a proficient in French and gaining a good knowledge of Latin. While there he returned nominally to the Protestant Church, though there is reason to believe that he had become and ever afterward remained an infidel at heart. In the course of a continental tour he found himself at Rome, and there, musing among the ruins of the capitol, as he tells us in his highly interesting and piquant " Memoirs" (his autobiography), he first conceived the thought of writing a history of the "Decline and Fall" of that stupendous power whose relics he saw scattered around him. He was then twenty-seven years old. Eight years were to pass by before the great history was begun, and twenty-three before the last words should be written. In the meantime, Gibbon travelled much and lived in various places. At one time he would be a member of parliament in his own country; at another, shut up in his library at Lausanne, where, in his fifty-first year, the book — a monument of industry — was at last completed. The amount of research required had been prodigious. He used no translations, but went directly to the originals of the books from which he drew his materials, and never rested until he had verified every statement. It has been said that the "Decline and Fall" is "the largest historic painting ever executed by a single hand." The conception is grand, the mode of treatment masterly. In particular, the historian excels in perspective—the art of giving to the different parts of his story their due proportion and importance. Nothing was too large and nothing too small to engage his attention, but he knew the relative value of each branch of his subject, and whether he was raising an arch of philosophic theory or laying a tesselated floor of florid description, his workmanship remains unrivalled. His style is open to criticism. Massive and magnificent as it is, it is sometimes almost oppressive from its wonderfully balanced evenness of structure, with the same cadence, the same rhythmic rise and fall, so frequently recurring. It is a style to admire, but not to imitate.

The most serious objection to the original work is its attitude toward Christianity. Candid on all other subjects, toward this he betrays a bitterness of feeling entirely at variance with the dispassionate utterances of the unprejudiced historian. Fortunately for young people, who in these busy days might not have time to read the whole of the voluminous record, an excellent abridgement exists in the "Student's Gibbon," in which all objectionable expressions are omitted, and the great mass of information is compressed into a space which makes it not impossible to attack.

CHAPTER XXXVI.

EIGHTEENTH-CENTURY MISCELLANEOUS WRITERS.

THE latter half of the eighteenth century was, with one magnificent exception, as poor in dramatic works as its early part had been brilliant. After the death of Congreve in 1729, the short list of David Garrick (1716–79), Samuel Foote (1720–77), Richard Cumberland (1732–1811), George Colman (1733–94), George

Colman the younger (1762–1836), this (omitting the name of Goldsmith, which has been already mentioned) brings us to the great master of modern comedy, Richard Brinsley Sheridan (1751–1816)).

Sheridan came of a noted Irish family, of which he was the third in direct descent who showed remarkable talents. His grandfather, Thomas Sheridan, an author and a wit, was the friend of Swift; his father, also named Thomas, was an actor as well as an author, and stood next to Garrick in his profession. His mother wrote both plays and novels; and so the boy had a literary inheritance to start with. He left school with the reputation of being a dunce; but this must have been only from laziness, for he showed in after life that he could learn what he chose to learn. He acquired information mainly by reading, for he was through life a pleasure‑lover, and liked no form of hard work. He made a secret marriage with the beautiful Miss Linley, a popular public singer, and daughter of Thomas Linley, the famous musical composer. The marriage proved a very happy one. Sheridan, although extremely poor at the time, and possessing scarcely anything but a small marriage-portion brought by his wife, would never allow her to sing in public or for money. Her fine voice was to be heard only at home or in friends' houses. Depending on success yet to come, Sheridan took a house in a fashionable quarter, and drew around him a brilliant circle, attracted by his wit and good‑fellowship and his wife's many charms. His first comedy, "The Rivals," was produced in 1775, and, strange to say, was considered a failure. This was owing partly to its great length, and partly to the poor acting of one of the principal characters. On the second night a good actor replaced the inferior one, and although little enthusiasm was shown, the play gradually grew in favor and the author had the satisfaction of seeing it established as one of the standard comedies of the English language. Bob Acres, Sir Lucius O'Trigger, Mrs. Malaprop, and Lydia Languish are types which the stage could not afford to be without.

Sheridan's next venture of importance was "The Duenna," an opera, for which his father-in-law, Mr. Linley, furnished the music. It was immensely popular, having a longer run than had even Gay's "Beggar's Opera." "The School for Scandal" followed, and afterward "The Critic," one of the most amusing burlesques ever written. The four pieces, with some minor ones, were produced within the space of four years. From this time he abandoned dramatic writing, except for one tragedy, "Pizarro," and betook himself to parliamentary life.

Here he proved himself greater as an orator than he had been as a dramatist. His splendid rhetoric and impassioned eloquence carried, while he was speaking, everything before him. For thirty-two years he sat in the house, filling meantime with credit several government positions. During all this time he had been living extravagantly, and though as an M.P. he could not be arrested for debt, when this protection was withdrawn he was constantly harassed by creditors and his house repeatedly occupied by bailiffs. He had, also, some unavoidable misfortunes, for Drury Lane Theatre, in which he had bought out Garrick's interest, was twice burned down during his proprietorship. Still, after making every allowance for him, we must regret that his magnificent talents were not accompanied with a sense of pecuniary honor, and that present enjoyment always seemed better to him than permanent good. When troubles began to press upon him he fell into intemperate habits which brought on disease, and his last days were as wretched as his earlier had been brilliant. He was arrested for debt while dying, and his creditors were only pacified by the kindness of a friend who advanced the money necessary to allow him to draw his last breath in peace. When he could no longer be gratified by attention, it was showered upon his lifeless remains; royal dukes were among the pall-bearers, and a place in the Poets' Corner of Westminster Abbey was with much difficulty found for his grave.

With the exception of Mrs. Aphra Behn, in the seventeenth century, we have not as yet met with the name of any woman novelist in England. The reading-world was surprised, one day in 1778, by the appearance of a novel called "Evelina," by an unknown author, whose secret was so faithfully kept that even the publishers were ignorant of the writer's identity. At length it turned out that the new star was Miss Frances Burney (1752–1840), daughter of Dr. Charles Burney, himself the author of a "History of Music," and an eminent musician. The young lady had had the plan of the book in her mind for ten years before finishing it. It gained an instant popularity, being the first novel of society written by a person in society; and it is, as we are assured, true to the life of the time. It is amusing now to read how the greatest literary men of the day were carried away with it. Dr. Johnson thought some parts of it as good as anything in Richardson; Edmund Burke sat up all night to read it, and Sir Joshua Reynolds could not be tempted to lay it down, even to eat his dinner. Her second novel, "Cecilia," was also very popular. Some years after writing this, she was appointed one of the keepers of the robes to Queen Charlotte, a post monotonous in itself and extremely distasteful to her, which the ambition of her father induced her to keep for five weary years. She was thirty-nine years old when she was at last released, with a pension, and two years later she married General D'Arblay, a French refugee, driven from his country by the Revolution. Her "Journal and Letters," describing a period of seventy-two years, are now more interesting to us than her novels. She is a sort of Boswell to herself, and gives us a minute description of the dreary life at the court of George III., which Macaulay has immortalized in his brilliant essay, "Madame D'Arblay." Her friendship with Dr. Johnson was a marked feature of her early years, though in later life she knew almost all the distinguished literary men of the time, and was a favorite with all. It will be encouraging, to those who think there is no hurry about teaching children to read, to be told that at eight years old she did not know her letters.

Mrs. Elizabeth Inchbald (1753–1821), a popular London actress, wrote several plays, and two novels, one of which, "A Simple Story," may be said to have introduced the novel of passion. It is very highly commended by the critics of her own time, as is also her second story, "Nature and Art." Mrs. Inchbald was possessed of great personal beauty and an unblemished character.

William Beckford (1760–1844), a wealthy and eccentric Englishman, was the author of "Vathek," an Eastern romance, which is one of the most extraordinary productions of its kind. His imagination, which ran riot amid the scenes of Oriental splendor, found a more practical expression in the superb piles of building which he successively erected for his residence. Beckford wrote accounts of his travels in Italy, Spain and Portugal, which are full of brilliant description and clever sarcasm.

Mrs. Ann Radcliffe (1760–1844) led the way in the novel of romance and wild adventure. Her "Flowers of the Forest" and "Mysteries of Udolpho" are examples of such elaborately woven plots as had never before been employed in any kind of fictitious writing. Whoever loves the terrible and the marvellous will enjoy Mrs. Radcliffe.

Until the eighteenth century no one had thought of writing especially for children. They read "Robinson

Crusoe," "The Pilgrim's Progress," and such romances and poetry as they could lay their hands on, but their range was limited. Mrs. Anna Lætitia Barbauld (1743–1825) opened the vast field, which is now so well covered with perennial harvests of juvenile literature of all sorts and qualities, by publishing her "Hymns in Prose for Children," and "Early Lessons"—these last for little ones. These became at once very popular. Later, she contributed many articles to "Evenings at Home"—a book by her brother, Dr. John Aikin, intended to bring scientific truths within the reach of unlearned readers, and especially of the young. Both Mrs. Barbauld and her brother were industrious writers, on historical, scientific and literary subjects, and Dr. Aikin's daughter, Miss Lucy Aikin (1781–1864) wrote several historical biographies—notably one of Queen Elizabeth.

Hannah More (1745–1833), distinguished for her piety and learning, wrote moral essays and dramas, many in the form of short stories, among which "The Shepherd of Salisbury Plain" has been most widely read. "Cœlebs in Search for a Wife," a religious novel, is her only attempt at sustained fiction. She wrote admirable letters, was clever and witty in conversation, and collected around her, even to extreme old age, the best society of her time. In her later years she became known as a practical philanthropist, and was unwearied in her efforts to improve the condition of the miserable, neglected children in the neighborhood. She was never married; though called "Mrs.," that being the equivalent for "Mistress," a title considered due to all mature women whether married or single.

Thomas Day (1748–89) is best known as the author of "Sandford and Merton," a story for boys which was the pioneer in that kind of literature. Leigh Hunt says of this book:

The pool of mercenary and time-serving ethics was first blown over by the fresh country breeze of "Sandford and Merton," a production that I shall ever feel grateful for.

Henry Mackenzie (1745–1831), born at Edinburgh, author of a novel called "The Man of Feeling," was much admired in a day when there were but few novels. He was editor of "The Mirror," and "The Lounger," periodicals after the plan of "The Spectator,"and wrote a life of John Home, author of the tragedy of "Douglas." He was an important person in literary society, and his opinion is often quoted by Scott, who looked up to him with much respect. He lived to be eighty-five years old, and to the last kept his place among writers and critics, taking an interest in all that was going on in the world of books, and prized as almost the sole survivor of the circle so intimately connected with the intellectual life of the eighteenth century.

CHAPTER XXXVII.

LITERARY FORGERIES.

BETWEEN fiction, published with or without an assumed name, artfully contrived to look like fact; and literary frauds and forgeries, it is hard to draw the line. The latter may be said to include such writings as are seriously and permanently ascribed by their author to another writer, and are represented to have fallen by accident into the possession of the one who gives them to the world. If the pretence is so obvious as to deceive no one, or if it is but temporary, and finally acknowledged by the free act of its originator, then it incurs no blame. But there are cases where it was perpetrated with the deliberate intention of deceiving the world, and these are the ones now to be described.

The chief persons whom history has indicted as literary impostors are James Macpherson (1738-96), Thomas Chatterton (1752-70) and William Henry Ireland (1777-1835).

Macpherson was a Scotch author of some repute who professed to have discovered the original poems of Ossian, a Gaelic bard who is said to have lived in the second century of the Christian era. Macpherson's story was that these poems had been handed down in Gaelic among the Scottish Highlanders, and that he had taken them down from the lips of old men and women who had learned them from their ancestors; and now gave them to the world translated into English prose. Their high quality, joined with their alleged romantic origin, caused them to be received with wonder and delight. The literary world made much of Macpherson, and naturally wished to pursue the search in such an interesting field; but when he was asked for his authorities he would say nothing, and resented any demand for proof of his claims. Then a "Highland Society" was formed of persons determined to probe the matter to the bottom under the pretext of seeking further material. The Highlands are not large nor the Highlanders many; and the search failed to show a trace of the oral poetry or tradition.

Macpherson was of gentle birth and good education and standing; and to the end of his days he persisted in the fiction of having taken these poems from the lips of persons who had in their youth heard them from their Gaelic forerunners. No such persons were ever pointed out by him or found by the careful searches for truth. So the world has come to the unwilling conclusion that the verses are no older than the day of their writing by Macpherson.

The poems were really full of wild and weird power such as would be the natural product of the age and place to which they were attributed. As a specimen we take the closing strain of "The Songs of Selma."

Such were the words of the bards in the days of song when the king heard the music of harps, the tales of other times! The chiefs gathered from all their hills and heard the lovely sound. They praised the voice of Cona, the first among a thousand bards! But age is now on my tongue, my soul has failed! I hear at times the ghosts of bards and learn their pleasant song. But memory fails on my mind.

I hear the call of years! They say as they pass along, Why does Ossian sing? Soon shall he lie in the narrow house, and no bard shall raise his fame. Roll on, ye dark-brown years; ye bring us joy on your course! Let the tomb open to Ossian, for his strength has failed. The sons of song are gone to rest. My voice remains, like a surf that roars, lonely, on a sea-surrounded rock after the winds are laid. The dark moss rustles there; the distant mariner sees the waving trees!

The story of Thomas Chatterton, whom Byron calls "the marvellous boy who perished in his pride," is more remarkable and far more pathetic than that of the well-born and prosperous Macpherson. Chatterton was the descendant of a family of sextons who had cared for the old church of St. Mary Redcliff, at Bristol, England, for more than a century. Thomas was placed at school at five years old, but was sent back to his widowed mother as being too dull to be worth teaching. He was of a masterful temper; and it is said that when asked what device should be painted on a plate which a friendly potter was making for him, he answered, "Paint me an angel with wings and a trumpet, to trumpet my name through the world!" His mother was fain to try to do something for her "stupid" son, and herself taught him until, at eight, he was admitted to a charity school.

As soon as he could read he got on rapidly; yet he took no part in the verse-making contests of his school. His first verses were made at eleven, and compare well with Pope's at twelve and Cowley's at thirteen; while Chatterton had not the advantages of the others, for he had to make his own way in a line foreign to the family habits and traditions. At fourteen he entered on a seven years' apprenticeship to a lawyer to learn to be a scrivener or copyist of law - papers. Here he used his ample spare time in desultory reading; getting books from a circulating library and dipping into one study after another as if each, in turn, was to be the passion of his life.

St. Mary Redcliff had a "muniment - room" where there were six antiquated chests or coffers, which of old were locked and double - locked; but during the time of Thomas's father had been broken open and the ancient documents exposed; and the old man (then schoolmaster as well as sexton) had helped himself to them unsparingly, using the parchment as book - covers in his school. The father having died at about the time of Thomas's birth, the latter had now easy access to the old muniments or documents, and conceiving the idea of taking them for his own use, removed all that were left to his room at the lawyer's house.

The next scene in the Chatterton tragedy was at the opening of a new bridge in Bristol, when there appeared in the Bristol "Journal" a description of the opening of the old bridge in the thirteenth century and the friars passing over it. The article was wonderfully well - written, but the printer could give no account of its origin, further than that the remarkable document had been left at the office by a boy. Chatterton was asked about it, but not liking the manner of the question — put to him as if he were a mere boy—he would say nothing. More artful persuasion induced him to speak, and he said he had got the manuscript with others, from his father, who had found them in the old chest before mentioned.

Then followed other manuscripts; chiefly poems ascribed to an imaginary monk named Rowley, said to have lived and written in the fifteenth century. The poems were not good enough to gain praise by their own merit; but as bits of antiquity they were highly prized; and poor Chatterton was on the top of the wave. He generally said that the document was destroyed; but he did occasionally show a parchment fragment that he had cut from some old deed; and written upon, and smoked and smirched into the appearance of antiquity. At the same time he produced and gave out without disguise some poems of his own which were very good, considering his age and opportunities.

A morbid vanity took possession of the unhappy boy; he thought he had fame and fortune in his grasp, and would promise his mother and sister great things as a part of his own future. Unfortunately his ambition led him to tire of his humble Bristol home and to cast longing eyes on London. He wrote to Horace Walpole offering services, asking help and enclosing specimens of the "Ancient" poems. Walpole (who had just been victimized by the "Ossian" fraud) replied kindly, advising him to stay at home, and saying that there was a suspicion that the poems were not genuine. Chatterton replied in such a tone that Walpole sent him back his letters and poems without a word. Chatterton sacrificed his business in Bristol and went to London, had a time of flattering though shallow success, then fell into adversity and want. Even now he retains a hold on our sympathy, for he sent home to his mother and sister and grandmother presents which he could ill afford.

His fierce pride never waned, and he starved rather than eat the food which kind friends, seeing his wan looks, pressed upon him. On the very day of his death he was offended at his landlady's urging him to share her dinner, and that night he took poison and died, alone in his room. He was not quite seventeen years old.

A favorable specimen of Chatterton's verses is the following, written when he was sixteen years old:

To Miss Hayland:

Count all the flowers that deck the meadow's side
When Flora flourishes in new - born pride ;
Count all the sparkling orbits in the sky ;

> Count all the birds that through the ether fly;
> Count all the foliage of the lofty trees
> That flies before the bleak autumnal breeze,
> Count all the dewy blades of verdant grass;
> Count all the drops of rain that softly pass
> Through the blue ether, or tempestuous roar;
> Count all the sands upon the breaking shore;
> Count all the minutes since the world began;
> Count all the troubles in the life of man;
>   *   *   *
> More are the beauteous charms that make my nymph excel.

The third member of this trio of literary impostors was William Henry Ireland, who, shortly before the year 1800, professed to have discovered some original and unpublished plays of Shakespeare. He was the son of a dealer in old books and prints who was a Shakespeare enthusiast; and William Henry, at about seventeen years old, presented his father with a forged autograph of the poet. This imposture succeeded so well that he was led on to other inventions which were generally accepted as valuable additions to the scanty stock of knowledge about Shakespeare. Growing bolder he produced an entire play which he called "Vortigern," and attributed to Shakespeare. Richard Brinsley Sheridan, himself a dramatist, went into raptures over the event, bought the play for his theatre (Drury Lane) and put it upon the stage, where its worthlessness was at once seen, and Ireland was loaded with the contempt which was his due. As is often the case, punishment fell, not on the wrong-doer but on the innocent; for Ireland's father, who had published the spurious works, was overwhelmed with shame and died not long afterward; while the son, after giving out a shameless account of his performances, became an ordinary "literary hack," or hired writer, and lived on well into the present century.

CHAPTER XXXVIII.

LATER MISCELLANEOUS POETS.

HREE poets of the latter years of the eighteenth century have been classed together from their common love of humanity and disregard of old poetical traditions. Two of these, Cowper and Burns, are reserved for a separate chapter; the third was George Crabbe (1754–1832). Born in poverty, he knew the trials and privations of the humble poor, and has depicted them with a truthfulness which would, in these days, be called realism, and which was utterly new in the world of letters.

Crabbe had a fairly good school education, and at the age of fourteen was apprenticed to a surgeon, in which position he had a hard life. He had his consolations, too; for while as a boy at home he had hoarded every scrap of poetry he could cut out of old newspapers, he now began to write it for himself; and, in the intervals of compounding drugs, filled a drawer with his attempts. At last he had the good fortune to gain a prize offered by a magazine; and considering his vocation to be plainly marked out, he determined, as did all country boys who wanted to be poets, to go to London. Once there, he was at his wits' end, and starvation stared him in the face.

A letter to Edmund Burke brought a kind reply. The great statesman looked over the manuscripts, made suggestions, took the poems himself to Dodsley, the famous bookseller, and Crabbe's fortune was made.

Burke's kindness did not stop here. He invited the young man out to his country-house and introduced him to men of distinction in literature who perceived his merits and admitted him into their circle. At a later time he entered the Church, and being "presented", as the English phrase is, with a small living, passed the rest of his quiet life as a country clergyman, employing his leisure in writing, and leaving to the world a collection unique in its literary value. The English poor, in all their various needs and interests, were his theme; their miseries, their pleasures, their struggles with poverty, their weaknesses and sins, all came out strongly depicted by his vigorous pen.

Though forcible, Crabbe's writings have defects of taste which have prevented him from becoming a popular poet. His descriptions are often repulsive; his diction is harsh and lacks polish. He is so determined to present things as they really are, that he becomes too minute, and we weary of his details, while recognizing their force and correctness. Sir Walter Scott, that generous and large-minded lover of all that was good, thought very highly of Crabbe, and in his last illness said to his attendant, "Read me some amusing thing — read me a bit of Crabbe." The most amusing thing to us in the connection of the two names is that when Crabbe read Sir Walter's imitation of him in an anonymous poem called "The Poacher," the former remarked of Scott, "This man, whoever he is, can do all that I can, *and something more.*" This is creditable both to his humility and his perceptive power.

Crabbe's first published poems — those which gained the approbation of Burke — were "The Library," and "The Village." Soon after this he produced "The Newspaper," and then wrote no more for twenty years, being occupied with the duties of his parish. After this came "The Parish Register," "The Borough" (considered by many persons as his best work), "Tales in Verse," and "Tales of the Hall." It has seldom fallen to the lot of a poet, in our own century, to be so much admired by his contemporaries and so entirely neglected by succeeding generations.

The minor poets of the latter half of the century we have been considering, do not require much space. John Home (1724–1808), a Scottish minister, wrote a tragedy called "Douglas," which with little change might have been made into the most unobjectionable narrative poem; but its being in the form of a drama so offended his brother - clergy that, to avoid being deposed from the ministry, he resigned his charge. After this he wrote several dramas, and a history of the Stuart rebellion of 1745. His chief claim to continued remembrance arises — half accidentally, one might say — from a certain speech contained in his tragedy of "Douglas" already mentioned; a bit of blank verse which happens to lend itself kindly to youthful declamation; and therefore was extensively studied and spouted by thousands of boys during the time it remained the fashion. It begins:

> My name is Norval. On the Grampian Hills
> My father feeds his flocks; a frugal swain
> Whose chiefest care was to increase his store
> And keep his only son, myself, at home.

Thomas Percy (1729–1811), afterward Bishop of Dromore, was the son of a grocer. He did a great service to English literature by collecting the old ballads, from Chevy Chase down, which were fast slipping from people's memories or were being thrown away as rubbish. His "Reliques of Ancient English Poetry" is a valuable storehouse of these ancient poems, and has inspired many a young student with a love for poetry. Bishop Percy also wrote original poems of much merit.

Erasmus Darwin (1731–1802), a physician, who has been called the poet - laureate of botany, wrote a long poem called "The Botanic Garden." He was the grandfather of Charles Darwin, author of "The Origin of Species."

James Beattie (1735 - 1803) demands more than a passing notice. Born in humble life, he secured for himself an education which enabled him to take rank with men of letters, and he was gifted by nature with the poetic faculty. His longest work, "The Minstrel," contains poetry of no mean order; a shorter one, "The Hermit," is (or was) in many school collections. The following beautiful stanza is from "The Minstrel":

> Oh, how canst thou renounce the boundless store
> Of charms which Nature to her votary yields,
> The warbling woodland, the resounding shore,
> The pomp of groves and garniture of fields;
> All that the genial ray of morning gilds,
> And all that echoes to the song of even,
> All that the mountain's sheltering bosom shields,
> And all the dread magnificence of Heaven,
> Oh, how canst thou renounce, and hope to be forgiven!

Sir William Jones (1746-94) was the great Orientalist of his century, and one of the greatest England has ever produced. His translations of Hindu law and literature opened the eyes of Englishmen to the wonders to be found in the study of the Asiatic languages in which he himself was so great a proficient. His claim to rank among poets is small; but his noble ode entitled "What Constitutes a State?" is worthy of being committed to memory by every patriotic citizen.

There are in every age (and in none more than in our own nineteenth century) writers of what is called "occasional poetry"— a few fine songs which touch the popular heart and are sung long after their authors' names are forgotten. Of such writers are Lady Anne Barnard (1750-1825), who wrote "Auld Robin Gray"; Miss Jane Elliot, author of the Scottish song quoted so effectively in "Marmion," called "The Flowers of the Forest"; and Lady Nairne (1766-1845), whose subjects extend from "Caller herrin'" and "The Laird o' Cockpen," to the exquisite "Land o' the Leal." The list might be much extended, did space permit.

Robert Bloomfield (1766-1823) was the son of an English tailor in Suffolk. While he was apprenticed to a shoemaker in London, he wrote the very remarkable poem called "The Farmer's Boy," which was then compared with the work of Theocritus. Its excellence was recognized at once, and it was translated into French, Italian, and Latin. Though 26,000 copies of this poem were sold, the author died in poverty.

Robert Fergusson (1750-74) possesses a special interest as being the person from whom Robert Burns, to a greater or less degree, drew his inspiration. In the circumstances of his life he differed from Burns, he having been born and bred in Edinburgh, and also never having been obliged to struggle with severe poverty. He was endowed with brilliant conversational powers, and had such a charm of manner that he was only too welcome in society; and, yielding to the temptations which social life brought with it, became dissipated and after a time partially insane.

Fergusson's poems give more promise of excellence than actual performance. Several of them are so evidently the prototypes of poems by Burns on similar subjects that we can well believe the generous acknowledgment of the latter that to Fergusson he owed his earliest inspiration to verse - making.

CHAPTER XXXIX.

COWPER AND BURNS.

TWO poets, whose names awaken in our minds feelings of tenderness and gentle, pathetic interest, remain to be mentioned before we close the record of the rich and varied eighteenth century. These are Cowper and Burns. With them came the new idea in poetry — that man, as man, and independent of worldly circumstances, is entitled to respectful consideration. Before their time, the poor had sometimes been spoken of as objects of charity when their lot was especially hard, but not as being made of the same clay with ourselves and sharing with us a common humanity. The lowly, in England, were looked on as a "class," and nowhere in the world was the distinction of classes more marked than there. The upper regarded the lower as from another sphere; individuals to be humanely—rather than humanly—treated; and persons to whom the greatest kindness lay in teaching them to "know their place;" that is, to be contented with inferiority. Pity was their due, not affection or sympathy. Now was dawning the day when riches were to be recognized as the gift of fickle fortune, and aristocracy as the accident of birth. As Burns says:

> The rank is but the guinea's stamp;
> The man's the gowd for a' that.

Of the poets named we will take the younger, reserving for a later page the one whose life closes the century.

Robert Burns (1759-96) was born to poverty. His father was a peasant of Ayrshire, Scotland, and had hard work to find bread for the mouths of his children, who were obliged, from their earliest youth, to share in the wearisome labor which scantily supported the family. He did not, however, neglect to give them the best education in his power, and Robert and his brother Gilbert used to be sent to school "week about" during the busy season when they could not both be spared from home. Of their religious training, Burns tells the story in that fireside classic, "The Cotter's Saturday Night." Of himself he says that his first inspirations toward poetry came from the singing of a young girl who was working with him in the harvest-field. He felt the power of song in himself, and labored long with it in secret before any one else knew what was struggling in his brain. After the death of the father, the brothers took a farm together at Mossgiel, and the old toil went on. The farm was not very successful, but the poetry kept growing in volume and fire, and Robert, whose appetite for knowledge was insatiable, spent every moment he could find in poring over books, and became a better read man than many a one of his age who had passed the same number of years at a university.

When the poet's fortunes were so low that it seemed useless to hope to make a living at home, Burns thought of going to Jamaica to try his luck, but had not the money to pay his passage nor any way to earn it; when by a happy thought some one suggested that his poems should be printed. A bookseller at Kilmarnock undertook to publish them, and Burns received twenty pounds for his share in the venture. With this he bought a steerage-passage to Jamaica and sent off his chest to the ship. It was with bitterness of spirit that he set out on foot for Greenock, where he was to take ship, leaving his dearly loved Ayrshire behind him, to try a possibly hopeless venture in a strange land. But on the way he was overtaken by a letter from the blind poet Dr. Blacklock, urging him to have a second edition of his poems issued, and prophesying that they would have "a more universal circulation than anything of the kind" yet printed. This changed the course of affairs. The Jamaica project was given up and the young farmer of twenty-seven went to Edinburgh to find himself a "lion."

His fame had preceded him, and people of all ranks were eager to invite him to their houses. He knew nothing of the ways of fashionable society, but his manly self-respect made his rustic plainness attractive. His appearance at this time was not without dignity, though hard work had bent his back and roughened his hands.

Walter Scott, then a boy of fifteen, once saw him, and thus describes him: "There was a strong expression of sense and shrewdness in all his lineaments; the eye alone,

I think, indicated the poetical character and temperament. It was large and of a dark cast, which glowed (I say literally glowed) when he spoke with feeling or interest. I never saw such another eye in a human head."

This happy time came to an end only too soon. Burns, who had already contracted that taste for drink which was to be his ruin, was tempted to still greater indulgence; and when he returned to country life, and, after an unsuccessful attempt at farming, settled down as an exciseman in Dumfries, there is little to tell except of a sad decline. The business of exciseman (taxer of spirits) ministered to his fatal taste; and its influence led him to vices of other kinds. Before this he spent a second winter at Edinburgh, as much neglected as he had been courted during the first. His proud soul rose in rebellion at this change, and many bitter expressions in his letters tell how he felt it. The poetic fervor did not fail him; the same pen which had written:

> O wad some power the giftie gi'e us
> To see oursel's as others see us!
> It wad frae mony a blunder free us,
> And foolish notion:

wrote also "To Mary in Heaven," "Tam o' Shanter," and "John Anderson, my Jo." But life was a disappointment. The poet's education, while it raised him far above the humble peasants and dissipated officials who were again his companions, had not fitted him to enter the fine society of that highly polished circle which he had learned to enjoy; and in the latter his pride continually met with mortifications which embittered and depressed, though they did not humiliate him. His few remaining years dragged out painfully. He had married a young woman of his own rank in life; the "bonnie Jean" of his early days; and while she made him a faithful and admiring wife, there could be between them none of the companionship founded on community of tastes. He failed in health and spirits; he had been too generous to his brother to lay up anything for himself; and in debt and poverty he passed away at the age of thirty-seven.

For several reasons, it is difficult to give a really illustrative quotation from Burns. His most characteristic poems are in Scottish dialect, so broad as to require a glossary with every verse; and they are, besides, so coarse as to be beyond the bounds of proper reading. Many of them are in praise of drink; the fatal vice which has dragged thousands of his countrymen to destruction, which drove him out of good society (where he was at first welcomed) and utterly ruined his whole life and caused his untimely death. Other poems are wild and ribald attacks aimed at religious narrowness and bigotry which, in their scurrility, come quite to the border of blasphemous assaults on religion itself.

Here is a single poem that shows the bard's hatred of cruelty:

ON SEEING A WOUNDED HARE LIMP BY ME.

Inhuman man! Curse on thy barbarous art,
　And blasted be thy murder-aiming eye:
　May never Pity soothe thee with a sigh,
Nor ever pleasure glad thy cruel heart!

Go live, poor wanderer of the wood and field,
　The bitter little that of life remains:
　No more the thickening brakes and verdant plains
To thee shall home, or food, or pastime yield.

Seek, mangled wretch, some place of wonted rest—
　No more of rest, but now thy dying bed!
　The shelt'ring rushes whistling o'er thy head,
The cold earth with thy bloody bosom press'd.

The life of William Cowper (1731–1800), which began twenty-eight years before that of Burns and lasted four years after it, is a mingled thread of joy and sorrow. No one who reads his lines on receiving his mother's picture

WILLIAM COWPER.

can fail to call up the image of the carefully tended boy, wrapped in his scarlet cloak by a fond parent and drawn to school in a mimic coach by the gardner Robyn, his rosy face shining with health and pleasure, and a sweet biscuit clasped in his little hand. At the next picture, our hearts burn with indignation. The now motherless child of six is sent to boarding-school, where for two years he is tyrannized over by a brutal boy of fifteen whose "fag" he is, and who singles out the delicate, helpless little fellow to vent his ill-temper upon. Of him Cowper says in his later years, "I conceived such a dread of him that I well remember being afraid to lift my eyes higher than his knees; and that I knew him better by his shoe-buckles than by any other part of his dress."

A little later he was sent to Westminster School, where he passed seven years of his life. As the law was to be his profession, he was articled to a solicitor and nominally lived in his house, but really spent much of his time at the home of his uncle, Mr. Ashley Cowper, whose daughters were nearly of his own age. He writes in after-life to Lady Hesketh, one of these daughters:

There was I and the future Lord Chancellor [Thurlow] constantly employed from morning till night in giggling and making giggle, instead of following the law. Oh fie, cousin! how could you do so?

Unfortunately he fell in love with another of the girls, his cousin Theodora; her father objected to the match, and he resigned himself very quietly to a bachelor life. He was a member of the "Nonsense Club," composed of several gay young men of his own circle, and, altogether, his life seems to have been a sufficiently easy and pleasant one.

On the death of his father (as anything which we call work seems never to have occurred to people of his stamp) his friends resigned themselves to the situation, and generously supported him for the rest of his life.

17

A period of religious mania made it necessary to place him under medical care; and when he left the asylum which had been his home for two years, he settled down as a boarder in the family of the Reverend William Unwin, at Huntingdon.   He had been the subject of very deep religious impressions; and while the piety and affectionate kindness of his new friends commended them to him, he became a welcome inmate of their family on account of his fine tastes and his literary accomplishments, the friendship with them ending only with life.

Upon the death of Mr. Unwin, who was killed by a fall from his horse, his widow removed to Olney, to which place Cowper accompanied her; and there he passed the rest of his days.   It was here that he became acquainted with the Reverend John Newton, and together they wrote the "Olney Hymns," many of which are still used in devotional collections.   In 1773, Cowper had a second attack of insanity, in which he for the second time attempted to take his life.   Upon his recovery, his good friend Mrs. Unwin recommended to him to occupy his leisure with poetry, and acting on her suggestion he wrote several grave satires which the more attractive works of his later time have caused to be almost forgotten.   His first volume of poems was published when he was fifty years old.

One of his friends and neighbors at Olney, Lady Austin, to relieve his melancholy, told him the story of "John Gilpin," which he turned into verse so easily that she pressed him to try another style, abandoning the heroic couplet in which his first poems were written, and composing something in blank verse.   "What shall I take for a subject?" "Oh, write upon anything," she replied.   "Write upon this sofa!"   Thus began his most famous poem, which he called "The Task," because he undertook it at the command of a lady.   The evolution of the sofa from a three-legged stool is told with much ingenuity and some humor; then the poet congratulates himself on not needing the languid repose afforded by a sofa while he has the strength and spirits to enjoy the open-air life of nature, tramping over hill and field and drinking in all the glorious freshness of the summer morning. His description of natural objects is breeziness itself, and fell upon the ears used to the formal couplets and quatrains of the previous age, like the voice of the lark after the singing of a caged canary-bird. He was a born lover of nature and wrote of it from the heart, with the observant eye of a painter, the musical ear of a poet, and the simplicity of one untrammelled by conventionalities.

Nothing in English poetry had as yet rung out like his "Apostrophe to Winter":

> Oh, Winter, ruler of the inverted year,
> Thy scattered hair with sleet like ashes filled,
> Thy breath congealed upon thy lips, thy cheeks
> Tinged with a beard made white with other snows
> Than those of age, thy forehead wrapped in clouds,
> A leafless branch thy sceptre, and thy throne
> A sliding car, indebted to no wheels,
> But urged by storms along its slippery way;
> I love thee, all unlovely as thou seemst
> And dreaded as thou art!

Cowper has been called the forerunner of Wordsworth, some of whose descriptions strongly resemble passages in "The Task."

The tranquil life at Olney was favorable to composition of all sorts, and especially to one beautiful branch of it in which Cowper excelled—letter-writing. His biographer, Southey, calls him the best of English letter-writers. He writes to his cousin, Lady Hesketh, when arranging for a visit from her:

I will not let you come till the end of May or the beginning of June, because before that time my green-house will not be ready to receive us, and it is the only pleasant place belonging to us. When the plants go out, we go in. I line it with nets and spread the floor with mats, and there you shall sit, with a bed of mignonette at your side, and a hedge of honeysuckles, roses, and jasmines; and I will make you a bouquet of myrtle every day.

In another letter he says, "Occurrences are as scarce as cucumbers at Christmas." We can imagine the pleasure of the winter evening from his well-known description:

> Now stir the fire, and close the shutters fast,
> Let fall the curtains, wheel the sofa round,
> And, while the bubbling and loud-hissing urn
> Throws up a steamy column, and the cups
> That cheer, but not inebriate, wait on each,
> So let us welcome peaceful evening in.

Having finished "The Task," Cowper was again in need of literary occupation, and some friend suggested a translation of Homer. This was good for the poet, as it furnished something to keep his brain from preying upon itself; but it did not add very much to the literary possessions of the world. The Odyssey is more interesting than the Iliad; but neither has the spirit and life of the later translations which have made the grand old Greek familiar to us. As compared with Pope's translation, Cowper's is the less polished, and the more exact and faithful; a difference to be expected from the fact that Cowper freed himself from the trammels of rhyme by choosing blank verse; that is, ten-syllabled rhymeless lines.

Not long after the completion of this work, Mrs. Unwin, his faithful friend and helper through many years of mingled trouble and happiness, was stricken with palsy, and, losing her mind, became in turn the object of his tender care. But the strain upon him was too great. After her death he sank into hopeless melancholy, and in this pitiable condition dragged out the remaining years of his life. With his death in 1800, we bring our sketch of the literary men of his century to a close.

CHAPTER XL.

WORDSWORTH. COLERIDGE.

WE have already spoken of Cowper, Burns and Crabbe as inaugurating a new school of poetry more natural and more human than the formal or artificial one which preceded it. In William Wordsworth (1770–1850) we find the humanitarian school joined to the philosophical, and bringing in the element of genius (which, except in the case of Burns, had been lacking in the preceding generation of poets) to illumine the new development.

The second group of contemporary writers, Wordsworth, Coleridge and Southey, have been improperly classed together as "The Lake Poets," until many persons are under an impression that they belong to one another from similarity of mind or style, instead of the unimportant fact that their dwellings were comparatively near each other on the Westmoreland lakes, and that they were friends. They have even been called by an amusing misnomer, "the lake school" of poets. However these names arose, they can not now be separated from the original subjects, and "the lakers" will go down to posterity together.

Wordsworth was born in Cumberland, another of the lake counties, and therefore not far from the scene of his later celebrity. He was early left an orphan, and was sent to college, as so many poets have been, by the kindness of relatives. After graduating at Cambridge he went to Paris, where the French Revolution was in full progress (1792–3). He was intensely interested in the republic, which he at first felt to be identified with the cause of human freedom; after a time he sympathized more with the moderate party, the Girondists, and probably escaped the wholesale destruction which overtook them in 1793, only by a timely retreat from the country.   At a later time, when the excesses of the revolution revealed its worst side, he become a conservative as to everything regarding church and state.

When Wordsworth was twenty-six, the smallness of his means made it necessary that he should do something toward getting a living; and his friends were much disgusted to find that he could not be induced to adopt any of the professions, nor any kird of business offered him, being determined to devote himself to poetry.   This appeared to them rank perverseness; though, as his mother was said to have pronounced him "stiff, moody and violent in temper" as a child, they were the less surprised at it. One person, however, stood by him; his sister Dorothy, a lovely, sensitive creature, herself of a highly poetic nature, who devoted herself heart and soul to his service. Wordsworth adhered to his determination to be a poet and nothing but a poet; and when his means were about exhausted, a friend whom he had nursed in his last illness left him a legacy of £900, saying that he did this in order that Wordsworth might devote himself to a literary life.   The brother and sister felt that they had inherited a fortune.   Dorothy had £100 of her own, and on the income of these united sums they chiefly lived, thanks to her excellent management, for several years.   They kept house in the humblest way, first at Racedown in Dorsetshire, and then, in order to be near Coleridge, whose acquaintance they had lately made, at Alfoxden in Somersetshire.   The two poets published together a volume of "Lyrical Ballads," which contained such incongruous material as Coleridge's "Ancient Mariner" and Wordsworth's "Idiot Boy."   The public laughed at both, and did not buy the book very freely, but the twenty guineas which fell to Wordsworth's share made it possible for him to take his sister to Germany, where they spent a quiet winter.   Here he began what is considered his most profound work, "The Prelude," a history of the growth and workings of his mind up to the point where he had matured his plan of life, and felt himself ready to begin what he took as his peculiar task—the development of a new standard in poetry. "The Prelude" was not completed for several years, and was not published until after his death—more than fifty years from the time of its commencement. It was dedicated to Coleridge.

On their return from Germany, the brother and sister settled at Grasmere, in Westmoreland; a place still so full of the associations of their lives that one seems almost to see and hear them while going over the little cottage. This is kept with pious care as a memorial of those beautiful days. "Plain living and high thinking," as Emerson calls it, was the order of the day; and to the many choice spirits who visited the poet's home, this was more agreeable than if the adjectives had been reversed. Thither Wordsworth brought his bride, the gentle Mary Hutchinson, and the three lived together in the closest of friendship during their lives.

From this time there was little variety in the poet's life. A sum of money due Wordsworth's father, which had been withheld through obstinacy on the part of the debtor, was paid, principal and interest, on the death of the latter, by his son, Lord Lonsdale; and the family from that time lived in comfort, without any puzzling questions as to ways and means.

Through Lord Lonsdale's influence, Wordsworth was appointed to the office of distributor of stamps, which gave him an additional £500 a year of income, with very light duties to perform, so that he could give his mind entirely to composition and to the study of natural things. He has been called a high-priest of Nature; he was rather one of her humble worshippers. By constant endeavor to know her secrets, he arrived at the closest communion with her that man can enjoy; and his delight in her companionship never flagged for a moment.

Mingled with this reverence was a lofty sense of the dignity of man; and the two ideas are blended in the magnificent poem called "The Excursion," the work of some of his ripest years of thought and observation. There are few reflective poems so abounding in quotable passages; and though at times its diffuseness makes it appear tedious, the general impression it gives is, as has often been said, like that of organ music.

Jeffrey, the dreaded critic of the "Edinburgh Review," began his famous notice of the "Excursion" with the words, "This will never do!" But the thinking world, even in Wordsworth's own day, discovered that it would do, and posterity has sustained the verdict. It is a poem written only for those who are able to reflect; to the frivolous it presents no attractions. The "Excursion" was meant to be only one of the three parts of a great life-poem, of which the "Prelude" (which name, by the way, was given to it by his wife after his death) was to be the first. The plan, however, was too vast, and the work was never completed. How slowly the world appreciated it is shown by the fact that the first edition of five hundred copies lasted six years, and the second, of equal size, still longer.

Wordsworth had some severe sorrows. The loss of two children in youth, of his sister, who overtaxed her more delicate frame in trying to keep up with his mountain-climbing, and of his beloved daughter Dora, Mrs. Quillilan, weighed heavily upon him, and he sank into apathy during the last years of his life. But his work was done; and every poet who has written since it began owes a debt of gratitude to Wordsworth.

Regarding his shorter poems, the "Ode on Intimations of Immortality," "The Daffodils," "Ode to Duty," "Tintern Abbey," and the exquisite sonnets,—we can only advise the reader to study them until he *feels* them and imbibes their spirit.   A mere reading is not enough.

Wordsworth wrote little prose except some excellent letters; but his "Essay on Poetry" embodies many exalted and elevating ideas.   He was made poet-laureate on the death of Southey (1843) and retained the position until his own death, when he was succeeded by Tennyson.

Samuel Taylor Coleridge (1772–1834) was by nature and habit a dreamer.   This must be kept in mind in endeavoring to set in order the events which made up that strange life, in the course of which we are constantly trying to make excuses for its subject.   He was the son of a clergyman, and was a precocious child; read his Bible at three years old and the "Arabian Nights" at six; was entered as a charity-boy at Christ's Hospital School (the "Blue-coat"), London; studied for two years at Cambridge; and then, mortified at owing a debt of £100 which he could not pay, he left college and enlisted as a private in a regiment of dragoons.   A young man passing through the town recognized him, and informed his friends, who soon obtained his discharge.   We next hear of him at Bristol, where he formed with Southey and Robert Lovell (the latter also a poet) a plan for emigrating to America, and there, on the banks of the Susquehanna, founding a social colony, where all property was to be in common, and where the labor of two hours a day was to supply all needs.   The government was to be a pantisocracy, or equal rule of all, and the funds — well, it was not so clear where the funds were to come from, but they thought so trivial a matter as the lack of money would not be a serious drawback to their plan. They invited a bookseller and publisher of Bristol, Joseph Cottle, to join their party, and he has preserved a delightful account of their simple-minded scheme in his "Reminiscences of Coleridge and Southey."   Without absolutely discouraging the visionaries, he quietly watched their proceedings, bought their poems, gave them good advice and suggestions, to which they paid no attention, and was finally much relieved when they came to him to borrow money to go into lodgings, for that meant that the pantisocracy was, for the time at least, given up.

It had been a condition of the pantisocracy that all who participated in the scheme should be married. Lovell had already married Miss Fricker of Bristol; Southey made a secret match with her sister Edith; and Coleridge, without secrecy, for there was no one to oppose him, married the third sister, Sarah.

The old question of ways and means was still an important one. Coleridge gave lectures, which were well attended, but to which he sometimes forgot to go; he began the publication of a paper called "The Watchman," but soon stopped it for want of subscribers; and in the year after his marriage he removed to Nether Stowey in Somersetshire, and devoted himself entirely to writing. It was while here that he made the memorable call on Wordsworth and his sister, which made the two poets friends for life. Dorothy Wordsworth, the lovely and gifted sister of the poet, has left a pen-portrait of Coleridge at the time. He was "thin and pale, the lower part of the face not good, wide mouth, thick lips, not very good teeth, longish, loose, half-curling, rough, black hair." But the moment he spoke, everything else was forgotten in his magical utterances. His conversation, to the end of his life, had a charm which fascinated all who met him. As has been said, he and Wordsworth published together the volume of "Lyrical Ballads," which included Coleridge's "Ancient Mariner." In 1798 some members of the Wedgwood family (of pottery fame) presented him with an annuity which enabled him to realize the wish of his heart and visit Germany, whither he went in company with the Wordsworths. He mastered the language with wonderful quickness, and on his return translated Schiller's "Piccolomini," two dramas of which Wallenstein is the hero. He continued to write, producing, amid some indifferent poetry, some of the most exquisite gems of which our language can boast.

For the first fifteen years of this century, the life of Coleridge is a miserable story of slavery to opium. He had been, as a young man, advised to take it as a medicine, which he did with the most satisfactory effect, and having thus acquired the taste for it, he had not strength of mind or will to break away from the habit of using it. He wandered from place to place, restless and unhappy, making now and then a brief return to social life. During these intervals he would give lectures, and enchant every one about him, as of old, with his wonderful conversation; then disappear again into mysterious obscurity, leaving his wife and family, meanwhile, to be supported by the generous, industrious Southey, whose house and heart were ever open to them. In 1810, Coleridge abandoned his family entirely, and five years later had the good fortune to be taken into the family of Mr. and Mrs. Gillman, at Highgate, who devoted themselves to him for the remaining nineteen years of his life. Mr Gillman was a medical man, and succeeded in restraining his patient's unfortunate propensity within such bounds as left him to some degree master over himself, and enabled him to live and die in tolerable comfort. Here he received his friends and indulged in the endless monologue to which all were so delighted to listen. There had not been such a talker since the days of Dr. Johnson; there has probably not been one since. Among his visitors was Thomas Carlyle, who has left a lifelike portrait of him in the "Life of John Sterling":

Brow and head were round, and of massive weight; but the face was flabby and irresolute. The deep eyes, of a light hazel, were as full of sorrow as inspiration; confused pain looked mildly from them, as in a kind of mild astonishment. * * * A lady once remarked, he never could fix which side of the garden walk would suit him best, but continually shifted, in corkscrew fashion, and kept trying both. A heavy-laden, high-aspiring, and surely much-suffering man.

Although most of his friends listened without criticism to his dissertations, there was occasionally one who took the liberty of quietly laughing at him. Hazlett says of him: "He did not cease [talking] while I stayed, nor has he since, that I know of." And Charles Lamb, when Coleridge asked him whether he had ever heard him preach, answered, "I never heard you do anything else!"

Coleridge's prose works are far more voluminous than his poetry, and are mostly of a highly philosophical cast. "The Friend" (a periodical), "Aids to Reflection," and "Biographia Literaria" are among the best-known of his prose works. His oldest son, Hartley Coleridge, a man of genius, a thinker and a poet, was ruined by intemperance. The second son, the Rev. Derwent Coleridge, wrote a memoir of his brother Hartley, and some theological works. Sara Coleridge, the poet's only daughter, who inherited much of his genius, wrote both prose and verse. She married her cousin, Henry Nelson Coleridge, who was, like the rest of his family, devoted to literature. He undertook a memoir of S. T. Coleridge, but dying before it was completed, it was finished by his widow. She was also the author of "Phantasmion," a prose fairy-tale, and of several other graceful literary works.

<hr>

CHAPTER XLI.

SOUTHEY. CAMPBELL. MOORE.

ROBERT SOUTHEY was not a great poet, but he was a fine prose-writer, and so admirable a man that one can scarcely separate what he did from what he was. In the midst of constant and engrossing occupation, he, like Scott, always found time for the claims of friendship, charity and civility; and his hospitable house was the constant resort of visitors, beside furnishing shelter, year after year, to his wife's widowed sister, Mrs. Lovell (who came, with her child, to live with him), and to the neglected family of his fellow-poet, Coleridge. Laborious, earnest and conscientious, his life was one of the busiest recorded among the literary brotherhood; and when at last his overtaxed brain gave way and the sad end came, we feel that his had been, like Scott's, a life nobly used.

Southey was the son of a linen-draper in Bristol, and was sent, at the expense of an uncle, to Westminster School, from which he was expelled, four years later, because he had taken part in the writing of an article against flogging. Afterward he spent two years at Oxford, where, according to his own account, he learned but two things— to row and to swim. While there he composed his first epic poem, "Joan of Arc," for which the generous book-seller, Cottle, gave him fifty guineas. His marriage, and the wild scheme of "pantisocracy," have already been spoken of in the sketch of Coleridge.

At the time of his apparently imprudent marriage, the same kind relative who had helped him before, remarked that he saw in him "everything you could wish a young man to have, except common sense and prudence;" and we, who see through to the end, know that these qualities were developed later.

A volume of poems, written jointly by Southey and his brother-in-law, Lovell, had appeared some time before the emigration plan was thought of. . Southey now produced "Thalaba," an oriental epic, and soon after settled at Greta Hall in Keswick, on one of the Cumberland lakes, not far from Wordsworth, where he spent the rest of his long life. In addition to the epics already mentioned, he wrote "Madoc," founded on a Welsh legend, and "The

Curse of Kehama." These long poems are now little read. Several of the short ones are still popular, such as "The Cataract of Lodore" (a burlesque), "My Books," "The Inchcape Rock," and "The Battle of Blenheim." The amusing fairy tale of "The Three Bears," so great a favorite with children, is of his invention.

The main part of Southey's work was in prose, in which his style was clear and vigorous, though he himself preferred his somewhat dull and feeble poetry. The list of his works includes writings on so many topics that we will not try to name them all. Biographies of Cowper, Wesley and Lord Nelson, histories of Portugal and the Peninsular War, the "Book of the Church," many volumes of essays, and a curious medley called "The Doctor," are only a part of his multifarious labors. A friend to whom he had been giving a list of his daily occupations asked, "But tell me, Southey, when do you *think?*"

In addition to the ordinary employments of a literary man, Southey was a scrupulous and voluminous correspondent. He made it a rule to answer, before going to bed at night, every letter received during the day; and as his kindness and obliging disposition were well known, he was subject to a continual drain on his time and strength, which a more selfish person would have managed to escape.

In 1813, he was appointed to the laureateship; an office which had been declined by Gray and Scott, and filled, since Cibber's time, by Whitehead (1757–85), Warton (1785 –90), and Pye (1790–1813).

He was offered a baronetcy, but declined it on account of the expense attending it. Bitter sorrow saddened his life. The loss of his only son, and of a daughter who is described by him as "the most radiant creature I ever beheld," seemed to take away his hope and spirit, and Greta Hall, the gay and hospitable home, became silent. This was not the heaviest trial. His wife, his beloved

Edith, the faithful companion of forty years, became insane; and after lingering for several years in this pitiable condition died, in 1837. Two years later he married Caroline Bowles, (a friend of twenty years' standing), whose poetical works are published under her name of Caroline Southey. A few months afterward, partial paralysis overtook him; the tireless hand and brain gave way, and a slow decay set in from which death came as a relief.

Thomas Campbell (1777–1844) was born to comparative poverty, but had a good education, and grew up an unpractical, sensitive, deep - feeling youth, quite dependent on love and friendship; the ideal nature for the development of a poet of his class. He served in various tutorships, and made his first serious effort in authorship in Edinburgh, a city always hospitable to literature, whither he carried his "Pleasures of Hope" and where it was well received. Scott, not yet famous, helped him to fame — and to the £60 that the poem brought. About 1800, he visited the continent and saw Hohenlinden and other battle-fields which inspired some of his splendid ballads; "On Linden when the sun was low," "The Soldier's Dream," "Ye Mariners of England," etc. He did not appreciate the value of these. Scott said to Washington Irving:

There's that glorious little poem of Hohenlinden—after he had written it he did not seem to think much of it—"drum and trumpet lines." I got him to read it to me and I believe that the delight I felt and expressed had an effect in inducing him to print it. The fact is, Campbell is a bugbear to himself. The brightness of his early success is a detriment to all his future efforts. He is afraid of the shadow his own fame casts before him.

Campbell tried editing, but was not successful. He engaged to do work for publishers at set times, and when the time came the work was not even begun. He could not live on fame and social popularity—especially seeing that he had married and that a son was born to him—and naturally got into difficulties which even a pension of £200, given him in

1806, failed to relieve. Then his wife died, and his son, in whom he had placed high hopes, lost his mind and became the inmate of a madhouse. So he fell into a state of continual melancholy and wrote very little poetry during the last twenty years of his life. His friends thought him the victim of an incurable indolence; but perhaps the vein was worked out. He delivered a course of "Lectures on Poetry," which were deservedly popular, and wrote two or three biographies, beside the addresses which his election as Lord Rector of the University of Glasgow made necessary. His social qualities were very brilliant, and he was always welcomed in the circle of wits and wise men, but as age drew on he shrank from society, partly from depression caused by domestic losses, partly from a feeling that his day was over — a sad waste of intellectual possibilities when we think of the fresh, vigorous men who at eighty are as delightful company as they were at forty. After a lingering illness, Campbell died, in Boulogne, at the age of sixty-seven. He was buried in Westminster Abbey.

Campbell's principal poem, "The Pleasures of Hope," is written in the heroic rhymed couplet of Pope, and shows an ear perfectly attuned to the melody of rhythm. Lord Byron pronounced it "one of the most beautiful didactic poems in our language." Here are some of the passages most frequently quoted:

> 'Tis distance lends enchantment to the view,
> And robes the mountain in its azure hue.
>
> * * *
>
> Without the smile from partial Beauty won,
> Oh what were man? A world without a sun.
>
> * * *
>
> The world was sad, the garden was a wild,
> And Man, the hermit, sighed till Woman smiled!
>
> * * *
>
> Eternal Hope! when yonder spheres sublime
> Pealed their first notes to sound the march of Time.
> Thy joyous youth began — but not to fade.
> When all the sister planets have decayed,

> When wrapt in fire the realms of ether glow,
> And Heaven's last thunder shakes the world below;
> Thou, undismayed, shalt o'er the ruin smile,
> And light thy torch at Nature's funeral pile!

Campbell's next longest poem, "Gertrude of Wyoming," is a narrative of the massacre perpetrated by Indians and their tory instigators in the Valley of the Wyoming, Pennsylvania, during our Revolutionary War. The poem was received with great enthusiasm. His fame must rest, however, on his unsurpassed lyrics, especially "Ye Mariners of England," "Hohenlinden," "Lochiel's Warning," "Lord Ullin's Daughter," "The Battle of the Baltic," and "The Soldier's Dream," which will be read as long as our language endures. Scarcely less admirable are the reflective poems, "To the Rainbow," "The Last Man," "Field Flowers," "The Exile of Erin," "To the Evening Star," etc. "A Thought Suggested by the New Year," contains the substance of a volume:

> The more we live, more brief appear
>   Our life's succeeding stages;
> A day to childhood seems a year—
>   A year like passing ages.
>
> Heaven gives our years of failing strength
>   Indemnifying fleetness,
> And those of youth a seeming length
>   Proportioned to their sweetness!

Thomas Moore (1779–1852) claims attention rather because of his success than of his eminence. Some one has shrewdly said "let me make the ballads of a people and I care not who makes the laws;" which is another way of expressing the idea that spontaneous poetry and what is called "folk-lore" operates on national character more than do its statutes. The ballad literature of a country, in this sense of the word, can not be restricted to the writings of any one man, but must include all the traditional verse which is the common heritage of the people. Still, each song has some author, known or unknown; and some of the rhyme-sters have written or rewritten many which go to swell the burden of "popular song." Such men are Béranger in France and Thomas Moore in Ireland.

Moore was born in Dublin, the son of a grocer. He went to Trinity College, where he made some progress in classics, and fitted himself for the study of the law; and at twenty went over to London to "keep terms," *i.e.* study law, in the Inner Temple. He had already made a translation of Anacreon, which he wished to publish by subscription; and such was his personal charm that his subscription list was easily filled, and included the rank and fashion of the town. He is described as the most fascinating of youths, his company sought and prized everywhere, and his sweet voice and charming songs (to his own accompaniment on the piano) the delight of old and young, high and low alike. The world seemed wait-ing for such a brightening, sweetening, softening influence, and fame and fortune flowed in upon him.

He began in 1807 his writing of words to fit old music, and for a very long time got for "Irish Melodies," from one publisher, £500 a year. For "Lalla Rookh" he received £3000, and for other works — his "Life of Byron," etc. —correspondingly handsome payment. He also obtained a profitable office from the government, that of Registrar in Admiralty in the Island of Bermuda, and he visited the United States on his way to that colony. He soon tired of his residence in the West Indies, his life in Lon-don having spoiled him for such an out-of-the-way place; so he left the office to a deputy, and contented himself for the next fourteen years with about £400 a year profit on its income.

Moore's warm, close and faithful friendship for Lord Byron was a marked feature in his career. Being made the greater poet's literary executor; and receiving Byron's memoirs with the leave to publish them, he consulted friends of taste and judgment, and, guided by their advice, decided that they were too scandalous to be preserved and therefore burned them all.

He certainly was a warm lover of Ireland. Nevertheless, the more earnest, serious and thoughtful patriots, who stayed at home instead of following his example of giving themselves up to London gayeties, are very far from ranking him among Erin's worthy sons; and think that his trivialities did his mother-land harm rather than good — made it beloved and pitied but not respected.

CHAPTER XLII.

LORD BYRON.

IF the question were to be asked, "Who is England's greatest poet?" the answers would vary as widely as the points of view from which such a subject can be approached; but if an inquiry should be made as to which of her writers of verse presents the most poetic personality, the general voice would probably be in favor of the handsome, lawless, brilliant, unfortunate Byron.

George Noel Gordon, Lord Byron (1788–1824) inherited his turbulence with his title, for the grand-uncle from whom the title descended had killed his neighbor and relative, Mr. Chaworth, in a drunken brawl, and well earned the name of "the wicked Lord Byron." His father was a profligate officer who married Catherine Gordon, the poet's mother, only for her fortune, and left her as soon as that was used up. Byron's better qualities seem to have come through his grandfather, Admiral Byron, who is said to have had the virtues without the vices of his race. Among the things told of the family are the circumstances that seven brothers fought in the battle of Edgehill, and that a later lord patronized literature and wrote verses.

Add to all these formative influences the fact that the family means had been wasted by the family spendthrifts (leaving nothing but the unprofitable estate of Newstead Abbey to support the title), and that the last lord, our poet, was born with a club-foot—all these things being considered, a part at least of his personality is fairly accounted for.

At the time of Byron's birth (which occurred in London) his father had squandered the maternal dowry, and Mrs. Byron, a fitful, passionate woman, went with her "lame brat," as she sometimes called him, to live in Aberdeen. At ten years old, the boy fell so violently in love with his cousin, Mary Duff, that when six years later he heard of her marriage, he "nearly went into convulsions." At fifteen he fell in love more seriously with Miss Chaworth, whose grandfather his great-uncle had killed in a duel. Her rejection of him was a matter of enduring grief, as testified in his poem "The Dream." He studied during this time at different private schools, making some progress in the classics and reading much general literature.

> The drilled, dull lesson, forced down word by word,

was not to his taste. Nothing could be so that savored of law or authority. His later utterance,

> Then farewell Horace, whom I hated so,
> Not for thy faults, but mine—

shows that he at least understood the cause of his repugnance. After five years at Harrow he went to Cambridge, where he stayed three years but took no degree. Still, he learned much beside the "swimming, riding, fencing, boxing, drinking, gambling and other occupations of idle undergraduates," which he says occupied his time.

The deformed foot, after many tortures, was at last so far

reduced that he was able to put on a common boot; yet an incurable lameness remained a bitter mortification. His poverty might have been cured by the large earnings of his genius, but unfortunately his unbridled extravagance and dissipation made any accumulation of wealth impossible. Debts, duns, flight from creditors and all the other incidents so common in English "high life" and so rare in American, were his constant miseries as long as he lived.

Byron had written verses while at Harrow; he wrote more during a year spent at Southwell during his college course, and had even printed a volume for private circulation; and in 1807, he put forth publicly (though of course anonymously) "Hours of Idleness," which was honored with much praise and also with a bitter and contemptuous critique in the "Edinburgh Review." This he met with the celebrated satire "English Bards and Scotch Reviewers," which brought him at once prominently before the public. It was a general assault on everybody worth assaulting. Scott was "Apollo's venal son," a "hireling bard," etc. Southey was "ballad - mongering Southey," producing "annual strains to take the field like armies." "Vulgar Wordsworth" is "the meanest object in the lowly group," with "verse of all but childish prattle void;" Coleridge, "the laureate of the long - eared kind." "Smug Sydney" is Sydney Smith. "Blundering Brougham" is he who afterward became the lord and prime minister. The few names he excepts from his slurs are as significant as the victims:

> Come forth, oh, Campbell! Give thy talents scope;
> Who dares aspire if thou must cease to hope?
> And thou, melodious Rogers! rise at last,
> Recall the pleasing memories of the past.
>
>   *   *   *
>
> Restore Apollo to his vacant throne,
> Assert thy country's honor and thine own.
> What! Must deserted Poesy still weep
> Where her last hopes with pious Cowper sleep?

> Yet still some genuine sons 'tis hers to boast,
> Who, least affecting, still affect the most:
> Feel as they write, and write but as they feel—
> Bear witness Gifford, Sotheby, Macneil.

In other words the furious satirist puts not only Campbell and Rogers, but Gifford, Sotheby and Macneil, above Scott, Southey, Wordsworth, and Coleridge! In later years he did what he could to atone for some of this, and the magnanimous Scott not only forgave the younger poet but asserted his superiority to himself.

In 1809, Byron traveled on the continent; departing in deep dejection, feeling friendless and alone as such unfriendly and unrestrained persons are apt to feel. His travels gave rise to his greatest poem, "Childe Harold." The profound melancholy that marks that poem reflects faithfully the state of the poet's soul, but he denies the imputation that its hero is, in truth, himself. Poverty, increased by revolting extravagance and dissipation, and made more trying by high rank (which he could not forget), exposed his pride and vanity to continued friction, and kept him in a state of morbid irritation which is wearying to read about and must have been still more unpleasant to meet with.

He assumed his place in the House of Lords and took part in the debates, having at this time some ambition for a political career. But, to use his own words, "I awoke one morning and found myself famous." This expresses the unexpected nature of the success of "Childe Harold," of which the first two cantos were published in 1811. Mrs. Oliphant says: "It is not too much to say that the public mind was moved by it to a sort of sudden ecstasy of interest such as is almost incredible in our calmer days. The first edition was sold out at once and a universal ferment of interest about the author flew through that society which, up to this time had known and cared nothing about him."

This put a sudden stop to his political views, which never,

in truth, had any grave or stable aim, being a mere speculation as to how he would appear to the world: "Lord H. tells me I shall beat them all if I persevere, and Lord G. remarked that the construction of some of my periods is very like Burke's."

He now concluded that his easiest way to "beat them all" was through his poetry; yet he rested for a while on his "Childe Harold" laurels, during which period he was the lion of London, the friend and intimate of the Prince Regent and all the fashionable circle which revolved around him, in which Tom Moore was the minstrel and Brummell the dandy. Then he resumed his pen, and put forth, within eight years, "The Giaour," "The Bride of Abydos," "The Corsair," "Lara," "Siege of Corinth" and "Manfred." Many others, produced in the following three or four years, have the same fierce strength and fervid beauty that marks those named.

In 1815 he married Anne Isabella Milbanke, a lady of fortune, with whom he lived for about a year, during which his debts were pressed for collection with renewed vigor, nine executions being levied in the house within that time. After the birth of a daughter, Lady Byron went on a visit to her father, and a few days later Byron received a letter from the father saying that she had resolved never to return to him, and a formal deed of separation followed. The causes of this separation have never been made clear, but they are easy to guess. There had been no love to begin with, on either side; on his side were indifference, perversity, selfishness and a brutal disregard of the ordinary courtesies of family life, while she seems to have been coldly correct, unsympathetic and unyielding. Her appreciation of his fame and glory can be judged from her asking him when he meant to give up his bad habit of writing verses!

After Byron's separation from his wife and his infant daughter, he sold Newstead Abbey and took a final leave of England, and by living abroad escaped the measures which his creditors took to collect what he owed them — measures which his biographers gravely call "indignities!" He lived at many places; always without the morality, decency and sterling honesty which have made illustrious the names of most of his brother poets, from Chaucer to Tennyson. Look at his insolent disregard of the rights of those who had trusted him, and compare it with Scott's noble self-martyrdom in the payment of debts from which he had drawn no gain!

In 1823 he gave his services to the cause of Grecian independence and entered heart and soul into the war with Turkey. While preparing for the siege of Lepanto he contracted the fatal illness which ended his life at Missolonghi, April 19, 1824.

Being so marked a figure, personally, we must make a place for his portrait as drawn by Lady Blessington, a year before his death :

I had fancied him taller, with a more dignified and commanding air. . . . His appearance is, however, highly prepossessing, his head finely shaped, his forehead open, high and noble; his eyes are grey and full of expression, but one is visibly larger than the other; his mouth is the most remarkable feature in his face, the upper lip of Grecian shortness and the corners descending, the lips full and finely cut. In speaking he shows his teeth very much, and they are white and even, but I observed even in his smile — and he smiles frequently — there is something of a scornful expression in his mouth that is evidently natural and not, as many suppose, affected. . . . He is very slightly lame, and the deformity of his foot is so little remarkable that I am not now aware which foot it is. . . . Were I to point out the prominent defect of Lord Byron, I should say it was flippancy, and a total want of that natural self-possession and dignity which ought to characterize a man of birth and education.

If one might venture to characterize in a few words so vast a genius as that set forth in Byron's poems, it may be said to be the embodiment of self; to show passion rather than affection, volcanic fire rather than homely warmth, noon and midnight without twilight, wit without genial humor, strength without sweetness, grief without sympathy, and joy without contentment.

CHAPTER XLIII.

SHELLEY. KEATS. HOOD.

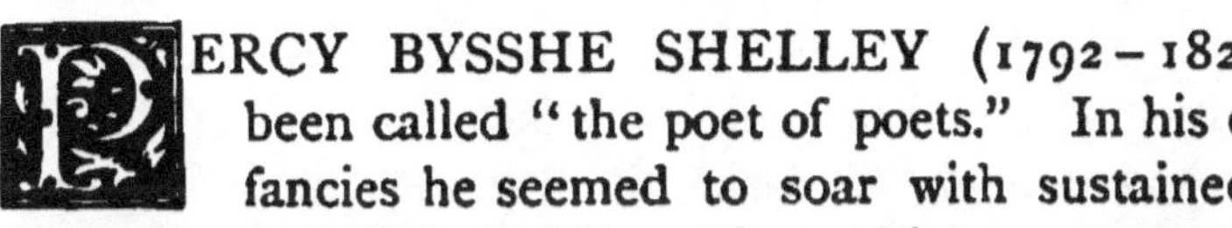ERCY BYSSHE SHELLEY (1792–1822) has been called "the poet of poets." In his ethereal fancies he seemed to soar with sustained flight, like his own skylark, in a region which common mortals rarely reach and soon abandon, sinking toward earth again from the rarer air above. Unhappily this delicately creative mind was marred by a lack of capacity to follow the path of morality and religion, a lack showing itself on the one hand in his irregular life, and on the other in the atheistical tendency of his writings.

Shelley was not, like so many of our poets, born to poverty. His father was a baronet, Sir Timothy Shelley, and expected his son to grow up into a respectable, commonplace person like himself; but nature, in endowing the boy with a sensitive and unmanageable soul, frustrated the father's intentions. Shelley was the victim of some tyranny and ill-usage at school, which increased his inborn hatred of law and control; and his life was one long rebellion against the established order of things, under whatever form it presented itself. After writing a pamphlet on atheism, for which he was expelled from college, and a poem in the same spirit entitled "Queen Mab," he brought his father's displeasure to a climax by a runaway marriage with Harriet Westbrook, the daughter of an innkeeper, a girl of seventeen, he himself being then still under twenty. Sir Timothy did not disown his son for this act of insubordination, but desired no more of his company, though he made him a small allowance to live on. After a time Shelley grew tired of Harriet—she "could not feel poetry or understand philosophy," he said—and, abandoning her and her two children, he went off to Italy with Mary Godwin, another girl of seventeen, daughter of Mary Wollstonecraft and William Godwin, who both entertained the same ideas in regard to marriage as did Shelley and the younger Mary. In the next act of this tragic drama poor Harriet drowns herself, and Shelley marries Mary Godwin. As one of his kindest biographers has said, "the fact that he ought to do a thing was enough to make Shelley set himself against it." The indulgence of the moment's desire was the only duty he acknowledged. A few years brought his strange, wayward life to a close. He was at Spezia, in Italy, and had gone out with his friend Williams, and a sailor boy, for a sail on the bay. A squall came up, the boat capsized, and all three were drowned. After much search, Shelley's body was found, and Lord Byron, with other friends, burned it upon the sea-shore, according to the old Grecian custom. In a pocket was a volume of Keats, who had died the year before, and to whose memory Shelley had written the exquisite poem of "Adonaïs." The ashes were laid in the Protestant cemetery at Rome. At the time of his death, Shelley was not quite thirty years old.

In the airy grandeur of his imaginings and the melody of his verse, Shelley has perhaps never been surpassed. His writing is unequal. Some of the longer poems, like "The Revolt of Islam," and "Alastor," are exceedingly obscure; "Prometheus Unbound," the most splendid effort of his genius, is marred by the impious daring of its sentiments; "The Cenci," a work of tremendous power, is repulsive from its subject; but the lovely "Skylark," the "Cloud" and the "Hymn to Intellectual Beauty" are pure poetry.

Shelley's personal appearance was in harmony with his mental graces. He was tall and slender, with wavy dark-brown hair, deep blue eyes and youthful face full of spirituality. His biographer, W. M. Rossetti, says of him: "He was generosity, unworldliness and disinterestedness personified," a dictum which his treatment of heartbroken Harriet Westbrook Shelley scarcely bears out.

John Keats (1795–1821) was the youngest of the group we have been occupied with, and the first to depart. Of humble origin (which meant then exclusion from the ranks of that higher class where culture is a matter of course), he was apprenticed to a surgeon, and tried bravely to do his duty in an uncongenial task. Poetry, however, was in his nature and would find its way out. His first collection of poems, published at twenty-two, contained nothing remarkable, except the glorious sonnet "On first looking into Chapman's Homer." The second, "Endymion," which came out the next year with a modest preface, gave early promise of a finer flight than it, as a whole, displayed, though it contained much that was admirable. In the third and last, the world saw a full-fledged poet, worthy to stand among the noblest.

To return to his early endeavors. Having published some poems in. Leigh Hunt's "Examiner," Keats was brought to the notice of literary men who recognized his merit and made him welcome among them. The drudgery of the mortar and pill-box was exchanged for more congenial occupation; and he devoted himself to writing poetry with the eagerness which characterized everything he did.

The great reviews attacked "Endymion" with fierce and contemptuous abuse, and the story was long current that the article in the "Quarterly" hastened Keat's death. He was undoubtedly deeply wounded and discouraged by it; but he came of a consumptive family, and his early death may not be chargeable to the strictures of "Blackwood" and the "Quarterly."

He answered the criticisms on his youthful work with a quiet dignity which must have put his savage critics to the blush:

J. S. is perfectly right in regard to the "slip-shod Endymion." That it is so is no fault of mine. No! though it may sound a little paradoxical to say so, it is as good as I had power to make it myself. * * * I have written independently *without judgment;* I may write independently and with judgment hereafter. The genius of poetry must work out its own salvation in a man. It can not be matured by law and precept, but by sensation and watchfulness. * * In *Endymion* I leaped headlong into the sea, and thereby have become better acquainted with the soundings, the quicksands and the rocks, than if I had stayed upon the green shore and piped a silly pipe, and taken tea and comfortable advice.

And then he went on to write the noble poem of "Hyperion," which remains a fragment because he felt unable to do the subject justice. Next followed in quick succession the terribly picturesque "Lamia," and "Isabella;" the "Eve of Saint Agnes," a poem perfect in its exquisite melody and tenderness; the "Ode to a Grecian Urn," breathing the very spirit of classic refinement and dainty grace; the "Ode to a Nightingale," almost overpowering in its intensity of feeling; several lovely sonnets, and much more that makes us regret that so fair a fruitage should be nipped and blasted before it arrived at its prime. At the age of twenty, the symptoms of consumption appeared. He went to Rome, hoping there to find at least some alleviation of his disease; but the change did him no good, and after a few months of suffering he was laid to rest, "Within the shadow of the pyramid of Caius Cestius."

On the tomb, by his own direction, are inscribed the words, "Here lies one whose name was writ in water." Shelley said of his burial-place, "It makes one in love with death to think of being buried in so sweet a place,"—little thinking how soon all that remained of his own mortal tenement would be laid beside him. Keats said, while lying in his last illness, "I feel the daisies growing

over me;" and those who visit his tomb now, find it covered
with daisies and violets.

The last of the group of poets of whom Wordsworth was
the first in poetic rank and Rogers the first in order of
birth, was Thomas Hood (1798–1845).   The death of his
father left the family poor, and it was by his own choice
that the son went early to work rather than burden his
widowed mother with his education.   At twenty - one he
became sub - editor of the "London Magazine," for which
(beside doing other work), he concocted humorous "Answers to Correspondents," etc.   This soon developed into
regular literary work in the magazine, which numbered
among its contributors such men as Lamb, Hazlitt, De
Quincy, Coleridge and others well-known.

At twenty-six Hood married.   It was a love-match; not
smiled upon by the young lady's family, yet productive of
great happiness.   The wife had literary taste and judgment,
and was the valued critic of all his later work.   He grew
so dependent on her that he could hardly write unless she
was at hand.   The charming little *jeu d'esprit* entitled
"Parental Ode to my Son, aged three years and five
months," shows, incidentally, his habits in this respect.

Hood's first book, published a year or two after his marriage, was a collection from his scattered pieces, called
"Whims and Oddities."   For seven years he produced
yearly the "London Comic Annual," and during this time
wrote his one entire work, "Tylney Hall," a novel.   The
rest of his collected works consist of poems, stories, travels and isolated bits of prose and verse, each good in its
time and place, but not adapted to continuous reading.
They seem, as they flash out from the pages of a periodical,
like successive discharges of fireworks at a fête; but collected in a mass and read at one sitting they somewhat
resemble the several pieces all ignited at once.

Hood's mind, being attuned to this species of composition,

seems to have run always toward jokes and puns. Nothing could meet his eye which was not instinctively scanned for its adaptability to a quip; he was the one great verbal humorist.   Mrs. S. C. Hall says of him:

I remember the first time I met him was at one of the pleasant soirées of the painter Martin; for a moment I turned away — as many have done — disappointed, for the countenance, in repose, was of melancholy rather than of mirth; there was something calm, even to solemnity, in the upper portion of his face, which in public was seldom relieved by the eloquent play of the mouth or the occasional sparkle of an observant eye. . . . Theodore Hook, perhaps, liked his celebrity. . . . He [Hood] was too sensitive, too refined to endure it; the dislike to being pointed at as "the man who is funny," kept him out of a crowd, where there were always numbers who honored his genius and loved him for his gentle domestic virtues. . . . . Although "social" in all his feelings, he never sought to stimulate his wit by the false poison of draughts of wine; nor was he ever more cheerful than when at his own fireside he enjoyed the companionship of his dear and devoted wife.

Hood was so great as a punster, a rhymester and a wit, that one is apt to forget that he was also a poet and a philanthropist.   The same hand which penned "Morning Meditations," gave the world also the "Song of the Shirt," and the "Bridge of Sighs."   Even in some of the poems most thickly strewn with jokes, like "The Tale of a Trumpet," and "Miss Kilmansegg," he had a lesson to teach, and taught it well.   Some of his sonnets, notably the one on "Lear," are pure pathos, and many of his shorter poems have a sad undertone which shows that the sources of laughter and of tears are not far apart.

The close of the long poem "Miss Kilmansegg and her Precious Leg" is interesting as a feat in rhyming as well as for its moral:

> Gold! gold! gold! gold!
> Bright and yellow and hard and cold,
> Molten, graven, hammered and rolled;
> Heavy to get and light to hold;

Hoarded, bartered, bought and sold :
Spurned by the young, but hugged by the old
To the very verge of the churchyard mould ;
Price of many a crime untold :
Gold! gold! gold! gold!
Good or bad a thousand fold!
   How widely its agencies vary—
To save — to ruin — to curse — to bless—
As even its minted coins express,
Now stamped with the image of good Queen Bess,
   And now of a Bloody Mary!

The "Tale of a Trumpet" contains, in spite of its stern
lesson, some delightful bits of fun.   A peddler is recom-
mending his ear-trumpet:

   There was Mrs. F.
   So very deaf
She might have worn a percussion-cap
And been knocked on the head without hearing it snap;
I sold her a horn, and the very next day
She heard from her husband at Botany Bay!

From the lighter efforts we turn to the more serious
strains of this tender - hearted, pitying, loving, lovable man;
to the lines by which he himself asked to be remembered;
for at his wish the record of one of his humane poems
is inscribed on his tomb in the simple phrase, "He wrote
the 'Song of the Shirt'."

   With fingers weary and worn,
      With eyelids heavy and red,
   A woman sat in unwomanly rags
      Plying her needle and thread.
   Stitch! stitch! stitch!
      In poverty, hunger and dirt,
   And still with a voice of dolorous pitch
      She sang the "Song of the Shirt."
       *   *   *
   Work — work — work
      Till the brain begins to swim!
   Work — work — work
      Till the eyes are heavy and dim!

> Seam, and gusset, and band,
> Band, and gusset, and seam,
>   Till over the buttons I fall asleep
> And sew them on in my dream.

Less known, though scarcely less worth knowing, is "The Lady's Dream." A single stanza near the close gives its key - note:

> The wounds I might have healed!
>   The human sorrow and smart!
> And yet it was never in my soul
>   To play so ill a part:
> But evil is wrought by want of thought,
>   As well as want of heart.

Late in life, Hood received through the influence of Sir Robert Peel an annual pension of £100. This was continued to his widow; who, with two children, was left unprovided for at his death, except by the pension. It is a sad commentary on the distribution of the world's rewards that service like his is so poorly paid — that those who, with the pen, lead the thought of the world, are so often left behind in the distribution of its bounties. A subscription was started for the benefit of Hood's family, the appeal for which opens with these words:

This distinguished writer, who has for upwards of twenty years entertained the public with a constant succession of comic and humoristic works, in the whole range of which not a single line of immoral tendency or calculated to pain an individual can be pointed out, whose poems and serious writings rank among the noblest modern contributions of our national literature and whose pen was the ever ready and efficient advocate of the unfortunate and the oppressed (as recently, for instance, in the admirable "Song of the Shirt," which gave so remarkable an impulse to the movement in behalf of distressed needlewomen), has left by his death a widow and two children in straitened and precarious circumstances.

Some relief was afforded by this friendly effort; and when Hood's son grew to manhood he became, like his father, a laborer in the world of letters, and made it the means of gaining an honorable livelihood.

CHAPTER XLIV.

SOME MINOR POETS.

CHARLES DIBDIN (1748-1814) excelled as a writer of sea-songs, which he set to music. Thomas Dibdin (1771-1841), son of the above, is said to have written more than one thousand songs, but none of them attained the popularity of his father's.

It is not often given to a poet to be a millionaire, but such was the case with Samuel Rogers (1763-1855). Born to a fortune, and increasing it by his business as a banker, his house became a centre of entertainment for all the literary celebrities of the day. Nor did he confine his good offices to the exercise of hospitality; his purse was always open for the encouragement of struggling authors, and many such an one has owed his relief from distress and encouragement to effort to the generosity of Samuel Rogers.

Of his own contributions to literature, the first was "The Pleasures of Memory," written in the last century, and in the style of that age. Polished and pleasing, and abounding in graceful thoughts, it lacks fire, and is now read mainly as a matter of literary history. His poem on Italy is a series of pen-pictures of that lovely country, mingled with legends and rich in historical illusions. "Human Life," and "The Voyage of Columbus," are his only other long poems. Some of the shorter ones are very charming.

Rogers lived to the good old age of ninety-two, preserving his faculties almost to the end. The art-treasures with which his house was filled were chosen with faultless judgment, and he possessed a remarkably fine library. He was never married.

As the world grows older and larger, the number of writers in each department of literature increases; and so it happens that in poetry several names of minor lights must be added to the list of eminent men already mentioned as flourishing near the beginning of the nineteenth century.

James Montgomery (1771–1854) was born in Scotland, though there is nothing about his poems to indicate the fact. His verse is mostly of a religious cast, "The World Before the Flood" being his principal long poem. He wrote several beautiful hymns, and all his writings show depth and tenderness of feeling, as well as a very agreeable power of description.

The opening of the reconstructed Drury Lane Theatre, after it was burnt in 1812, gave an opportunity to the brothers Horace and James Smith to do an excellent bit of burlesque. The managers had offered a prize for the best poetical address (to the audience) sent in on the occasion, and afterward the Smiths published a volume of pretended "Rejected Addresses," in which the styles of Coleridge, Wordsworth, Byron, Scott, Crabbe, and other well-known writers are so cleverly reproduced that some of the persons "taken off" declared they could scarcely believe that they did not write the verses themselves. Horace, the younger brother, wrote also many historical novels, some essays and a few poems, of which the best are, "Address to a Mummy," and "Hymn to the Flowers."

The verses to the mummy have always been great favorites:

> And thou hast walked about (how strange a story!)
>   In Thebes's streets three thousand years ago,
> When the Memnonium was in all its glory,
>   And time had not begun to overthrow
> Those temples, palaces and piles stupendous,
> Of which the very ruins are tremendous.
>
> *   *   *
>
> Perhaps that very hand, now pinioned flat,
>   Has hob-a-nobbed with Pharaoh, glass to glass;
> Or dropped a half-penny in Homer's hat;
>   Or doffed thine own, to let Queen Dido pass;

> Or held, by Solomon's own invitation,
> A torch at the great temple's dedication.
> *   *   *
> Since first thy form was in this box extended
>   We have, above-ground, seen some strange mutations;
> The Roman empire has begun and ended—
>   New worlds have risen—we have lost old nations;
> And countless kings have into dust been humbled,
> While not a fragment of thy flesh has crumbled.

Ebenezer Elliott (1781–1849) is the poet of the people. To apply his own words:

> His teachers were the torn heart's wail,
>   The tyrant and the slave,
> The street, the factory, the jail,
>   The palace—and the grave!

His "Corn-Law Rhymes," vehemently urging the repeal of the duty on grain, produced a great effect in England during the long political agitation which preceded the repeal of the ancient "protective" statutes framed to enhance the price of food.

Henry Kirke White (1785–1806) was a poet of much promise, whose short life came to an untimely end through over study. He was the son of a butcher in Nottingham, and after various efforts to earn a living in other ways, decided to cultivate poetry. A volume of his poems attracted the notice of Southey, who was very kind to him, and with other friends helped him to enter college. There he worked so hard, being determined to win honors, that his health gave way, and he died at the age of twenty-one. Southey edited his poems, with a kindly and appreciative memoir.

Reginald Heber (1783–1826), Bishop of Calcutta, wrote the prize poem, "Palestine," while an undergraduate at Oxford. He wrote a great number of hymns, many of which are of remarkable beauty. Appointed to the Diocese of Calcutta in 1823, he traveled extensively in India, and his "Journal through India, with notes on Ceylon," was pronounced by Lord Jeffrey to be the most instructive and important work that had up to that time been written on the condition of the British Empire in India. Bishop Heber's personal qualities were charming. With all his learning and elegant acquirements, he was remarkable for his modesty, tolerance, and the most scrupulous consideration for others. He lived but three years after his arrival in India, and his death was deplored as a national loss in that country.

Another English divine of piety and learning, noted as being one of the leaders in the "Tractarian" or "High-Church" revival at Oxford (1833) was the Rev. John Keble (1792–1866), author of the series of devotional hymns known as "Christian Year," which has already passed through more than fifty editions. The latest of the colleges in Oxford, Keble Hall (opened 1870), testifies to the reverence felt for his memory.

Among the lesser poets whose pleasant writings diversified the early part of the century was Bryan Waller Procter (1787–1874), better known to us by his *nom de plume* of "Barry Cornwall." His bright, breezy song beginning,

The sea! The sea! The open sea!
The blue, the fresh, the ever free!

has given pleasure to many thousands of readers. It is somewhat singular that in his long life of eighty - seven years his poetical work should have been confined to about fifteen years, closing when he was little more than forty years old. He wrote, beside poems, "Dramatic Scenes," a tragedy called "Mirandola," and several essays and literary biographies.

Adelaide Anne Procter (1825–64), a daughter of "Barry Cornwall," was also gifted with poetic talents, and left a volume of poems entitled "Legends and Lyrics," some of which are very beautiful. When about twenty - five years old Miss Procter became a Roman Catholic. An earnest tone pervades her works, corresponding to her character, which was of the loveliest type of womanly excellence.

Among the poets whose names were familiar to readers of the early part of this century is Felicia Dorothea Hemans (1794–1835). Her versification is pleasing, possessing simplicity and melody, though without any great depth of thought; and her expression is often singularly felicitous. Such poems as "The Landing of the Pilgrim Fathers," "The Graves of a Household," and "Casabianca," are not likely soon to go out of date, though Mrs. Hemans's long poems are already almost forgotten. Lord Jeffrey calls her poetry "infinitely sweet, elegant and tender." Something more than sweetness, elegance and tenderness must be accorded to her verses on the landing of the Pilgrims:

> The breaking waves dashed high
>   On a stern and rockbound coast;
> And the trees against a stormy sky
>   Their giant branches tossed.
> And the heavy night hung dark
>   The hills and waters o'er,
> When a band of pilgrims moored their bark
>   On the wild New England Shore.
>   *   *   *
> Amidst the storm they sang
>   And the stars heard, and the sea;
> And the sounding aisles of the dim woods rang
>   To the anthem of the free.

The poems of Letitia Elizabeth Landon (1802–38), better known by her *sobriquet* of L. E. L., were very much the fashion in the early part of the century. Though far inferior to Mrs. Hemans as a writer, she enjoyed a great popularity in London literary society. She married the governor of Cape Coast Castle, Africa, and died from an overdose of prussic acid, a drug which she was accustomed to take for headache.

William and Mary Howitt, husband and wife for fifty - six years, were more closely connected in literary work than often falls to the lot of members of the same family.   They were married in 1823, when he was twenty‑eight and she nineteen years old, and their first joint work, "The Forest Minstrel," a volume of poems, was published in the same year.   From that time until the death of Howitt in 1879, literature was the main business and pleasure of their lives. The husband wrote mostly prose.   Among his works are, "The Aristocracy of England," and "The Homes and Haunts of British Poets."   He wrote also several books of descriptive travel.   Mrs. Howitt was the first to bring to the notice of English readers the novels of Fredrika Bremer, which she translated, as well as the works of Hans Christian Andersen.   Her "Tales for Children," are still popular, and many of the poems are great favorites with the little people.   Mrs. Howitt survived her husband nine years, dying in 1888.

Winthrop Mackworth Praed (1802–39) was a writer of graceful *vers de société*, and especially of poetical charades. His poems abound both in fun and wit, and are expressed with elegance and propriety.   The following charade (on the name Campbell) is a good specimen of them:

> Come from my First, ay, come!
>   The battle‑dawn is nigh,
> And the screaming trump and the thundering drum
>   Are calling thee to die!
> Fight as thy father fought,
>   Fall as thy father fell.
> Thy task is taught, thy shroud is wrought,
>   So — forward! and farewell!
>
> Toll ye my Second! toll!
>   Fling high the flambeau's light;
> And sing the hymn for the parted soul
>   Beneath the silent night!
> The wreath upon his head,
>   The cross upon his breast,
> Let the prayer be said and the tear be shed:
>   So take him to his rest.

> Call ye my Whole, ay, call
>   The lord of lute and lay;
> And let him greet the sable pall
>   With a noble song to-day:
> Go, call him by his name;
>   No fitter hand may crave
> To light the flame of a soldier's fame
>   On the turf of a soldier's grave.

Caroline Elizabeth Norton (1808–77) was one of the three lovely daughters of Thomas Sheridan, son of Richard Brinsley Sheridan. They were called "The Three Graces." Mrs. Norton's poems show smoothness of versification, and an uncommon wealth of illustration. The principal long ones are "The Sorrows of Rosalie," "The Undying One," and "The Child of the Islands." She also wrote several novels, of a somewhat gloomy tendency. Her married life was unhappy, and she was for many years separated from her husband. Two years before her death she was left a widow, and the next year married Sir W. Stirling-Maxwell.

Richard Monckton Milnes (1809–85), afterward Lord Houghton, was an author both in prose and verse. His "Memorials of a Tour in Greece" are a record of his travels in that country; he edited "The Life and Letters of Keats," and wrote "Monographs, Personal and Social." His principal volumes of verse, "Palm Leaves," and "Poems of many years," contain very graceful and pleasing pieces. "I Wandered by the Brookside," is the best of his songs.

Martin Farquhar Tupper (1810–89) was a poet whose enormous success (so far as an immense sale of his poems betokens success), it is difficult to account for except on the supposition that the great mass of humanity loves the commonplace. His "Proverbial Philosophy"—a series of somewhat trite observations couched in irregular blank verse—ran through forty editions in his life-time, and is always to be found on booksellers' counters. His other works are not worth mentioning, except a pretty story called "The Crock of Gold."

Charles Mackay (1812–89), a Scottish poet and song-writer, was born in Perth. His songs are vigorous, and his voice was always raised on the side of freedom and the rights of the poor. His most popular song is "There's a good time coming!"

William Edmonstoune Aytoun (1813–65), a Scottish poet and miscellaneous writer, is best known by the "*Bon Gaultier* Ballads," humorous satires on popular follies, and "Lays of the Scottish Cavaliers," spirited mementos of the persecutions of Covenanters in Scotland. He was son - in - law of John Wilson (Christopher North), and for many years contributed regularly to "Blackwood's Magazine." He was professor of rhetoric and belles-lettres at the University of Edinburgh.

Arthur Hugh Clough (1819–1861) was an English poet who chose Scottish characters and scenery for the subjects of his verse. He tried a "new departure" in the "Bothie of Tober - na - Vuolich," a Highland legendary poem which received warm praise from the critics, and which is written in hexameters, somewhat in the style of Longfellow's "Evangeline," but without the smooth and correct rhythm of that delightful poem. Various shorter poems and some prose pieces have been published since his death.

Coventry Kearsey Dighton Patmore (1823–83) was for many years assistant librarian in the British Museum. "The Angel in the House," a domestic poem in four parts, is the favorite among his poetical works.

Dante Gabriel Rossetti (1828–82), one of a singularly gifted family, was by profession an artist, but is known in literature by his "Early Italian Poets" (prose), and by his two volumes, "Poems," and "Ballads and Sonnets." His poetry, like his art, is full of the loftiest romance and sentiment.

Alexander Smith (1830–67), a Scottish poet, was, like Burns, a native of Ayrshire. When very young he published "The Life Drama," a poem which was at first over-praised, and then correspondingly abused, with charges of spasmodic writing, plagiarism, and so forth. The truth was that having had access to but few books, he had studied Keats and one or two other poets until his style produced the effect of an echo. Had he lived longer, it is probable that he could have done better work. His prose-works, "Dreamthorpe," "A Summer in Skye," etc., are written with a picturesque vigor and a delicate sympathy with nature which betray the poetic spirit. He was a close friend of Sydney Dobell (1824–74), himself a poet of no mean order, and they published together a volume of war-sonnets called forth by the Crimean War.

It is now generally known that "Owen Meredith" is only the pseudonym of Edward Robert Bulwer - Lytton (1831-92), son of the celebrated novelist, and himself in later life Lord Lytton. His chief poem is "Lucile," a romantic tale written in anapæstic verse, perhaps the most popular single poem of its class since Scott's. His shorter poems are marked by strong passion expressed in melodious verse. Most of his life was passed in diplomatic service.

Travelers have been busy during this stirring century, and have left most interesting accounts of the wonders they saw. Of the great number who might be mentioned, we select a few as typical ones. David Livingstone (1817–73), a native of Scotland, was up to his time the greatest of African travelers. He began life as an operative in a cotton-factory, and obtained his early education in an evening - school. Afterward he studied both medicine and divinity, and in 1840 was sent to Africa as a medical missionary. His "Missionary Travels and Researches" belong to this period. The details of his later work are to be found in his very interesting "Last Journals," which include his wanderings and discoveries in Eastern Africa from 1865 to within a few days of his death. He was buried in Westminster Abbey.

CHAPTER XLV.

WALTER SCOTT.

MANY great writers have we passed in review, feeling for them interest, gratitude, admiration, reverence, wonder and delight; now we greet one with a glow of all these sentiments and, in addition, a rare personal affection. His poetry entranced our early years; his romances delighted our maturer taste; his personal character and history claim our undying sympathy and respect.

Walter Scott (1771–1832) was born in Edinburgh, both his parents being of "gentle" though not "noble" birth. An illness of his infancy left him partly paralyzed, and though he recovered his general health, he remained lame through life; a trial made the greater through his being by nature of active temperament and much bodily strength. He made the best of his lameness—as he did of all troubles —and by his wonderful vigor pushed his way through the world in a fashion that left behind many a man whose limbs were free from any defect.

He became a great walker, and in his prime often tramped, with his stout stick, twenty or thirty miles a day. In youth he was sensitive about his disability, but not morbid, as is shown by the fact that when the play of Richard III. was acted by the young folks he volunteered to take the part of Richard, saying that the limp would do well enough to represent the hump.

He was, as in duty bound, a sturdy Briton, and at five years old, heard of Washington's defeat at Long Island with keen delight. At school he learned but little, lacking the perseverance and self-denial for hard study. He did however, shadow forth his future greatness in one way; he was a good story-teller. His fine memory helped him out with his lessons, but it was "easy come, easy go," and he never became an exact scholar in any branch. He was an omniverous reader and describes himself as "driving through a sea of books like a vessel without pilot or rudder."

Scott entered the University of Edinburgh, but, as his college course was interrupted by a severe illness, he began the study of law (his father's profession) without taking a degree. After serving his apprenticeship to his father, a "Writer to the Signet," he was admitted, at twenty-one, to the bar. Five years later he married Charlotte Carpenter, the daughter of French parents living in England. They began their married life at Lasswade, where they were poor but happy, Mrs. Scott proving a loving and lovable wife, though by no means the wisest and noblest of her sex. Their winters were passed in Edinburgh.

Scott seems to have developed into an author very slowly. When he was twenty-five years old, a lady friend to whom he showed some pieces he had written had occasion to tell him that it sounded odd to say "the little two dogs," instead of the "two little dogs." Yet his style in later years, though far from faultless, was quite up to the standard of his time. His first publications, translations of Bürger's "Lenore," and "The Wild Huntsman," produced a marked sensation in Edinburgh. The Scottish people had just lost their national bard, Robert Burns, and were ready to welcome a new light whenever it should rise.

The first work worthy to foretell Scott's future in any degree was his "Minstrelsy of the Scottish Border," in which he did for Scotland all that Bishop Percy had done for the ballad poetry of England in his "Reliques," by rescuing from fast-following oblivion a mass of folk-lore of unmistakable value and interest.

Scott was thirty-three (1804) when he moved to Ashestiel, a lovely place on the Tweed, where a small farm gave him the rural life so dear to his nature as long as he lived. There his first original work took shape. It was the splendid poem, "The Lay of the Last Minstrel." The reading public was familiar with poetry in many styles, but a poet of historic romance was still unknown, and the enthusiasm was boundless. "Marmion" and "The Lady of the Lake" followed in quick succession, and, as Macaulay says, all the world, from the peer in his ermine to the beggar in his rags, went wild over the new departure in the world of letters. It would have turned the head of a less well-balanced man, but Scott was only surprised and gratified by it; not unreasonably elated. When his daughter Sophia was about eleven years old, a gentleman asked her how she liked the "Lady of the Lake." ¡She said, very simply, " Oh, I have not read it. Papa says there is nothing so bad for young.people as reading bad poetry."

The poems poured forth, volume after volume, until 1813; then as if one matchless triumph were not enough for one man, the novels began to appear. "Waverley," "Guy Mannering," "The Antiquary," were only the beginning of that splendid series which continued to be written and printed, year after year, until "Count Robert" and "Castle Dangerous" closed the long list, and the life of this world's wonder ended, itself the greatest romance of all. Beside the novels, the mighty master gave forth histories, biographies and essays, attended to his official duties, performed all social obligations, including that of a generous hospitality, and kept up a most onerous correspondence.

Before Scott began to make literature the business of his life, his friendship for James Ballantyne, an old schoolmate, induced him to lend some money to establish him in the printing business in Edinburgh. This led to a secret partnership, which later included Scott's publisher, Archibald

Constable.   It was, on Scott's part, a fatal step, seeing that he had no business capacity or education,   As time went on he began to feel as if his income was inexhaustible, and to act as the possessor of millions might do — but seldom does.   His ordinary living-expenses, though liberal, would never have troubled him; but in an evil hour his love of nature and the romance of antiquarianism led him to buy an estate on the banks of the Tweed, near the lovely ruins of Melrose Abbey, which purchase afterward expanded into the country-seat of Abbotsford, and cost its owner, in the end, more than $325,000 of our money.   The overwhelming, heart-rending, ruinous bankruptcy which ended this dream of delight is generally attributed to the ill-advised speculations of Constable and Ballantyne.

It is hard to tell now just how much of the blame rests with each actor in the sad drama; but the fact remains that Scott's visions of wealth and splendor had vanished forever and a mountainous load of debt had taken their place. How he met this blow we shall learn hereafter.

The consideration of these sordid matters has led us away from the strictly literary part of Walter Scott's life.   It was just when "The Lay of the Last Minstrel" was in its fresh burst of fame and popularity that he wrote the first few chapters of the novel now called "Waverley," embodying, as he says, some of his recollections of Highland scenery and life.   Its original title was, "'Tis Sixty Years Since;" and as it was written in 1805, that places its scenes in 1745 — the year of the last Stuart rebellion.   He showed these chapters to a friend, and meeting an unfavorable judgment on them, laid them away in a drawer and forgot them.   Nine years later, as he himself tells, he found the original fragment while rummaging through an old cabinet, took the fancy of finishing it, and wrote so fast that the last two volumes were written in three weeks.   He withheld his name, partly for fun, to see what people would say of it, and partly to evade the notoriety which was already becoming burdensome to his busy, modest habits of life. The general public did not recognize his hand in the work, though a few personal friends saw through the mystery.

The sale of "Waverley" was enormous, almost an edition a month being called for; but Scott's well-balanced mind was not disturbed by the praise which resounded on all sides. When he found that "The Lord of the Isles," the last of his great poems, was not as well received as the others had been, he merely said that it was wonderful that his popularity had endured even so long, adding, "Since one line has failed, we must just stick to something else." He at once began "Guy Mannering," which was finished in the incredibly short space of six weeks. It was received with the same wild enthusiasm as the other, and "The Great Unknown," as the novelist began to be called, had an assured future before him. He wrote his first poem at thirty-four, and his first novel at forty-two; and it adds to our wonder to consider how comparatively late in a not long life he entered on his monumental work.

The methods which made it possible for him to keep up the tremendous speed of his production can not be described here, but must be sought for in the delightful memoir written by his son-in-law, Lockhart; a book of the greatest interest and value. .

On the death (1813) of the poet-laureate, an obscure person named Pye, the laureateship was offered to Scott by the prince regent. He declined it, but when, some years later, the prince (then King George IV.) offered him a baronetcy, he thought best to accept, for the sake of his wife and children; so he became "Sir Walter Scott."* He was by nature a "Tory"—that is, an adherent of kingly

---

* In pronouncing this and all similar names, good usage requires that the word "Sir" should *not* be accented. Well-bred people say "S'r Walter Scott," "S'r Robert Peel," etc.

power with all the prerogatives sanctioned by history and tradition—and thus it appeared to him that an acquaintance with the prince regent was the crowning glory of his life, though we should feel that the glory of such a friendship flowed the other way.

In 1825 he began to keep a diary. The little book, withheld until lately out of respect to the feelings of the families named in it, has been almost completely transcribed and published within the last two or three years. At almost the same time with the commencement of the diary began the financial storm which was to overwhelm him, and among the saddest things in all the biography are the early entries marking the advent of trouble. The acme of pathos is reached when he asks, wonderingly, if, when he dies, some one will take the diary out of the ebony cabinet at Abbotsford, and friends will whisper to each other, "Poor old gentleman! A well-meaning man—nobody's enemy but his own; thought his talents would never wear out. Family poorly left. Pity he took that foolish title!" He records also his gratitude toward those who showed him sympathy in the hour of his distress, and they were many. All offers of assistance were declined with heartfelt thanks, and at fifty-five he started on the stupendous work of paying off the mountain of debt (£150,000) by his own labor. And when he drew his last breath the task was essentially done.

Troubles and sorrows overshadowed his path. His wife was taken from him after a close companionship of nearly thirty years; his darling grandson, John Hugh Lockhart (to whom the fascinating "Tales of a Grandfather" were addressed, under the name of Hugh Littlejohn, Esq.), son of his daughter Sophia, sickened and died; his unmarried daughter Anne lived on, a hopeless invalid, and survived him but a few months; his own strength began to show the effect of the terrible draughts he had made upon it—but yet the ceaseless labor never flagged!

In 1830 there came a slight paralytic shock from which he partially recovered, but rheumatism in the hand made it needful that he should have a permanent amanuensis, and he kept him at work from six in the morning until six at night, stopping only for meals. When friends and doctors protested against this extravagance of toil, he only said, "As for bidding me not work, 'Mollie might as well put the kettle on the fire and say, 'Now, don't boil!'"

A second paralytic stroke followed in a year after the first, and his speech became so much impaired that even his friends could scarcely understand his words; and in this condition the last "Tales of My Landlord," "Count Robert of Paris," and "Castle Dangerous" were finished! These with some other completed works, closed the list, closed his life, and closed his account with the world; for the last penny for which he was liable, directly or indirectly, was paid from the proceeds of his writings within a few years after his death. He himself had the satisfaction of believing, at his last moment, that the whole load of debt had been already cleared off by his exertions; and his friends did not disturb the pleasing illusion.

When further resistance to the inevitable became impossible, the English government put a naval vessel at Sir Walter's disposal, to enable him to spend in Italy the winter of 1831–2.* At the close of the winter he was

---

* It is in memory of the journey that Wordsworth's exquisite sonnet "On the departure of Sir Walter Scott from Abbotsford for Naples," was written. "Eildon" is a three‑peaked mountain (said to have been divided by magic), visible from Abbotsford; "Parthenope" is the old name for Naples.

> A trouble, not of clouds, or weeping rain,
> Or of the setting sun's pathetic light
> Engendered, hangs o'er Eildon's triple height.
> Spirits of power, assembled there, complain
> Of kindred power departing from their sight;
> And Tweed, best pleased in chanting a blithe strain,

seized with a feverish desire to see home once more, which increased as, traveling through Venice, Switzerland and Germany, he approached his native land. On the way he had an attack of apoplexy, and in journeying northward from London he lay in a stupor most of the time, but when he neared Abbotsford and saw the familiar towers, it was hard to keep him in the carriage. Months of slow decay followed, during which the most noticeable thing about Scott was his habitual courtesy. As Lockhart says, "the gentleman survived the genius." His last words were, "God bless you all."

So peacefully passed away this great - hearted man, on September 21, 1832, in the sixty - second year of his age. His two sons died without issue, and now the only surviving descendants are a granddaughter of his daughter Mrs. Lockhart, and her children. Her husband, Mr. Maxwell, took the name of Scott on his marriage, and the family still own Abbotsford.

The only way to gain an estimate of Scott's vast and varied genius is to read, and read largely, his illustrious prose and poetry. To his work is familiarly applied a couplet in which he himself described the power of magic, witchcraft, necromancy, which forms so large a part of his romance. He says its touch can make

> A nutshell seem a gilded barge,
> A shieling [cottage] seem a palace large.

In keeping with this suggestion is his best known sobriquet, "The Wizard of the North."

Saddens his voice again, and yet again.
Lift up your hearts, ye mourners, for the might
Of the whole world's best wishes with him goes;
Blessings and prayers in nobler retinue
Than sceptred king or laureled conqueror knows,
Follow this wondrous potentate. Be true
Oh winds of ocean, and thou midland sea,
Wafting your charge to soft Parthenope.

Partly for their literary importance, and partly for the lesson they teach of unflagging industry and heroic devotion to a noble object, a list of the works which the world owes to the pen of Walter Scott is given below. The magnitude of the array will strike every reader; but it is only those who have written and published a book, and so have learned by experience the toil, mental and physical, which it involves, who can come to anything like an appreciation of Scott's colossal achievements.

Poetry: "Lenore," "The Wild Huntsman," "Goetz von Berlichingen," etc. (translations). "The House of Aspen" (a tragedy), "Lay of the Last Minstrel," "Marmion," "Lady of the Lake," "Vision of Don Roderick," "Rokeby," "The Bridal of Triermain," "The Lord of the Isles," "Harold the Dauntless," ballads, songs, lyrical pieces, etc.

Novels: "Waverley," "Guy Mannering," "The Antiquary," "The Black Dwarf," "Old Mortality," "Rob Roy," "The Heart of Midlothian," "The Bride of Lammermoor," "The Legend of Montrose," "Ivanhoe," "The Monastery," "The Abbot," "Kenilworth," "The Pirate," "Fortunes of Nigel," "Peveril of the Peak," "Quentin Durward," "Saint Ronan's Well," "Redgauntlet," "The Betrothed," "The Talisman," "Woodstock," "Chronicles of the Canongate" (including "The Fair Maid of Perth"), "Anne of Geierstein," "Count Robert of Paris," "Castle Dangerous."

Works of History, Biography, etc.: "Minstrelsy of the Scottish Border" (compilation, with copious notes), "Paul's Letters to his Kinsfolk," "Life and Works of Dryden," "Life and Works of Swift," "Lives of the Novelists," "Life of Napoleon," "Letters of Malachi Malagrowther," "Tales of a Grandfather," "History of Scotland," and "History of France." To these might be added a large number of essays and contributions to the reviews.

CHAPTER XLVI

THE MINOR NOVELISTS.

AFTER naming Scott, all contemporary novelists seem to shrink into very small dimensions, and yet there were others who wrote good novels, notably three ladies, of whom Sir Walter Scott said, "Edgeworth, Ferrier, Austen, have all given portraits of real society far superior to anything vain man has produced of like nature."

Maria Edgeworth (1759-1849) was born in Berkshire, England, but early removed with her father to his ancestral home in Edgeworthstown, Ireland, where she lived during the greater part of her life. She did not begin her career as an author with novels, but published first a "Treatise on Practical Education" and an "Essay on Irish Bulls," both of which were highly successful. Her first novel (1801) was "Castle Rackrent;" after which appeared "Belinda," "Patronage," "Helen," and others. Her collection of short stories called "Moral Tales," has delighted thousands of children since her day; and her "Parents' Assistant," with its charming stories of "Simple Susan," "Waste Not, Want Not," and a score of others, is a welcome addition to any child's library.

Richard Lovell Edgeworth, father of the authoress, was a writer on various scientific and practical subjects.

Jane Austen (1775-1817) was the daughter of a clergyman, and lived a life so simple and retired that there is not much to be said of her. She began writing when she was a mere child, though her first novel, "Pride and Prejudice," was not published until she was twenty-one. "Sense and Sensibility," and "Northanger Abbey," which followed, could not at first find a publisher; the latter, with "Persuasion," were not printed until after her death. Her remaining novels were "Mansfield Park," and "Emma," published, like all those which came out in her life-time, anonymously. Scott said of her, "That young lady had a talent for describing the involvements and feelings and characters of ordinary life, which to me is the most wonderful I ever met with. The Big Bow - wow strain I can do myself like any now going; but the exquisite touch which renders common things and characters interesting is denied me. What a pity so gifted a creature should die so young!"

Susan Ferrier (1782–1854) was born in Edinburgh. Three novels, "Marriage," "The Inheritance," and "Destiny," were all that came from her pen, and were published anonymously. She was a keen satirist, but showed up the follies and vices of society more from an overpowering sense of humor than from any intention to be a reformer. Her pictures of contemporary Scottish life and character are most amusing. She, like Miss Edgeworth, was a personal friend of Scott, and visited him at Abbotsford. He calls her "a most gifted person," and says she was the least *exacting* of any female author he had ever seen. He quotes from one of her novels the advice, given by an old lady, never to let a visit exceed three days — "the *rest* day, the *dressed* day, and the *pressed* day."

Mrs. Opie (1769–1853), born Amelia Anderson, married the distinguished artist James Opie, and afterward wrote several novels, "Father and Daughter," "Temper," etc. Her most popular work, however, was a collection of tales called "Illustrations of Lying," written after she became a member of the society of Friends. After that, she wrote little except one or two religious works.

Jane Porter (1776–1820) was born at Durham, but early removed to Edinburgh, where she became acquainted with the young Walter Scott; and thus, perhaps, nourished the taste for tales of war and romance which led to her writing "Thaddeus of Warsaw," and "The Scottish Chiefs." She wrote many other novels, but no others that have kept the public favor. Her sister, Anna Maria Porter, was the author of nearly twenty novels, the best known of which is "Don Sebastian." Their brother, Sir Robert Ker Porter, is famous for his books of travel.

Matthew Gregory Lewis (1775–1818), familiarly known among his friends as "Monk" Lewis, was the author of a romance called "The Monk," of no great merit, but sufficiently original to give the author a literary reputation in those days, when literary reputations were more easily earned than they were later. He was intimate with most of the celebrities of the day, and his genial nature and real kindness of heart made him welcome everywhere. He was rich and fashionable, and made a journey from London to Edinburgh with the Duke of Argyle in the duke's landau. In Edinburgh he met Walter Scott, then newly married, and only a dabbler in letters. Scott describes him as a "martinet in rhymes and numbers," and adds that his criticisms were "severe enough, but useful eventually." So they were, if they influenced Scott's poetry, the first bits whereof ("The Eve of St. John," "Glenfinlas," etc.), were *kindly* included in Lewis's next book, "The Tales of Wonder."

John Galt (1779–1839), one of the most characteristic of Scotch novelists, was an unsuccessful man of business, who at last found a more congenial sphere in writing. His characters have a sharply‑defined personality, and the pictures of Scottish life portrayed in his novels are remarkably true to nature. The best among them are "The Ayrshire Legatees," "The Annals of the Parish," "The Entail," and "Lawrie Todd"—the latter showing the Scotchman in America, where Galt spent several years in a vain search after fortune.

Theodore Hook (1788–1841), a brilliant wit and humorist, endowed with a wonderful faculty for improvisation, was for many years the delight and marvel of London society. As a dramatist he had an instantaneous success. His novels, popular in their day, are mostly forgotten; but it is impossible to take up any book connected with the literary men of his time wherein he does not figure as the life of the social circle where he happens to be; scattering puns, practical jokes and drollery of all sorts from an apparently exhaustless treasury. His name was coupled with that of Thomas Hood, as a humorist, though the fine honesty and purity of the latter shows more of contrast than of likeness to the loose and conscienceless character of Hook. Hook gained large sums by the immense popularity of his writings and of the magazine, "John Bull," which he published (and in which he was shamefully distinguished as the scandalous detractor of the unfortunate Queen Caroline), yet he left his debts unpaid; and died, as he said near the end, "done up in purse, in mind, and in body too, at last"—a victim to drink. His books were numbered by the score; and are all absolutely lost sight of.

Thomas Love Peacock (1785–1866), a writer whose works have lately risen into notice after a long period of comparative neglect, can scarcely be ranked with the novelists, although it is customary to speak of "Headlong Hall" and "Nightmare Abbey" as novels. They are rather a series of brilliant imaginary conversations and discussions strung on the lightest thread of narrative. Peacock was a friend and benefactor of Shelley when the latter was in trouble in early life, and is said to have sketched the poet's character, as it appeared to him, in that of the hero of "Nightmare Abbey." Peacock's other novels were "Crotchet Castle," "Melincourt," "Gryll Grange," etc. For many years he held an important position in the India House — the same great commercial office in which so much of Charles Lamb's life was passed.

Lady Morgan (1786–1859), the daughter of an Irish actor, wrote several romances, of which "The Wild Irish Girl" was the most popular. The Countess of Blessington (1790–1849), also an "Irish Girl," wrote several novels, and "Conversations with Lord Byron." She was noted for her beauty and accomplishments; and her residence, Gore House, Kensington, was for many years the resort of cultivated people, both English and foreign.

A noteworthy literary curiosity is the tale of "Frankenstein," unique in its conception, and most remarkable as having been written by a girl of seventeen. Several friends, among whom was "Monk" Lewis, were gathered together, one rainy day, in Byron's villa near Lake Geneva, and, after amusing one another with ghost-stories and the like, it was proposed that each of the party should write a story, making it as horrible as possible. Byron began one called "The Vampyre," which was afterward finished by his physician, Dr. Polidori. The only other person who carried out the plan was Mary Godwin, afterward the wife of the poet Shelley. She produced the story of "Frankenstein," where a student, anxious to fathom the mysteries of life, forms and causes to live a creature with the form of man, who, by circumstances, becomes a terror to others and a burden to himself, and whose creation is described with a hideous realism that has no exact parallel in literature. Mrs. Shelley wrote several novels, and after Shelley's untimely death (1822) she edited his poems with explanatory notes by her own hand.

Samuel Lover (1797–1868) was a man of varied talent, being an artist, musical composer, and poet, as well as a writer of novels. In the latter capacity he wrote "Legends and Stories of Ireland," and the inimitable "Handy Andy," while "Rory O'More," "Molly Bawn" and "The Low-backed Car" attest his skill as a song-writer.

George Payne Rainsford James (1801–60), was one of

the most successful writers of historical novels. From the time when he published "Richelieu," at the age of twenty-four, until he was well past fifty, he wrote between seventy and eighty books, most of them being in the form of the English three-volume novel. Without attaining a very high rank even among second-class novelists, James's novels have always commanded a great sale for circulating libraries, and are still eagerly sought by the omnivorous novel-reader. He had a pleasing gift of narrative, and contrived always to interest the reader in his personages, though they lack the reality which we have in later years grown accustomed to demand from writers of fiction. James spent several years in America, as consul at Richmond, and afterward filled a similar position at Venice up to the time of his death. He is said to have had reason to complain that his name was given to books which he never wrote and which were unworthy of and even discreditable to him.

Captain Frederick Marryat (1792–1848) is a name dear to the heart of every schoolboy who has ever felt the magic of his portraitures of boy-life. "Peter Simple," "Jacob Faithful," "Japhet in Search of a Father," "Mr. Midshipman Easy," "Masterman Ready," "Settlers in Canada," "The Children of the New Forest," and "Snarley-Yow," are only a few of his two dozen stories, all written within twenty years. Many of his works are sea tales. He had a passion for the sea, and, after having tried several times to run away, was allowed at the age of fourteen to enter the navy. In the wars with Napoleon, he was present at more than fifty naval engagements, and often received "honorable mention" for his gallantry. His novels are full of fun, incident, adventure and feeling, and have a freshness which, at the time he wrote, was unknown to the novel-reading world. His "Diary in America" (1839) was unpopular in this country from the excessive severity of his criticisms.

The literary life of Benjamin Disraeli (1805–81), better known now as Lord Beaconsfield, is divided into two widely separated parts. From his twenty-second to his twenty-seventh year he produced half a dozen novels, including "Vivian Grey," "The Young Duke," and "Contarini Fleming," beside other works. He then entered political life, and for nearly forty years wrote nothing further except parliamentary speeches and state-papers. At the age of sixty-five he again tried his hand at novel-writing in "Lothair," and ten years later published his last work of fiction, "Endymion." It is as a statesman rather than as an author that Lord Beaconsfield will be most honorably remembered. He was the son of Isaac Disraeli (1766–1848), an essayist of the preceding generation, whose name will be found in a later chapter.

William Harrison Ainsworth (1805–82) was a prolific writer of fiction. He chose for his early novels "Rockwood" and "Jack Sheppard," heroes from the criminal classes. The later tales, among which are "Admirable Crichton" and " The Tower of London," are less objectionable in subject and sentiment. Whatever is of a historical nature in his novels shows great research and industry.

Charles Lever (1806–1872), a native of Ireland, was a brilliant and successful novel-writer, taking for his subjects, mainly, the depicting of Irish character. His early novels, " Harry Lorrequer" and "Charles O'Malley," are full of stirring incident and boisterous fun; the later stories are more subdued in tone and show more refinement. Lever was for several years editor of the "Dublin University Magazine."

Dr. Samuel Warren (1807–77) was a distinguished physician, and wrote, beside many short tales, the extremely popular novel of "Ten Thousand a Year." He had few of the higher qualities of a novelist, but excelled in caricature, of which his characters, "Tittlebat Titmouse" and "Oily Gammon" are specimens. His "Mr. Quicksilver" is said to have been intended for Lord Brougham. Among his shorter stories, those collected under the title of "Diary of a Physician," are the most powerful. They were published anonymously, and were written with such evident medical skill that the unknown author was accused by the faculty of betraying the secrets of their profession.

Mrs. Elizabeth Cleghorn Gaskell (1810–65) was one of the most distinguished of England's women novelists. Her mother died at the time of her birth, and her studies were pursued under the direction of her father, who was a man of cultivation.   After his death she lived with an aunt until her marriage to the Rev. William Gaskell of Manchester.   In her new position she was a most efficient help to her husband, devoting herself to ministrations among the poor, and interested in everything that concerned the factory-hands, especially the young girls.   It was to relieve the depression caused by the loss of her only son that (urged by her husband) she began to write, in order to turn her thoughts from her own grief. After one or two short stories she produced "Mary Barton," a tale of Manchester life.   It sprang at once into favor and has always held its place as a standard work of fiction. The publisher to whom it was first sent rejected it without reading; the next one kept it a year without acknowledgment, and then gave her £100 for the copyright. It was published anonymously, and she was entertained by hearing the various opinions expressed in Manchester, for and against it. After the appearance of "Mary Barton" (1848) she visited London, and became acquainted with many of the great authors of the day—among others with Charlotte Brontë, whose biographer she was afterward to become. From this time her pen was never idle; "North and South," "Cranford," and "Wives and Daughters," (which last she was just finishing at the time of her sudden death) are generally considered the best of her novels; while her "Life of

Charlotte Brontë," who was for years her dear friend, is as interesting as a novel, and may be called one of the most fascinating biographies ever written.

CHAPTER XLVII.

THE REVIEWERS.

THE first of the great quarterly reviews to be established was the "Edinburgh," begun, in 1802, by a company of dashing young writers, who said what they thought without caring whom they pleased or offended. Among the original contributors were Sydney Smith, Jeffrey, Scott, Brougham and Horner. All (except Scott) were liberals, and they enjoyed cutting and slashing away at their opponents. Francis Jeffrey (1773–1850) was the sharpest critic, and was its first editor (except for a very brief term of Sidney Smith), continuing to hold that position for twenty-seven years. He was a Scotch advocate, afterward raised to the bench and peerage as Lord Jeffrey, by which name he is now known. He had a quick eye for seizing the weak points of an author, and great power of sarcasm; but he was not so ready to acknowledge excellence, and sometimes made woful failures in judgment. What he wrote was always readable, however, and he was not behind the others in creating the popularity of the "Edinburgh."

Henry Brougham (1779–1868), afterward Lord Brougham, is known as an orator and statesman as well as an author. His versatility was amazing. Physical science, international law, educational reform, biography, all engaged his attention and had been made the subjects of deep thought and study. His prodigious industry is shown by the fact that as lord chancellor of England he left not a single case, when he retired, in arrear for judgment. His contributions to the Edinburgh Review, political, historical and miscellaneous, have been published by themselves.

Francis Horner (1778–1817), a distinguished lawyer, orator and statesman, was the fourth member of the brilliant group whose names have been associated with the first quarterly periodical. His career was cut short by ill health, and his articles in the Edinburgh, chiefly on political economy, form his only contributions to literature.

The Edinburgh was not begun as a strictly political review; but its whig tendencies after a time became so prominent that Scott, who was himself always a tory, and at first was a contributor to it, induced a set of conservative writers to set up (1809) an opposition review, the "Quarterly," in order to counteract its tendencies. The first editor was William Gifford (1757–1826), who in the previous century had produced two satires, the "Baviad" and the "Mæviad," aimed respectively at the "Della Cruscan"* writers and the corruptions of the drama. He was for a time editor of the "Anti-Jacobin," for which Canning, one of its contributors, wrote the famous satire, "The Knife-Grinder." As a critic he was acrid, delighting in abuse rather than praise, though perhaps scarcely deserving the saying of Southey, that he regarded authors "as a fishmonger regards eels, or as Isaac Walton regarded worms, slugs and frogs." He retired in 1824, and was succeeded by Sir John Taylor Coleridge, the eminent jurist, nephew of the poet; and he, in 1826, by J. G. Lockhart, of whom we shall speak hereafter. Before this time, however, the Scotch tories had started a magazine of

---

* So named from the Della Crusca Academy in Florence, after which certain verse-makers living there called what they tried to erect into a "School of Poetry." They published their inanities in the "Florence Miscellany," and actually found admirers and imitators for some of the most absurd, affected, insipid and fantastic bathos that ever appeared in verse.

their own, the famous "Blackwood's" (1817). The first numbers were dull, but from the next year, when the contributors' staff was joined by Lockhart, the poet Hogg, and John Wilson, the world was electrified by such a display of wit, satire and brilliant personal attacks, as far exceeded anything the Edinburgh had been able to show. The magazine, which included articles of a lighter and more sparkling kind than its older competitor, sprang at once into popularity and has held its own ever since.

John Wilson (1785–1854), better known to us under his pen-name of Christopher North, was, like Jeffrey, Brougham, and Horner, a Scotchman. Having inherited a fortune he bought a place at Lake Windermere, where he enjoyed the society of the "Lake Poets." Here he wrote his first poem, "The Isle of Palms," which was followed after several years by "The City of the Plague." Having lost most of his large fortune through the dishonesty of a relative, he went to Edinburgh (though without giving up his home at Elleray), and applied himself to earning a living. His literary labors did not bring much pecuniary reward, but he entered the law, and political influence secured him the professorship of Moral Philosophy in the University. His varied abilities and splendid physical health enabled him to accomplish an immense amount of work. The "Noctes Ambrosianæ" are his contributions to Blackwood, in which, under the form of conversations, he poured out witty and brilliant thoughts on almost every imaginable subject, beside writing special essays on some of the poets. His "Lights and Shadows of Scottish Life," and "The Trials of Margaret Lindsay" are his main efforts in fiction.

John Gibson Lockhart (1794–1854), the fellow countryman and son-in-law of Scott, was a fine scholar and a most attractive man. He was one of the noted contributors to Blackwood; wrote "Peter's Letters to his Kinsman," a pungent satire on the Scottish society of the day, and "Valerius," a classical novel, and made an admirable translation of the best "Spanish Ballads." He was editor of the Quarterly from 1826 to 1853; and, as his crowning piece of work, has left us that inestimable "Life of Sir Walter Scott," which is a precious possession to all lovers of literature. Lockhart was no Boswell; he did not photograph, with laborious minuteness, every feature of his idol; he wrote of him tenderly, reverently, truthfully, dwelling on what was great and noble and neither obtruding nor suppressing the imperfections inseparable from all human lives.

Lockhart's domestic life was checquered by keen sorrows. His eldest son, the "Hugh Littlejohn," for whom Sir Walter wrote "The Tales of a Grandfather," died first, and the deaths of Sir Walter, Miss Anne Scott and Mrs. Lockhart followed in the course of five years. Some fifteen years later, the loss of his surviving son, Walter, broke down what remained of his once high spirits and keen enjoyment of life. He left a daughter, Mrs. Hope Scott, the mother of the present Mrs. Maxwell Scott of Abbotsford.

Sydney Smith (1771–1845) was one of the wits of the early part of the nineteenth century. Son of a country gentleman of ability and eccentricity, he was carefully educated and ultimately became a "fellow" (salaried instructor) of New College, Oxford. His fellowship not being sufficient to support him while reading for the bar, he was compelled, against his will, to enter the church, and all through his life to be a clergyman rather in spite of himself than by natural bent. While curate in a small parish on Salisbury Plain he chanced to be invited to dinner by the squire of the parish, who was surprised and captivated —as men always were—by the charm of his talk and manners. The squire engaged him as traveling tutor to his son, and the two started for Weimar; but they were turned back by threatenings of war on the continent (1797) and found themselves in Edinburgh, where Smith, as usual, began to make numberless friends. Among the number was Francis Jeffrey (afterward Lord Jeffrey), and Henry Brougham (afterward Lord Brougham), and after some years spent there they together established the "Edinburgh Review," of which he was editor for one number and contributor for the next twenty-five years. His articles were the very life of the great magazine; not merely brilliant and readable but solid, serious and consistent. So gay and good-natured was he even as a controversialist that his opponents as well as his friends laughed with him. He is perhaps the most brilliant of reviewers, though not the greatest.

In 1803 he went to London, where he was highly prized as a preacher, a lecturer and a social favorite. There was often not standing-room in his church; and when he lectured on moral philosophy at the Royal Institution, the London world crowded to hear him. When the whigs came into power in 1806, he was presented with the living of Foston-le-Clay, in Yorkshire, and in 1809 most reluctantly moved from the gay metropolis to this out-of-the-way place, where he was embargoed by muddy roads and was, as he says, "twelve miles from a lemon."

Nevertheless, he served there for twenty years with the utmost cheerfulness and efficiency. Then his high qualities won preferment, even from an adverse government, the tories, against whose tenets he had always used his trenchant pen. He became a canon of Bristol Cathedral and exchanged Foston for Combe Florey. Either because of his reputation as a humorist and wit, or because of his uncompromising spirit, of which persons having partisan ends to gain were afraid, he was never made a bishop, much to the surprise and regret of his friends.

His best-known book is "Peter Plymley's Letters on Catholic Emancipation" whereof he was a warm advocate. His sermons are also much read; but the delightful "Life and Letters," edited by his daughter, will always be the favorite reading for those who wish to know the man "in his habit as he lived."

One of the innumerable "good things" attributed to him —some doubtless without reason—is a reply said to have been made by him to a friend who suggested that he should sit for his portrait to Landseer, the celebrated animal-painter: "Is thy servant a dog that he should do this thing?"

CHAPTER XLVIII.

MISCELLANEOUS WRITERS.

WILLIAM WILBERFORCE (1759–1833), the philanthropist who spent his life in efforts to promote the abolition of slavery in the British colonies, belongs to literature only as the author of a "Practical View" of the contrast between real and professed Christianity, which passed through five editions in six months, and was translated into four foreign languages. His life was written by his sons, of whom Samuel (1805–73) became successively Bishop of Oxford and Bishop of Winchester, and was the author of several ecclesiastical works, notably a "History of the American Church." He was an eloquent preacher, as is shown by his published sermons, and a man of great breadth and activity of mind. He died in consequence of a fall from his horse.

The sermons of Robert Hall (1764–1831), a Baptist minister, rank among the most perfect specimens of pulpit oratory. An eloquent writer has remarked that what Hall said of Burke might be applied to himself—"his imperial fancy laid all nature under tribute," and that "he collected riches from every scene of the creation and every work of art."

Of the religious writers of this age, the number is so great that we can only glance at them. John Henry Newman (1801–90) studied at Oxford, entered the Church of England, and was one of the leaders of the Tractarian or High Church movement at Oxford in 1833. Twelve years after this, he was formally received into the Roman Catholic Church, and he was made a cardinal in 1879. He was the author of a great number of theological works, both before and after his withdrawal from the Anglican Church, and of several fine hymns.

John Frederick Denison Maurice (1805–72), and Frederick William Robertson (1816–63) were among the leaders of what is called the Broad Church movement, were preachers of remarkable eloquence, and both have left volumes of sermons. To the same school belong Arthur Penrhyn Stanley (1815–81), Dean of Westminster, and author of the "Life of Dr. Arnold" already mentioned, and Charles Kingsley (1819–75), who will again be noticed among the novelists of the century. Dean Stanley, besides many religious books, wrote a book on "Sinai and Palestine," "Lectures on the Jewish Church," "Essay on Church and State," and "Historical Memorials of Westminster Abbey,"—the latter invaluable as a companion while going through that home of the great dead. Dean Stanley may be considered the leader of the Broad Church party, and he ranked high in the opinion of all bodies of Christians, from his large charity, great acquirements, and generous, sympathetic spirit.

Dr. Thomas Chalmers (1780–1847), one of the most learned and distinguished of Scottish divines, was also a man of science. His "Political Economy," and "Astronomical Discourses" (the latter of which had a larger sale than any volume of sermons, before or since), are his principal works in these directions. His theological and ecclesiastical works are very numerous, his "Institutes of Theology" being among the most prominent. He was at the head of the movement which broke up the National Church of Scotland and resulted in the establishment of the Free Church.

"Guesses at Truth," by the brothers Hare, Augustus William (1793–1834) and Julius Charles (1796–1855) was an extremely popular work. Its authors were both clergymen of the most liberal or Broad Church party. Each of the brothers wrote other books, though none which achieved the success which attended their joint-effort. The younger brother wrote "Memorials of a Quiet Life" which relates to the Hare family.

John Foster (1770–1843), a Baptist clergyman, was an essayist of great power and originality. His essay on "Decision of Character" and that on "The Evils of Ignorance" (a plea for the education of the masses) attained great celebrity. He was for many years the principal writer in the "Eclectic Review." His "Life and Correspondence" is extremely interesting.

John Payne Collier (1789–1883) one of the earliest commentators and critics on Shakespeare of the present century, is best known for those commentaries and criticisms; but his most valuable work is unquestionably the "History of English Dramatic Poetry to the Time of Shakespeare, and Annals of the Stage to the Restoration." He began his literary career with "The Poetical Decameron," a work of no great merit.

Isaac Disraeli (1766–1848) was a man of large wealth, who chose to devote himself to literature. His special interest was in personal anecdotes connected with authors, and his titles, "Curiosities of Literature," "Calamities of Authors," "Quarrels of Authors," and "Amenities of Literature," sufficiently indicate the nature of his works. Of these the first named is the most interesting, and has passed through many editions. Lord Byron says of himself that he had read Disraeli's works "oftener than perhaps those of any English writer whatever."

Richard Chenevix Trench (1807–86), Archbishop of Dublin, is well known in America for his delightful critical volume "On the Study of Words," of which twenty-two editions were printed in this country within a dozen years of its first appearance in England. The companion work "English, Past and Present" is in its way equally valuable, and the lectures "On the Lessons in Proverbs," originally delivered before societies of young men, is excellent reading. He wrote also several theological works, and published two volumes of poems, some of which have been widely copied and circulated.

Mrs. Anna Jameson (1797–1860), the most important art-critic of her sex and time, was the daughter of Robert Murphy, an Irish artist. Early in his life, they removed to England, which was thenceforward her home. At sixteen she became governess in a family, and in a tour with one of her pupils she spent some time in Italy, giving the results of her observation, later, in the "Diary of an *Ennuyée.*" Her marriage with Mr. Robert Jameson, a barrister, was not a happy one, and after a few years she separated from him. Her first work of importance was "The Characteristics of Shakespeare's Women," in which she displayed a fine critical insight and great delicacy of handling. Her style is remarkable for its elegance and simplicity. After a journey to Canada, in which a reconciliation with her husband was fruitlessly attempted, she turned her attention to art, and after much study began a series of works on "Sacred and Legendary Art" which extended over many years and of which the last volume was completed after her death by Sir Charles Eastlake. Not less valuable in its way was her book on "The Relative Position of Mothers and Governesses," a subject which she was able, from her own experience, to treat with knowledge and discrimination. She was especially interested in all that concerned the well-being of women, though every form of philanthropic effort claimed her hearty sympathy, and the memory of her devoted labors is still kept green in many of the charitable institutions of London.

Douglas Jerrold (1803–58), was a dramatist, a novelist, a humorist and a wit. His "Black-eyed Susan" still holds the stage, though, like most of the old-fashioned comedies, it is now seldom played. He wrote several novels and character-sketches; among them the "Chronicles of Clovernook," "St. Giles and St. James," and the world-famous "Caudle Lectures;" the last having become classic as a satirical fling at the relations of weak-minded husbands with strong-minded wives. It was first published in "Punch," of which he was one of the original writers and a long-time brilliant light.

His son, William Blanchard Jerrold, was a noted writer in London newspapers and periodicals, and after his father's death edited an excellent and amusing biography of him. He also wrote several novels, not particularly noteworthy; and some books of travel and sketches of social life, particularly among the poor in large cities.

Sir Arthur Helps (1817–75) was an essayist somewhat after the pattern of Lamb and Leigh Hunt, though thoroughly original in thought and matter. His "Friends in Council," and "Companions of my Solitude" were seized upon eagerly by the reading world, which saw in them the native humor, delicate satire and polished grace of style which had distinguished the earlier essayists, combined with greater depth of thought and seriousness of purpose. These books make excellent fireside company. "Realmah"— a singular work of fiction attempting to describe life in one of the old lacustrine cities*— has not the charm of the

---

* Cities built over certain European lakes, wherein their remains are now to be found.

others, but is full of inspiring thoughts. Ruskin, in speaking of Helps, in connection with others, as "a true thinker, who has practical purpose in his thinking," says that he is "in some sort a seer, and must be always of infinite use in his generation." Beside the works already mentioned, Helps wrote the tragedy of "Catherine Douglas," and some other dramas, and several historical works in relation to the Spanish Conquest in America.

CHAPTER XLIX.

MISCELLANEOUS WRITERS.

JOANNA BAILLIE (1762–1851), ranked by her contemporaries as among the chief dramatists of her day, was born in Scotland. Being left an orphan in early life, she and her sister Agnes removed to Hampstead, near London, to be with their brother, Dr. Matthew Baillie, a distinguished physician and writer on medicine. Miss Baillie's dramas, "Plays of the Passions," "The Family Legend," "De Montfort," and others, while showing great poetic talent and being highly applauded by the first critics of the age, proved not very successful as acting plays. Her poems show fine feeling and will probably be read longer than will her tragedies. Her house at Hampstead was the centre of a delightful circle of friends, whom she charmed by her simple good breeding and unaffected dignity. She lived to the age of eighty-nine, retaining to the last her faculties and her power of pleasing.

The plays of James Sheridan Knowles (1784–1862) were eminently suited for acting, and were for many years extremely popular with the public. Like his relative, Sheridan, he was born in Ireland and went on the stage. His first play he produced at twelve years old. At fourteen he wrote a ballad called "The Welsh Harper," which, being set to music, became a popular favorite and procured for him the acquaintance of such men as Hazlitt, Lamb and Coleridge. He was educated for a physician, but preferred to become an actor. His first published plays, "Leo," and "Brian Boroihme," drew crowded houses, but he made so little money by acting and authorship that he was glad to betake himself, for a time, to school - teaching, first in his father's academy at Belfast, and afterward at a school of his own at Glasgow. His most successful pieces were, "Caius Gracchus," "Virginius," "William Tell," "The Hunchback," "Love," and "The Wife," several of which still hold the stage. In later years he became a Baptist preacher.

Sir Thomas Noon Talfourd (1795–1854), lawyer, dramatist and essayist, is best known as the author of the exquisite drama of "Ion," and as the loving biographer of Charles Lamb. In "Ion" he has caught wonderfully the spirit of the old Greek tragic poets; and in reading it one is carried back to the times when the oracle was a power in the land and a relentless fate disposed of the destiny of men.

Talfourd wrote other plays which were not so successful, and many essays for the reviews and magazines. Having attained some distinction in the law and on the bench he entered Parliament, where he was for several years a hard - working member. His chief speeches were made on the copyright bill; and, in his law - practice, whatever pertained to literature he worked at with especial zeal. His death took place while he was sitting in the court as judge.

The lines from "Ion" given below have been often quoted, appealing as they do to a feeling deep - seated in human nature:

> 'Tis a little thing
> To give a drop of water; yet its draught
> Of cool refreshment, drained by fevered lips,
> May give a shock of pleasure to the frame
> More exquisite than when nectarean juice
> Renews the life of joy in happiest hours.

Sir Henry Taylor (1800–86) is, like Talfourd, better known as a dramatist than as a poet, though he figures in both capacities. His beautiful tragedy, "Philip Van Artevelde," takes a high rank in English literature, although not suited to dramatic representation. "Edwin the Fair," a drama of which St. Dunstan is the hero, is full of historical interest, and contains carefully studied historical portraits.

Mary Russell Mitford (1786–1855), like so many other writers destined to win fame in prose, began by writing verse. She read, early in life, Bishop Percy's "Reliques" of early English poetry; and her later education seems to have been of a desultory kind, likely to lead to poetic efforts. She had a face of the utmost intelligence and sweetness, but without beauty, being too fat to be comely; yet there are few women who have won so much love and admiration. Her letters to her family, preserved in a memoir, are full to overflowing with fun, goodness and affection.*

It was in 1808, when she was twenty-two, that her verses were first mentioned, and in the next year she wrote some lines on the burial of Sir John Moore which are pleasing and spirited. They close as follows:

> A hurried grave thy soldiers' hands prepare;
> Thy soldiers' arms the mournful burden bear;
> The vaulted sky to earth's extremest verge
> Thy canopy; the cannon's roar thy dirge!

---

* They have many journeys about England in the early stage-coaching days, and to read them seems like a sojourn in the land of Pickwick and Sam Weller.

The poor girl had a gambler and spendthrift for a father, and all through her early life was writing bright, loving letters to the man who was slowly but surely wasting the little fortune his wife had brought him, together with all the dutiful daughter could earn with her pen; and at last, in 1820, when Mary was thirty-four, she and her mother were in actual want of bread.* They moved from their fine home, yet she writes gaily from the little cottage they have rented:

My objection to a small room is its extreme unbecomingness to one of my enormity. I really seem to fill it, like a blackbird in a goldfinch's cage! The parlor looks all me.

In 1823 we find her selling a play to Charles Kemble, for which she gets £220 — a much-needed help. At the same time she is writing acceptably for the "Lady's Magazine," and, as she describes it, is chained to the desk, eight, ten, twelve hours a day.

From this time forward she supported herself by her pen; and never was there shown a more captivating sight of unquestioning, uncomplaining filial devotion—largely undeserved, as the reader can not help perceiving. Having nothing to stake, her father could no longer gamble, but he could live on through years, accepting the self-sacrificing devotion of his daughter; she, meanwhile, not only loving but admiring him to the end.

Her best work was a delightful book called "Our Village;" three volumes of narrative, incident and description, based on so simple and homely a theme as a country village with its surrounding walks. It ran through many editions and is still ranked among the classics of the "naturalistic" school.

Agnes Strickland (1801–74) was an industrious historical writer, who did much to bring the lives of great people

---

* His gambling was not unknown at home; for we find Mary writing to him (when he complained of being cheated at whist) urging him at least to play *only* at a certain club where he "would meet only gentlemen."

within the range of the young. She was so enthusiastic an admirer and partisan of royalty that her "Lives of the Queens of England" must be received with some allowance; but she made careful studies from history of the manners and customs of the times represented, and her various books contain many interesting personal details.

Harriet Martineau (1802–76) wrote on so many subjects that it is difficult to place her in any class. Her own favorite among her writings was a series of tales entitled "Illustrations of Political Economy." Of her novels, the best known are "Deerbrook," and "The Hour and the Man," the latter a historical fiction of the negro insurrection in St. Domingo (1791–1801), of which Toussaint L'Ouverture, the patriot and liberator, is the hero. Miss Martineau spent two years in the United States (1835-37), visiting among other places, Chicago, then a mere village, and on her return, published "Society in America," a book containing many hard hits at the crudities which she observed here, but written on the whole with candor and fairness. Some charming tales for children — "Settlers at Home," "Feats on the Fiord," "The Crofton Boys," and others — are from Miss Martineau's pen. She wrote in all more than a hundred books, many of them, however, being scarcely more than pamphlets. All topics connected with political and social reform interested her. Her "Autobiography," written many years before her death, was published after it.

CHAPTER L.

INTERMEDIATE HISTORIANS.

THE first name on the long list of historians who succeeded the brilliant triad, Hume, Robertson and Gibbon, was William Roscoe (1753–1831), a native of Liverpool. His father was a market-gardener, and at twelve years old young Roscoe, having learned all that his master knew, left school and worked with his father in the garden, giving his spare hours to study. In looking back to this time, he says, "If I were now asked whom I consider to be the happiest of the human race, I should answer, those who cultivate the ground with their own hands." In the course of time he became a banker, and showed the world one of those examples of the "merchant prince" who uses his money in the service of art and letters, and his leisure for intellectual pursuits. He had the courage to write and talk against the slave - trade at a time when much of the wealth of his own city came from it. His studies were largely in the direction of Italian literature and history; and in 1796 he published his "Life of Lorenzo de' Medici, called the Magnificent," which at once took its place among the standard historical works of the English language. The Italian historian Fabroni, who had written the life of Lorenzo in Latin, was about to translate it into Italian, when he saw Roscoe's work, and he engaged a friend to make an Italian version of Roscoe's book instead of his own. The "Life of Leo X.," a natural sequence to that of Lorenzo, is not quite as interesting; but both together form a valuable contribution to our literature.

After many years of prosperity, Roscoe, through the fault of others, lost his property. His costly library and the works of art with which his house was filled, were sold; but his friends bought the books he most cared for, and placed them in a public library in Liverpool, where he could still have access to them.

The charming little poem called "The Butterflies' Ball," which has delighted thousands of children, was written by Roscoe. He had four sons, all of whose names figure as authors in Lippincott's "Cyclopedia of Biography."

Sir James Mackintosh (1765–1832), was born in Scotland, but spent most of his life in England, or in India, where for seven years he held the office of Recorder of Bombay. His chief works were the "History of England to the Establishment of the Reformation," "Dissertation on Ethical Philosophy," and the "Vindiciæ Gallicæ," a defence of the French Revolutionists. Mackintosh was a man of immense learning and of brilliant conversational powers; a peculiarity which has been characteristic of many historians.

John Lingard (1771–1851), a Roman Catholic priest, wrote a History of England up to the abdication of James II. The work is interesting as being the only one of the kind written from a point of view hostile to the Reformation. Its style is calm and dispassionate, and there is much valuable information in regard to the Anglo-Saxon period. Lingard remained voluntarily, all his life, in the humble position of a Catholic village priest; and is said to have declined a Cardinal's hat with the remark, "It would quite put a stop to the progress of my history!"

James Mill (1773–1836), a philosopher and writer on political economy, gained a place among historians by his great work, "A History of British India." Beside many articles of great weight in the reviews, he wrote "Elements of Political Economy," "Analysis of the Phenomena of the Human Mind," "Law of Nations," etc.

Henry Hallam (1778–1859) has been called "the most judicial of our modern historians." His "View of the State of Europe during the Middle Ages" is remarkable for its insight into the development of that complex period. The "Constitutional History of England from the Accession of Henry VII. to the Death of George II." shows immense industry, acuteness and impartiality. His third great work, "Introduction to the Literature of Europe in the 15th, 16th and 17th Centuries," the Edinburgh Review called the most important contribution to literary history received by English libraries for many years.

Three histories of Greece appeared during the first half of our century. That of William Mitford (1744–1827) is quite spoiled by his almost insane hatred of democracy, which makes valueless his undoubtedly studious research. Dr. Connop Thirlwall (1797–1875), Bishop of St. David's, wrote an excellent history, but was cramped in his work by having engaged to bring it within a certain compass, required by "Lardner's Cyclopedia," for which it was furnished. It was reserved for George Grote (1794–1871) to produce a really complete history of that fascinating country, with no limitations as to space except as his own sense and taste exacted. Impartial, scholarly and philosophical, his work remains a standard one among those treating the entire subject, though many most instructive books exist dealing with certain portions or aspects of it.

Henry Hart Milman (1791–1868), Dean of St. Paul's, was a poet, historian and divine. His two principal works are the "History of Christianity from the Birth of Christ to the Extinction of Paganism," and the "History of Latin Christianity," both valuable storehouses of information. As a poet, he is best known by his tragedy of "Fazio." He wrote also some fine hymns.

For thorough investigation of the Anglo-Saxon period of our history we are indebted to Sharon Turner (1768–1847) and Francis Turner Palgrave (1788–1861).

Col. Sir William Napier (1785–1860) is the historian of the bloody Peninsular War (that wherein the British helped Spain to throw off the Napoleonic yoke), he having himself taken part in the struggle. As a military historian he has been compared to Thucydides and Cæsar, both of whom, like himself, had been soldiers in the wars they describe. Napier worked with intense fervor and spirit, and re-wrote the first volume of his history six times in order to insure accuracy as to details. He wrote also the life of his brother, Sir Charles James Napier, "the acknowledged hero of a family of heroes."

Patrick Fraser Tytler (1791–1849) wrote a "Universal History," for many years a standard text-book until more modern methods of dealing with that vast subject superseded his work.

Sir Archibald Alison (1792–1867), son of a Scottish clergyman, was the author of a "History of Europe from the Commencement of the French Revolution to the Restoration of the Bourbons, 1815," a work which commanded a great sale by reason of the fullness of its details, dealing, as it did, with a subject up to that time imperfectly treated by historians—the wars of Napoleon. More recent researches have discovered many and glaring mistakes in the book; the style is faulty, and the author's conservative bias prevents him from being impartial.

A continuation of the history, carrying it on for the forty years succeeding the Bourbon restoration, did not meet with the same success as the earlier part.

Dr. Thomas Arnold (1795–1842) was a man about whom much might be said, and it is with regret that we are forced to treat the subject so briefly as is necessary in "a short history" of an illimitable subject. As a historian, his "History of Rome," (which he had carried only through the Second Punic War when death overtook him) is his greatest work. This, as well as his "Lectures on Modern History" and "Manual of English Literature," grew naturally out of his occupation as a teacher. For fourteen years he was head-master of Rugby School, familiar to most of our young readers as the scene of Thomas Hughes's "Tom Brown's School-days," in which Dr. Arnold figures. It is not too much to say that, while occupying this position, Arnold changed the character of boys' schools throughout England. By putting his pupils upon their honor instead of watching them, and by living before them a life of utter devotion to duty, he gained such an influence over them as no master had ever had before. Those who wish to know the whole story of that grand, symmetrical life, should read the memoir of it by Dean Stanley.

Dr. Arnold was appointed, a few months before his death, to the professorship of modern history at Oxford, a post exactly suited to his abilities and tastes.

Five volumes of Dr. Arnold's sermons have been published, and he wrote much for reviews and periodicals that has not been preserved. Whatever affected the well-being of his fellow-creatures was of interest to him, and his work in every good cause that presented itself to him was untiring, while at the same time his methods were so practical that every effort told in favor of the object for which it was put forth.

CHAPTER LI.

LORD MACAULAY AND OTHER HISTORIANS.

THOMAS BABINGTON MACAULAY (1800–59) was born at Rothley Temple, Leicestershire, England, son of Zachary Macaulay, a well-known philanthropist, and grandson of the Rev. John Macaulay who is mentioned by Dr. J hnson in his "Tour to the Hebrides." His mother was of Quaker descent. He was a precocious boy and his remarkable character and attainments attracted the notice of Hannah More, who mentions them in her letters. At eighteen he entered Trinity College, Cambridge, where he made a brilliant record, gaining medals and scholarships almost at will. He did not care for mathematics, but read deeply in classics and literature. At twenty-four he wrote his fine poems "Ivry," and "The Spanish Armada," and at twenty-five made his mark as a master of critical writing by his article on Milton, published in the Edinburgh Review. He read law and was admitted to the bar, but never practised, having determined on politics as a profession. He entered Parliament as a pronounced liberal, and his first speech was in favor of removing the disabilities of the Jews in England; his second in favor of abolishing slavery in the British West Indies. He favored the great Reform bill of 1832. He was sent to India by the Government to reform the courts of law, and while holding his office there he kept up his historical studies and wrote many brilliant articles for English magazines. Returning to England he was made, at forty, a member of the Cabinet, or governing council of England.

Even in these great trusts his ability was not fully employed, for at this very time he wrote and published his stirring "Lays of Ancient Rome," which will move the hearts of English readers as long as the language exists. From the ballad "Horatio at the Bridge," a stanza or two will give the style and the sounding swing of the poet's verse:

> Now from the rock Tarpeian
> Could the. wan burghers spy
> The line of blazing villages,
> Red in the midnight sky.
> The fathers of the city
> They sat all night and day,
> For every hour some horseman came
> With tidings of dismay.
>   *   *   *
> Then out spake brave Horatius,
> The captain of the gate:
> "To every man upon this earth
> Death cometh soon or late.
> And how can man die better
> Than facing fearful odds,
> For the ashes of his fathers
> And the temples of his gods?

Later in life he gave himself up to his greatest work "The History of England." His plan of writing history was almost the direct opposite of Carlyle's, for as the latter always kept the heroes and the great in view, Macaulay set himself avowedly the task of recording the condition and disposition of the larger mass of the people, their manners, their progress and their well - being.

He gloried in the practical, and held Lord Bacon the greatest of philosophers, because he cared nothing for abstract theories; everything must come to the test of actuality.   The following fierce denunciation of Charles II. and James II. illustrates his hatred of baseness in high places, and shows also the eloquence of his prose as compared with the music of his verse:

The government had just ability enough to deceive, and just religion enough to persecute.   The principles of liberty were the scoff of every grinning creature, and the Anathema Maranatha of every fawning dean.   In every high place, worship was paid to Charles and James, Belial and Moloch; and England propitiated those obscene and cruel idols with the blood of her best and bravest children.   Crime succeeded to crime, and disgrace to disgrace, till the accursed of God and man was a second time driven forth to wander on the face of the earth, and to be a byword and a shaking of the head to the nations.—*Essay on Milton.*

A main feature in the history is its clearness. His style is lucidity itself, and his method is the statement and re-statement of what he wants his reader to understand, so often and so variously that he can not help comprehending it.

On this great matter of literary style, Macaulay himself speaks with no uncertain sound: "How little the all - important art of making meaning pellucid is studied now! Hardly any popular writer except myself thinks of it."

By all these means he makes his immense history as interesting as any novel. Of the second volume 30,000 copies were ordered before publication.

The best and most impartial critics now say that Macaulay was too fond of dramatic and pictorial statements; that he used only the brightest of lights and deepest of shadows. When he wished to condemn a man who deserves blame, he painted him of an unnatural blackness, without

·any redeeming feature; while for his heroes, no praise was too great; and if a flaw appeared it must be palliated, excused or explained away. This criticism is no doubt true, for no thing or person is ever quite one-sided. Good and bad exist everywhere, with all gradations between them.

In 1857 he was made a peer of England, under the title of Baron Macaulay of Rothley; and consequently is properly spoken of in history as Lord Macaulay. No doubt he was proud of the title, though one is apt to think that he reflected more honor on the peerage than he received from it. As he left no children, dying unmarried, his peerage died with him. He lies buried in Westminster Abbey.

In social life he was immensely admired. There seemed no subject on which he did not have some knowledge; for his study was broad and his memory prodigious. He talked readily and fluently, casting into the shade nearly every other talker in every company. One of the friendly critics acknowledged his splendor and supremacy; but added with some bitterness: "Macaulay would be faultless if he would only give us a few brilliant flashes of silence!"

Most of the great historians of the present century (always excepting Macaulay) are Americans, and therefore do not come within the scope of the present work.

The "Popular History of England," by Charles Knight (1791–1873), a richly illustrated work, gives an excellent idea not only of historical incidents, but of the· manners, customs, constitutional changes etc., of the country up to the time of finishing the history (1860). Mr. Knight was a most industrious writer and compiler, and as he was also a publisher, he was able to do much to promote extensive popular reading. The "Library of Entertaining Knowledge," the "Penny Magazine," the "Penny Cyclopedia," with many similar undertakings, came from his press, and he devoted himself to the spread of literature with an unselfish enterprise which merits the highest praise.

The lamented Edward Augustus Freeman (1823–92), who has but just passed away from among us, made most valuable contributions to historical literature, mostly in the way of studies of detached portions of it. The subjects which came under his attention were extremely varied. Immense learning and perfect accuracy of statement are his strong points; diffuseness and unnecessary multiplication of details his weak ones. Whatever he wrote, however, is worth reading.

The finest piece of philosophical writing which takes in the whole history of England, is that of John Richard Green (1837-83), whose "Short History of the English People" has already become a standard work. More than a hundred thousand copies of it were sold in England, during the author's life, and nearly as many in the United States. Encouraged by this reception he added to his materials, broadened the scope of his work and produced the "History of the English People," in four volumes. He afterward wrote "The Making of England," and at the time of his death was engaged upon "The Conquest of England."

Mr. Green achieves, more perfectly than did Macaulay, the task which the latter set for himself; namely, the depicting of the life of common people. He says in his preface:

It is with this purpose that I have devoted more space to Chaucer than to Cressy; to Caxton than to the petty strife of Yorkist and Lancastrian; to the Poor-Law of Elizabeth than her victory at Cadiz; to the Methodist revival than to the escape of the Young Pretender.

His English style differs broadly from the flowing periods of Macaulay, with their splendid display of contrast, antithesis and strong lights and shadows. Mr. Green deals in extremely short sentences, the paragraph devoted to a single event being so broken up by periods as to seem almost "jerky." Yet this, if a fault, is better than its opposite, for the short phrases are simple; more easy to read, to comprehend and to remember.

CHAPTER LII.

SOME GREAT ESSAYISTS.   CARLYLE.

ALTER SAVAGE LANDOR (1775-1864) was a poet and a prose - writer, great in both characters but admirable to brother poets and prose-writers rather than to the world at large. He inherited a large fortune and was educated with the utmost care at Rugby and Oxford. Latin was as familiar to him as English. Yet he was of so rebellious and intractable a nature that he disdained to compete for college honors, and (like many of the literary men of his generation) left Oxford without completing his course, being expelled for some insubordination. He and other fiery young enthusiasts were interested in favor of liberty, and much moved by the dawning of free government in America and by the French Revolution. Wigs and hair-powder were the mark of the old order of conservative gentlemen, while the revolutionists wore their own hair, long and powderless; and Landor boasted of having been "almost the first student who wore his hair without powder."

Soon after leaving college he wrote the first — perhaps the best — of his poems, "Gebir;" and his utter indifference to popular appreciation is shown by the fact that he wrote it partly in Latin. It is so overloaded and involved in style and thought as to be extremely obscure, and Southey likens the more comprehensible passages to "flashes of lightning at midnight." No wonder that scarcely a hundred copies of it were sold! He afterward wrote another poem, "Count Julian," which the publisher to whom he offered it declined to publish even at Landor's expense; which so excited his rage that he threw in the fire a third which he had begun.

Mrs. Oliphant describes his life thus:

The career of Landor was full of storm and tumult, and, it must be added, of the strangest sincere braggadocio, vanity, generosity and extravagance throughout. . . . He quarreled with all his surroundings and did everything that in him lay to make the neighborhood too hot to hold him. . . . After throwing away the greater part of his fortune he went off in profound offence and bitterness to Italy, where he lived for most of the remainder of his life. . . . He married, rather, apparently, because he had been lucky enough to find a perfectly unsuitable person than for any other motive.

Landor was about forty when he went to Italy, and while there he wrote the best known of his works — the "Imaginary Conversations." These are fanciful talks in which the author puts into the mouths of dead great men speeches supposed to be characteristic of them. They require, therefore, much scholarship in the reader to appreciate their aptness. To the average reader, the most charming of his writings is his "Pericles and Aspasia," which consists largely of letters supposed to be written from Athens by Aspasia to a friend at home, and breathes the very spirit of classic Greece.

The poet lived to a great age, and the end of his life was filled with the love and respect of younger men of letters.

Near the end of the eighteenth century, a gentle, pathetic presence comes upon the scene; that of Charles Lamb (1775–1834). He was of the humblest origin, his father, John Lamb, having worn livery as "servant companion" to a London dignitary; while Charles himself got his education as a "Blue-coat boy," or inmate of Christ's Hospital, where he was schoolfellow of the poet Coleridge, who became his lifelong friend. At eighteen he began a service in the accounting office of the great East India Company which lasted thirty - three years. The hundred thick business volumes which he filled with his delicate hand - writing in this long service he used to call his true "works;" his few published essays and poems bearing to them but a very small proportion.

While living at home with his family, consisting of his invalid father, mother and aunt, himself, and his elder sister Mary (the latter the unwearied care-taker of them all), a dreadful calamity fell upon them. Mary, who had already had slight attacks of insanity (as had Charles also) but who was supposed to be quite free from danger of mania and was the tenderest and gentlest of persons, suddenly became seized with madness, and snatching a knife from the dinner-table stabbed her helpless mother to the heart. The poor Mary was placed in a mad-house, where she would have passed the rest of her days but for the fact that her brother, with the help of influential friends, obtained her release on condition that he would be answerable for her safe-keeping for life. Afterward, for nearly forty years, they lived together; she subject to relapses which he always watched for and foresaw; on which occasions she and he wended their way together to the asylum which she willingly entered and where she stayed until the return of her poor senses.

This necessarily changed, governed and saddened Charles's whole life. He was engaged to Miss Alice Winterton, but gave up the hope of marriage, and devoted his life, cheerfully, to the duty which had thus come upon him. Both he and his sister being endowed with fine literary faculty, they worked together or separately in producing the books that bear their names.

The "Tales from Shakespeare," are the product of their joint labor. "Mrs. Leicester's School" was Mary's alone. "The Essays of Elia," all by Charles alone, were written for the "London Magazine," and became at once noted and popular. They remain now the main source of his fame, and will be so, probably, in the future.

Lamb was of delicate frame and feeble health; and among other small infirmities, made puns and stuttered in his speech. As a letter-writer he was almost inimitable. His letters and memoirs were published by Thomas Noon Talfourd.

After thirty years of service in the India House, Lamb retired on a pension of about £450. His deprivation of the constant employment which had been his so long was a direct loss to him; and he did nothing in the literary way during the rest of his life. His tendency to indulgence in stimulants grew upon him and he died of erysipelas brought on by a fall; his sister, then hopelessly mad, outliving him some ten years.

William Hazlitt (1778–1830), one of the most distinguished of English critics and essayists, was the son of a Presbyterian minister, and formed one of the intellectual circle of which Coleridge, Lamb, Leigh Hunt and Godwin were members. At the outset he determined to devote himself to art, and studied it sufficiently to make himself a renowned art - critic, though he never made any success as an artist. He was also deeply interested in metaphysics, a somewhat incongruous line of thought ; but his remarkable boldness and acuteness of mind were to appear neither in art nor in abstract musings, but in critical, suggestive and instructive essays on literature, men and manners. All subjects touched by him he treated with an ingenuity and felicity of illustration and expression never surpassed. As has been said, "Other men speak like books, but Hazlitt's books speak like men."

His private life was as eccentric and discreditable as his literary course was distinguished and admirable. He seems to have lacked good common sense, and his last years were clouded, and his death perhaps hastened by anxieties and disappointments about money.

Thomas De Quincey (1785–1859) has a curious, discordant, anomalous place in literary biography. He was a profound and brilliant essayist, an almost unequaled master of the English tongue, and a recorder — the only recorder — of the phenomena of opium - eating from the point of view of the victim to the fatal vice.

Born to a competency, he read and studied under the most advantageous circumstances and became almost a prodigy of classical learning. His mastery of Greek was phenomenal; as one of his teachers said: "That boy could harangue an Athenian mob better than you and I could address an English one." Wild and erratic, he twice ran away from school; the second time hiding himself in London where he stayed for a year or more and then became reconciled to his guardians. At nineteen he went to Oxford, where he studied five years, but, unruly as usual, went away without his degree.

While at college he became enamored of the poetical movement which owed its being to what are called the "Lake Poets"— Wordsworth, Southey and Coleridge. He showed his appreciation of them by giving the latter £300 through Cottle, the Bristol publisher; Coleridge being, as usual, in want, and De Quincey not having yet dissipated his patrimony. Soon afterward he took up his abode in that haunt of poverty and poetry, Grasmere, where he lived eleven years.

The most famous of De Quincey's works is the "Confessions of an Opium-eater." He had begun the use of opium during his college course, to allay neuralgic pains, and, being ungoverned and self-indulgent, the taste grew to a habit, the habit to a passion, and the passion to a consuming vice. The drug was beside him at meals in a decanter, and he drank it by the wineglassful, as others did wine. As one result of this suicidal course he was what Mrs. Oliphant calls "an odd, sensitive, abstract little man, light and shivery as a bird upon the bough, full of dreams and visions, a being with as little flesh and blood as possible—sufficient and no more to house his soul in." Speaking of himself he says: "I can not face misery, whether my own or not, with an eye of sufficient firmness, and am little capable of surmounting present pain for the sake of any recessionary benefit." In spite of economical habits and great industry, he managed to make away with his patrimony, and died, almost unnoticed, at the age of seventy-five.

James Henry Leigh Hunt (1784–1859), son of a West-Indian minister by an American wife, was a "blue-coat boy," that is, a pupil at Christ's Hospital, London. He began his literary life as a writer for the London Examiner, and was so "liberal" in politics and so unbridled in his treatment of "the powers that be" that he brought himself under the ban of the law, and was imprisoned for two years and heavily fined for one of his articles which called the prince regent "a fat Adonis of fifty." His imprisonment was not very hurtful, as it made him a kind of martyr to a political persecution, and he was the object of popular sympathy. "He hid the prison bars with flowers, and received visits from Byron, Shelley and Keats."

After putting forth his first volume of poetry, containing "The story of Rimini," and "Abou Ben Adhem," he did little for many years but struggle with want and ill-health and quarrel with his friends and relatives. He went to Italy, with Byron and Shelley, to establish a quarterly magazine for English readers. Shelley was drowned, Byron went to Greece, and the magazine lived but a single year. He had a lawsuit with his brother and this brought him back to England, where he had the bad taste to publish "Lord Byron and His Contemporaries," a bitter attack on men who had been his friends and benefactors. The book contained wholesome truths, but such as should have found some other narrator.

He was an industrious worker, but always at a disadvantage; he having no business ability and no tact in dealing with his fellow men. At last, when he was sixty-three, the Shelley family came to his rescue with an annuity of £120 and, three years later, Lord John Russell procured him a pension of £200. Fortunately he had still enough of vitality to write and publish his most charming books, "Wit and Humor," "Imagination and Fancy," "Men, Women and Books," etc.; and an admirable autobiography which portrays him in all his unconscious weaknesses.

Thomas Carlyle (1795–1881) was the son of James Carlyle, a village mason. He was born at Ecclefechan in Annandale, Scotland, and began his education at that small hamlet. Later he was sent to a grammar-school, and when he was fourteen he entered the University of Edinburgh with a view of becoming a minister of the Scotch Presbyterian Church, a purpose which was never carried out. He studied irregularly, but with amazing eagerness, and the stories of his immense reading are almost incredible. For a while he tried teaching, from time to time writing articles for the magazines; also translating Legendre's Geometry, mathematics having been his favorite branch of study. His "Life of Schiller" and his translation of Goethe's "Wilhelm Meister," showed indications of the towering genius he was afterward to make so conspicuous; but it was in a series of essays called "Sartor Resartus" (the Patcher Re-patched), that his strength and the peculiar novelty of his style made itself fully felt. The title is a rough translation of that of an old Scottish song, "The tailor done over." The book has been well called an indescribable mixture of the sublime and the grotesque. He was at heart a cynic, regarding mankind always as on the downward path; and in his "Sartor" he storms and scolds at poor humanity under the cloak (and other garments) which it wears. He asks:

To the eye of vulgar Logic what is man? An omnivorous Biped that wears Breeches. To the eye of Pure Reason what is he? A Soul, a Spirit, and divine Apparition. Round this mysterious ME, there lies, under all these wool-rags a Garment of Flesh (or of Senses) contextured in the Loom of Heaven, whereby he is revealed to his like and dwells with them in UNION and DIVISION; and sees and fashions for himself a Universe, with azure Starry Spaces and long Thousands of Years.

His next book (the first that bore his name) is his "History of the French Revolution;" more interesting than the other, because it treats of the doings of certain men instead of making a general assault on all mankind. He looks upon that awful reign of terror as the work of Nemesis (Fate), which in the fullness of time destroys the falsehoods and avenges the wrongs of centuries. This was followed by papers of less mark, and they again by his "Heroes and Hero Worship," wherein he upholds the right of strong men to use their strength whether for good or ill, and defends the tendency of the weak to worship them for so doing. The saying,

> O it is excellent
> To have a giant's strength, but tyrannous
> To use it like a giant:

he agrees with only as to its first part; disregarding the second and more humane sentiment.

This tendency of his mind is manifest in all his later works. He collected Oliver Cromwell's letters and speeches and connected them together by a most able and valuable narrative of the events of the great revolution of which Cromwell was the hero. The last and most striking and celebrated of his historical books was his "History of Frederick II. called the Great;" a monument of laborious research, of brilliant imagery and of impassioned language.

At the age of thirty-one years, Carlyle married Jane Baillie Welsh, and after living at several places in Scotland (among others for seven years at Craigenputtock, a moorland farm in Dumfriesshire), they settled down in London at Number Five Cheyne* Row, living there during the rest of their married life, and he afterward until his death.

Turning now to the memoir of Mrs. Carlyle, written by Mr. Froude but included in the "Reminiscences" left by Carlyle to his friend Froude to be edited, we find much of

---

* Pronounced "Chaney."

interest, chiefly sad. Miss Welsh was born in Haddington, Scotland, in 1801. She was a charming little genius, excelling all about her in beauty, wit and spirit. She wanted to learn Latin "like a boy," and when that painful privilege was denied her she got some boy to teach her a noun of the first declension, and then hid herself under the dinner-table when supposed to be in bed. "In a pause in the conversation a little voice was heard, *Penna*, a pen; *Pennæ*, of a pen; etc., and as there was a hush of surprise, she crept out and went up to her father saying, 'I want to learn Latin; please let me be a boy!'" This is only one of many such anecdotes, all tending to make us love the brilliant and happy little girl—and deplore the fate which married one genius to another.

Their married life was long and childless, and marred by dyspeptic ill-humor and neglect on his part, invalid querulousness on hers. He grew to be a great and much courted man—a distinction which she naturally did not always fully share—and their domestic unhappiness was no secret to their most intimate friends. Mrs. Carlyle died suddenly and almost unaccountably (1866) in her carriage in Hyde Park, and Carlyle spent the rest of his life in agonized self-reproach for his conduct toward her; evidently exaggerating its character, as was his habit regarding everything in life.

If the world rolls on very much as of old, in spite of Carlyle's lurid prophecies of impending chaos, it seems likely that many of his utterances will be forgotten, or kept alive only as curiosities of literature.

CHAPTER LIII.

MISCELLANEOUS WRITERS.

OF scientific writers, our century has had a vast array; concerning whom a history of literature can not have much to say, except so far as their works enter into general reading. First comes Mary Somerville (1780–1872), the wonderful scholar of whom Laplace said that she was the only woman who understood his works. She was born in Scotland and was the daughter of Admiral Fairfax. Her parents thought that a very little education was enough for a woman, and discouraged her wish for the more advanced branches; but she took the matter into her own hands and studied mathematics by herself, in secret, without a teacher. She was twice married, and her second husband, Dr. Somerville, entered with zest into her aspirations and did everything he could to facilitate her studies. She translated and popularized Laplace's great work under the title of "Mechanism of the Heavens," upon which she was at once elected a member of the Royal Astronomical Society. Of her other scientific works the best known are "The Connection of the Physical Sciences" and "Physical Geography." Her delightful "Personal Recollections," written in old age, looking back over a life which lasted for ninety-two years, are excellent reading for old and young.

Sir David Brewster (1781–1868) was one of those men who know how to make science attractive to the non-scientific. Of his claims to attention as a natural philosopher we can not here speak. His "Letters on Natural Magic," "Martyrs of Science," "More Worlds than One," and "Life of Sir Isaac Newton," are valuable contributions to literature.

Archbishop Whateley (1787–1863), a native of Dublin, was the author of treatises on logic and rhetoric, which for many years were the received text-books on those studies. He wrote also "Lectures on Political Economy," and a handbook of "Christian Evidences," which has been translated into more than a dozen languages.

Sir Charles Lyell (1797–1875), one of the greatest geologists of modern times, is chiefly known in literature by his "Travels in North America," which, though primarily devoted to the science of which he was a master, contain much of interest to the general reader. Another work, "A Second Visit to the United States," is especially interesting from its just appreciation of American institutions. His other works are exclusively geological.

Hugh Miller (1802–56), was born at Cromarty in Scotland, and worked there as a mason, in a quarry of the geological formation known as the "old red sandstone." He studied constantly, and after engaging in various occupations became editor of a religious paper. His book called "The Old Red Sandstone, or New Walks in an Old Field," established his reputation both as a geologist and a writer. "There was nothing in his works," says the Edinburgh Review, "which so much surprised the public as their mere literary merit. Where could this Cromarty mason have acquired his style?"

Miller afterward published "Footprints of the Creator," "My Schools and Schoolmasters," and other works. Excessive study caused his brain to give way, and in a paroxysm of insanity he killed himself. He had just finished a powful book called "The Testimony of the Rocks."

Charles Darwin (1809–82) was the boldest and most noted naturalist of his century. He gave his name to a theory, not absolutely novel, but never before so ably stated and argued out. It is called "The Darwinian theory of the origin of species," and teaches that the various orders of plants, and animals have sprung not from special acts of supernatural creation but from changes, wrought in a single original type of being, by the various agencies in which, in the succession of uncounted ages of time, it has been placed. "Natural Selection," according to Darwin, has caused "the survival of the fittest;" that is to say, any individual (animal or plant) which happens to be best adapted to thrive in the particular circumstances which surround it, is the one most likely to live and grow strong, and perpetuate its like in other individuals inheriting like peculiarities.

Darwin followed, of course, the Baconian method of philosophy; that is, he observed facts and from them deduced theories.   In his observance of natural phenomena he was perhaps the most humble, patient and industrious seeker after truth who ever lived.   He was graduated at Christ College, Cambridge, at twenty-two, and at once started (as naturalist) in H. M. S. Beagle, on a scientific voyage around the world ; concerning which he wrote several books.   But the work which made him famous and attached his name to one whole. branch of scientific speculation is, " The Origin of Species by Means of natural Selection ; or the Preservation of Favored Races in the Struggle for Life."   He did not even except humanity itself from his general tracing of the characteristics of every race to its surroundings; and a subsequent book " The Descent of Man; and Selection in Relation to Sex" stated still more emphatically the doctrine that the human race, like all others in the animal kingdom, has progressed from lower forms to higher, instead of having degenerated from higher to lower.   "Darwinism" has become a name for the system embodied in his researches and reasonings of progress from cause to effect.

Sir William Hamilton (1788–1856), one of the greatest metaphysicians of modern times, may be considered in some respects as a successor of Reid, Stewart, and Brown, though superior to all of them.   He was, like them, a Scotchman, and for the last twenty years of his life he was professor in the University of Edinburgh.   His chief works are his lectures on logic and metaphysics, and "Discussions on Philosophy and Literature, Education and University Reform."

John Hanning Speke (1827–64), at one time an officer in the India service, was the first white person to see the great Victoria Nyanza, the lake later known as the source of the Nile. His books, "What Led to the Discovery of the Nile," and "Journal of Discovery," tell the story of his travels and adventures. He was killed in England by the accidental discharge of his gun, while out shooting.

Alexander William Kinglake (1802–91), a prosperous lawyer, made a tour in Syria and other Oriental countries, which he described in a vivacious book entitled " Eothen, or Traces of Travel Brought Home from the East." His other important work is a history of the " Invasion of the Crimea," prepared during the twenty-five years following 1862. It is written with a strong prejudice against the French emperor; perhaps too strong to allow the history to rank as an authority.

George Barrow (1803–81), author of "The Bible in Spain," has given in that book a very entertaining description of the country, while relating his personal adventures, imprisonments, etc., experienced in the attempt to distribute the books confided to him by the Bible Society. His next work was "Lavengro," which is generally supposed to be autobiographical, though with a large infusion of fiction. " The Romany Rye," a sequel to "Lavengro," though widely read, did not add to his reputation.

John Stuart Mill (1806–73), the son of James Mill, author of a history of India, was educated at home, and spent some time in France studying languages and political economy; that is, the general laws governing the relations of mankind. At seventeen he went into the service of the English East India Company, and began as a clerk in the India House, London. His branch of duty was the political, which had to do with the transactions between the company and the native East Indian rulers. At fifty he became head of that department, and so continued until, two years later, after the great and terrible Sepoy mutiny, the control of East Indian affairs was transferred from the company to the British government.   After this he became a member of parliament, being classed among the liberals; those who pay especial attention to the interests of common people rather than to those of the privileged classes—crown, nobility, gentry and capitalists.

Most of his works appeared first in the shape of essays in the "London and Westminster Review" (of which he was an editor and proprietor), and various other periodicals.   His first noted book was a system of logic, which remains a standard work.   Then came two on certain branches of political economy and one on liberty, and later one on the subjection of women; all these being more or less associated with the study of political economy.   No writer on this class of subjects holds a higher place than does Mr. Mill. · He left, also, an autobiography which is a model of interesting personal annals.

George Henry Lewes (1817–79) was a writer of most varied abilities.   His "Life of Goethe" is perhaps the most widely read of his works.   If he had been either exclusively an editor, scientist, novelist, essayist, dramatist or historian, instead of being all these, he would have made a more permanent and conspicuous mark in literature; but probably would have been less noted and popular in his own day and generation.   Although he worked in so many fields, he was excellent in each.   A happy and discriminating characterization of Mr. Lewes is that given in the "International Cyclopædia:"

An intellect clear and sharp, if not remarkably strong; a wit lively and piquant, if not very rich; sympathies warm, if not wide; and a style as firm as it is graceful, made Lewes one of the best of critics and biographers.

Mr. Lewes's connection with Marian Evans, "George

WILLIAM MAKEPEACE THACKERAY.

Eliot," and her overshadowing genius, have associated his name with hers in a way that perhaps puts him at some disadvantage.

Matthew Arnold (1822–88) was a noted writer of our own times. He was the son of Dr. Thomas Arnold, head master of Rugby, and after going through that school and Balliol College, Oxford, he was elected a fellow of Oriel, and later was for ten years professor of poetry at Oxford. His poetical works came first (as is so often the case with men who write both poetry and prose) and we may cite "Tristram and Yseult" as the best known of his poems. In prose he published many books; chiefly lectures on certain scholarly subjects, collected into book form after use in his course of college-instruction. At about fifty, however, he subjected himself to much criticism through a new departure in religious writing in an essay called "Literature and Dogma;" which subjected theology to criticism from a new point of view. He traveled in America (quite late in life) and lectured; attacking, among other things, the system of governing by popular majorities. His last three books are all on American subjects.

Henry Thomas Buckle (1822–62) is one of the very few writers who have earned an enduring place in history by the production of only a single book. He was a delicate youth and got his education by his own efforts. He came into a large fortune when only eighteen years old, and at once devoted himself to literary pursuits; getting together one of the finest libraries in the world. At the age of thirty-five he, published the first volume of his "History of Civilization in England" and after a few years his second; the two being only the beginning of a work which death cut short before any more was done. The book, so far as finished, is really an essay on history in its reference to civilization, rather than a statement of the steps by which Englishmen became civilized. Therefore it is not possible to say that the narrative comes down to such or such a date. There is no sequence of dates; it merely goes a certain way toward exhausting the subject, and stops short of doing so.

The untimely death of this admirable and praiseworthy writer occurred at Damascus, where he chanced to be, having journeyed so far in search of health.

CHAPTER LIV.

NINETEENTH-CENTURY NOVELISTS. THACKERAY. DICKENS.

IN the brilliant Victorian period of English literature the names of Dickens and Thackeray are closely and constantly connected. In the earliest of their novels appear the very last of the wearers of hair-powder and small-clothes, and they were both still writing when the war of the American Rebellion was fought. Thus their scenes embrace the emergence from the old and slow things to the new and rapid; from stage-coaches and wooden sailing-vessels to steamboats, railways, telegraphs and ironclads, not to speak of friction matches, penny-postage and postage-stamps, gas-lights, power printing-presses, and a thousand things more or less connected with life and literature.

William Makepeace Thackeray (1811–63) was born in Calcutta, and was the son of an officer in the East India Civil Service. His father dying, his mother married Major Smyth, and during Thackeray's childhood the family moved to England. He was sent to the Charter-House School, afteward made famous in "The Newcomes" as "Gray Friars." Of his recollections about this a schoolfellow remarks:

His change of retrospective feeling was very characteristic. In his earlier days he always spoke of the Charter House as Slaughter House and Smithfield. As he became famous and prosperous his memory softened, and Slaughter House was changed into Gray Friars, where Colonel Newcome ended his life.

The unlucky breaking of his nose, which spoiled his good looks and marked him for life, occurred in one of the school-fights which were in those days (perhaps are still) a recognized part of a boy's experience at great English schools. At seventeen he was entered at Trinity College, Cambridge, but stayed there less than two years. During this time he wrote for a Cambridge periodical called "The Snob," thus early turning his attention to a subject pursued afterward in his "Book of Snobs."

After leaving college, while his mother and step-father were living in Devonshire, he went to Weimar and Paris; his aim being to make himself an artist. He achieved no success except in caricaturing; and even this he did not do well enough to rely on it for a living. In looking over the sketches with which he illustrated his earlier works, one wonders whether it was that his mental picture was not clear, or that his hand did not answer to his imagination. It was probably the former, as all his figures have the same faults; and none of them look exactly like human beings; yet after all, they do give the feeling of the text, and at any rate, so associated are they with his beloved personality that one prizes them as they are and would not exchange them for the best work of the art illustrative.

When he succeeded to his fortune — about £500 a year — he very promptly lost it, interest and principal. Perhaps this was really a blessing in disguise, for the rule seems almost invariable that the highest literary achievement must spring from the stony ground of necessity. At about this time, Dickens, already on the high wave of success (he being then twenty-three and Thackeray twenty-four), received a call from the would-be artist, who brought a portfolio of his sketches and vainly sought the privilege of illustrating Dickens's next publication.

Thackeray's literary life began in London, at about the same time when Dickens refused his drawings. He wrote short stories for various periodicals—among them "The Great Hoggarty Diamond," and "The History of Samuel Titmarsh"—and (as he told long afterward) met with so little appreciation that the editor warned him that the latter story was running too long; it must be shortened!

He married at twenty-six, showing by this assumption of new responsibilities, a certain degree of confidence in the future.   It certainly added to his chance of success by giving a spur to counteract his lifelong tendency to indolence and procrastination.

"Punch" was Thackeray's main source of income for the ten years following 1843; and though his work on it was necessarily anonymous, his name gradually became identified with the "Thackeray" style of humor, which embodied fun and philosophy, satire and sense. During this period appeared "Vanity Fair, a Novel without a Hero," published in twenty-four weekly numbers. The first publishers to whom it was offered declined it; Bradbury & Evans (the owners of "Punch") took it up, and it made fortune for them and fame for him.

The serial method of publication, necessitating as it does sharp and continuous attention to the interest of articles each coming to the test of public approval at the end of the week which gave it birth, was doubtless of immense worth to Thackeray, and helped to give the uniformity of value to "Vanity Fair," "Pendennis," and the "Newcomes." In such work there could be no more of the old prosaic methods; though they did very well in the early days of fiction when a dull and spiritless chapter could be atoned for by its fresh and vigorous successor. The "Punch" articles, the Snob papers and ballads, furnished also excellent material for later publication in book form, when the greater books had given their author a name under which any word was sure of an audience.

"Vanity Fair" (though not a caricature) is essentially a

satire, and therefore an exaggeration. We turn from it with pleasure to "Pendennis," "Esmond," and "The Newcomes," where satire is only an incidental ingredient and exaggeration unneeded. The novels were incomparable; the appearance of each number was an event in the reading world; the chief catastrophe in the last-named book the finest bit of pathos in English prose. To many readers, these novels mark, to this day, the high tide of fiction.

It was in 1851 that Thackeray entered upon a course of public readings, unlike those of Dickens, because he did not read from his published works, but prepared entirely new lectures, with infinite care and study. The researches needed for his historical novel of "Henry Esmond," paved the way for the course upon "The English Humorists of the Eighteenth Century;" and in the same general line of exploration came the material for that treating of "The Four Georges." Both were highly profitable in England and America. "The Virginians" is a sequel to "Henry Esmond," carrying on the lives of its characters, and varying the scene to the Virginia of the colonial period. It should be, therefore, of the highest interest to American readers.

At forty-eight he became editor of the "Cornhill Magazine," and contributed to it "Lovel the Widower," and "The Adventures of Philip." But he was too tender-hearted to be a good editor. The rejection of manuscripts, with the consequent pain given to contributors and reflected on the editor, he called "thorns in the cushion," and made them the subject of one of his delightful "Roundabout Papers."

Thackeray's verses — poems he would never call them unless in jest — were written at various times and as fancies struck him or the call for "copy" found him at a loss. The pieces were chiefly ballads — if that name can be applied to verses not intended for singing. Sometimes they were fun, pure and simple; sometimes written to kill, by sharp ridicule, some abuse, imposture or imposition. The most effective are those where humor gives way to pathos; there they touch the line of true poetry.

"The White Squall" is one of the best bits of meteorlogical descriptions ever penned, in fun or in earnest. After several scores of short seven - syllable lines, ingeniously rhymed and queerly conceived, descriptive of a steamer's deck in a sudden squall, he suddenly changes his tone and ends:

> And when, its force expended,
> The harmless storm was ended,
> ' And as the sunrise splendid
>   Came blushing o'er the the sea,
> I thought, as day was breaking
> My little girls were waking,
> And smiling, and making
>   A prayer at home for me.

Thackeray was engaged on a new novel, "Dennis Duval," when he died.   On a December morning, in 1863, he was found dead in his bed, from apoplexy.   He had been for ten or twelve years subject to spasms of pain of which he made as little as possible.

He had more than replaced, in his manhood, all he had lost in his youth; and left to his daughters property yielding £750 a year.   The elder one, Anne, became Mrs. Ritchie, and, following in the footsteps of her father, ranks among the best of English novelists since his time.   The younger, Harriet, married Leslie Stephen (also of the literary guild), and died after a few years of married life.

However jaded and dulled by the multiplicity and variety of literary subjects already presented, our hearts warm as we come to the name of Charles Dickens (1812–70).   With all his imperfections, he has taken a hold on the hearts of the readers of English such as perhaps no writer of any time or quality has ever exactly matched.   Humor, Pathos, Philanthropy, Comedy, Tragedy, Farce and Melodrama all joined hands in a circle around him as he wrote, and his quick eye glanced from one to another, catching inspiration from each in turn; most frequently and fondly accepting from Humor a smile and from Pathos a tear — often blending them together as he penned the thought they suggested.

Charles was the son of John Dickens, a clerk in the navy pay-department at Portsmouth, and later a parliamentary reporter for a London daily. The family was poor and embarrassed, the father at one time in the debtor's prison at Marshalsea, and the boy pasting labels on blacking-boxes for about a shilling a day. The circumstance has been made the occasion of a good deal of maudlin sympathy; although to the thousands of self-made men, from Abraham Lincoln down to the ordinary run of successful toilers who started without fortune, it seems to be quite in the course of nature. His biographer, Forster, calls it his "humiliation."

His parents he later caricatured in the "Micawbers" of "David Copperfield," making them to rank among the greatest fools that can possibly be imagined. Yet they seem to have tried quite hard — however unwisely — to furnish him such education as came within their power.

In his early youth he was small and sickly, and played little with other boys. He found somewhere the novels of Fielding and Smollett, the "Vicar of Wakefield," "Don Quixote," "Gil Blas" and "Robinson Crusoe," which, with the "Arabian Nights," formed the basis of his general reading. At about fourteen he wrote some small stories which a small club of boys read and circulated, and also took part in some youthful theatricals, all of which shows the formative character of his early experiences. After leaving school he studied short-hand, the difficulties of which are comically set forth in "David Copperfield," said to be to some extent a recounting of his early life. Then he began reporting for the newspapers, and as it was just at the end of the old coaching days and the old inns that belonged to them, he gained an intimate knowledge of the peculiarities of life on the road that make "Pickwick" so delightful.

His first published article (not paid for) was in the old "Monthly Magazine" for January, 1834. After this, he became a contributor to various papers under the name of "Boz," that being an abbreviation of the nickname "Moses" (Boses), which he applied to his brother Augustus.* Later he collected the "Boz" sketches into two volumes, and began the publication, in shilling numbers, of the "Posthumous Papers of the Pickwick Club." The success of these was so great that he gave up reporting and turned his attention to literature. In the meantime he had married Miss Catherine Hogarth, daughter of one of his newspaper friends and fellow - laborers.

Of the first number of "Pickwick" the binder prepared 400 copies: of the fifteenth number, 40,000. "Oliver Twist" was coming out at the same time, and before that (or even "Pickwick") was finished he had begun "Barnaby Rudge," both published in the "Miscellany," of which he was editor. His stories possessed him in a remarkable fashion, the characters being self-constructive, as it were, and seeming to have an individual existence independent of the brain which gave them birth. This perhaps partly explains why and how he was able to keep so many going at once. "Nicholas Nickleby," as a serial, followed "Oliver" in the "Miscellany," and reached a sale of 50,000 on the day of its publication.

His manner of life at this time—and always—was convivial; though perhaps not yet particularly so. He worked with speed and energy and took his mental rest in great

---

* Augustus Dickens ("Boz") spent the closing years of his life in Chicago, where (1855-60) he filled an humble office in the land department of the Illinois Central Railway. He shared some of his brother's characteristics, but none of those which made Charles a genius. The convivial bowl was his invincible enemy.

bodily activity; walking and riding many miles almost daily; often in company with Mr. Forster, afterward his biographer. Nearly every road leading out of London must have been familiar to his footsteps, and the hostelries where the best chops, wine and ale were to be had were always kept in view.   Even as a child he regarded his beer as one of the necessaries of life, though the cost might lessen the sum that should be spent for food; and at twenty-six, after one of his numerous illnesses, he says: "You will imagine how queer I must have been when I tell you that I have been compelled for four-and-twenty mortal hours to abstain from porter or other malt liquor!!! I have done it though — really."

In all his earlier works, unforced, spontaneous humor was the mainspring; and it seems really doubtful if in the history of literature so much of genuine, irresistible fun ever flowed from human pen.   True, it was not like anything on earth.   Dickens created the characters and inspired them with the breath of life.   No such people have existed or ever will exist; but if they did they would be *so* funny! Mrs. Nickleby with her love-scenes vanquished even the disapproving Sydney Smith and he writes: "*Nickleby* is *very good*.   I stood out against Mr. Dickens as long as I could, but he has conquered me."   The humor, too, was usually — not always — good; directed against shams and abuses, and when it was so aimed it was apt to be fatal. The workhouse, the cruel school, the debtors' prison and other plague-spots found their St. George in Charles Dickens.

"Master Humphrey's Clock" was a series of tales in which the "Old Curiosity Shop" led the way.   "Little Nell" was always one of his favorite creations — creatures, they became to him.   In our younger days she drew floods of tears from our eyes; but to our maturer judgment the intention to draw tears becomes manifest, and the eyes weep no more. As some wit has phrased it, "Dickens is always raising an altar to Pathos, and sacrificing a *kid* upon it!"

In 1842 came Mr. Dickens's famous visit to the United States. The whole American people "went wild" over him, and many made themselves troublesome and ridiculous. A greater man than Dickens might have excused the annoyance for the sake of the cordial love for his writings which underlay it. But Mr. Dickens saw only the surface of the strange, informal, inelegant, democratic society; a society imperfect, but growing better by its own strength, then as now. Of the "American Notes," published after his return, he learned to be ashamed; of the anger they excited among Americans we learned to be ashamed; therefore they may well be forgotten, bright though the "notes" were and many the unpalatable truths they told. When he came again, twenty-five years later, he was again received with cordial welcome, and his readings from his own works were extremely profitable, the amount cleared by thirty-four of them being near £11,000. One can not but rejoice at this as being in some sort, though imperfectly, an offset to the fact that the millions of his books sold in America had yielded him no income, because of the absence of international copyright. This righteous measure, fruitlessly urged by Mr. Dickens upon the American people and government, has at last, forty years after his visit, been enacted, and is the law of the land.

Unfortunately, Mr. Dickens's health was unequal to the strain of such a campaign as that of his lecturing winter. As to his manner of living, it may be judged from a letter to a friend in which he speaks of having been "reduced," by ill-health, to such a regimen as the following:

At seven in the morning, in bed, a tumbler of new cream and two tablespoonsful of rum. At twelve, a sherry cobbler and a biscuit. At three (dinner-time) a pint of champagne. At five minutes to eight an egg beaten up with a glass of sherry. Between the parts [of his reading] the strongest beef-tea that can be made, drank hot. At a quarter past ten, soup and any little thing to drink that I can fancy.

Indeed the matter of drink is continually cropping up, in all his letters.

After the first American tour came "Martin Chuzzlewit," a poor and weak recalling of the trip; next "Dombey and Son," with its rather grim pathos, and then "David Copperfield," the most artistic work he ever did; the most natural, heartfelt and satisfactory; the favorite among all his novels. "Bleak House," and "Little Dorrit" were written before the memorable year when he removed to the fine Gadshill property; a change which reminds one painfully of Scott's taking up the fatal burden of Abbotsford. The occasion was simultaneous with his separation from his wife; they afterward living apart, the children being free to come and go as they pleased.

It was in this year (1858) that he finally took up the long-considered plan of giving public readings for his own profit; the cost of Gadshill drawing heavily upon him. The place itself was far from costly, but his living expenses were large and his benevolent outlays most generous. He seems to have supported his parents almost entirely, and other members of his family largely; and every charitable and philanthropic work that appealed to his sympathy was the recipient of boundless help. The receipts at his readings for charity were enormous.

"The Tale of Two Cities," which appeared about this time, showed much of Dickens's old power, but was lacking in the humorous — a sad deficiency. This novel, "The Uncommercial Traveller," and "Our Mutual Friend," all appeared serially in "All the Year Round" (a periodical with which he was then connected), before being issued in book form. He wrote nothing more except the unfinished "Edwin Drood." Paralysis was near. He had to give up dinner-parties. At the last meeting between him and Mr. Forster they recalled their old jolly companions, now all gone, and as he said "none beyond his sixtieth year, very few beyond fifty."

He died at Gadshill on June 9, 1870, aged fifty-eight, evidently a victim to the pace at which he lived. He may be said to have burned his candle not only at both ends but also in the middle. He walked hard, wrote much and lived fast.

Few men have ever written who moved the minds and hearts of their fellow-men as greatly as did Charles Dickens. And his voice was in favor of charity, justice, benevolence, manliness, brotherhood, morality. If one could add temperance, the circle of beneficent influence would be complete. But to those who find in drink the fruitful source of all evil, the feeling intrudes itself (even while wondering at and admiring the boundless power and kindly impulses of the man) that his constant reference to the delights of convivial excitement, making it the inseparable companion if not the absolute foundation of joy and gladness, has been and must remain a fatal defect in the fabric of his teachings.

CHAPTER LV.

BULWER. READE. COLLINS. THE TROLLOPES.

THE earlier writings of Edward George Earle Lytton Bulwer-Lytton (1806–73), Baron Lytton, appeared under the writer's family name of Bulwer, and by that name he is better known than under his title of Lord Lytton.*

He was one of the most versatile of men; novelist,

* He was over sixty when, in reward for political services, he was raised to the peerage.

dramatist, poet, essayist and politician. Poetry was his earliest ambition; he published a volume of poems at fifteen, and at twenty won a prize for a poem on sculpture. His first noteworthy novel was "Pelham," which was very successful, and is a remarkable production for a young man of twenty-two. From this time until the rise of Charles Dickens, ten years later, he may be said to have been the leading English novelist, writing in that time "The Disowned," "Devereux," "Paul Clifford," "Eugene Aram," and "Godolphin." The most noted is "Eugene Aram," written to illustrate how a man of fine nature may be led, step by step, into the deepest villainy.

His greatest and best work is "The Last Days of Pompeii," a historical novel, its time being the first century of the Christian era, and its place the Roman city buried during the terrible eruption of Vesuvius in the year 79 A.D. It is by far the most popular and most valuable English novel dealing with times so remote, and has become and will remain an English prose classic.

As a playwright, Bulwer is greater than as a novelist. He achieved the rare success of writing three plays — "The Lady of Lyons," "Richelieu," and "Money,"— which hold the stage to this day. This is more than any other modern playwright has done who was not himself an actor; and it is said that the great actor, Macready, helped him to make the plays what they are.

After Bulwer's earlier novels, several of which are open to the charge of great immorality, a change came over the manner of his writing, and his later works, "The Caxtons," "My Novel," "What Will He Do With It?" and others, are entirely free from this blemish. In his first novels, also, he seemed to write for the purpose of inculcating a theory rather than telling a story; later, he tried to meet the popular demand for real-life pictures; and if we had not had such humorists as Dickens, such satirists as Thackeray, such realists as Anthony Trollope, and such character-painters as Charlotte Brontë and George Eliot, he would have stood at the head of the English novelists of his generation. His greatest deficiency was the lack of a sense of humor. Otherwise, he had many of the requisites of a successful novelist. His training was perfect, his aim exact, and his industry untiring.   In his fifty productive years he published at least fifty separate books, and beside all the work mentioned, he was a politician, a parliamentary orator and a member of the British cabinet.

Charles Reade (1814–84) has been characterized by Trollope as "almost a genius." If it were true, as is alleged, that "genius is only infinite capacity for work," he would take rank as not almost but quite a genius, for he was one of the most painstaking and indefatigable of writers. He called "no day without a line," the eleventh commandment.

Like many another man destined to make a name with his pen, he took to it only after trying in vain to succeed in other lines.   The law (for which his fine education especially fitted him) and playwriting having both failed him, he took his rejected drama, "Masks and Faces," and after succeeding in producing it by the help of the dramatist, Tom Taylor, he worked up the same plot and characters into the romance of "Peg Woffington," which established him as a novelist.   He followed this up by "Christie Johnstone." At this early stage in his career, he maps out its course in a diary, thus:

June 20. The plan I propose to myself in writing will, I see, cost me undeniable labor. I propose never to guess where I can know. For instance, Tom Robinson is in gaol. I have therefore been to Oxford gaol and visited every inch, and shall do the same at Reading. Having also collected material in Durham gaol, whatever I write about Tom Robinson's gaol will therefore carry (I hope) a physical exterior of truth.

George Fielding is going in a ship to Australia. I know next to nothing about a ship, but my brother Bill is a sailor. I have com-

missioned him to describe, as he would to an intelligent child, a
ship sailing with the wind on her beam — then a lull — a change of
wind to dead aft, and the process of making all sail upon a ship
under that favorable circumstance. Simple as this is, it has never
been done in human writing so as to be intelligible to landsmen.
. . . Now, I know exactly what I am worth. If I can work
the above great system there is enough of me to make one of the
great writers of the day; without it, NO. NO.

The information obtained by these laborious methods, he
embalmed in voluminous notes, and used with scrupulous
exactitude. His books abound in facts and truths, medical,
surgical, nautical, agricultural, financial, industrial, educational, historical, political, economical, statistical, theological — in short nearly all the adjectives ending in al. The
most marked of his works beside the two already mentioned
are "Never too Late to Mend," "Love Me Little, Love Me
Long," "The Cloister and the Hearth," "Hard Cash," "Put
Yourself in His Place." The novel called "Foul Play," written in connection with Dion Boucicault, was aptly characterized by some newspaper in the following jingle:

> If you wish me to say
> What I think of "Foul Play,"
> I can very conveniently do so;
> It's a simple re-hash
> Of "Very Hard Cash,"
> With a seasoning of "Robinson Crusoe."

Reade himself preferred dramatic writing, and made
some success in that line; while his novels, beside being
instructive and picturesque, are essentially dramatic in
their treatment.

Personally he was one of the most quarrelsome of
men. When he was unfavorably reviewed he rushed into
print to defend himself, and into libel-suits to punish his
critics. When he thought himself wronged in business he
appealed to the courts under the copyright laws and others.
Like other men of that stamp, he made himself extremely

disliked by enemies, and to a corresponding degree loved and admired by friends. And it must never be lost sight of that he was strongest in defence of the weak and most pronounced in aid of those who can not speak for themselves. He never, in his writings, glorified drink; and (considering his times and surroundings) was a temperate man. He lived in generally rugged health to the allotted limit of three score years and ten, and died leaving many loving and mourning hearts behind him.

William Wilkie Collins (1825–89), usually called Wilkie Collins, was born in London, the son of a distinguished landscape painter. His first literary work was a well-written memoir of his father, which he followed up by several romances of which the best known are "After Dark," "The Dead Secret," "The Woman in White," "No Name," "Armadale," and "The Moonstone."

His particular characteristic is intricacy of plot. He made his denouement a secret, and covered it up with such a mass of deceptions that the reader is at a loss to guess the outcome until the very last chapter is reached. In these days, those who read "The Dead Secret," or "Armadale" (which is also a "dead secret") can simply turn to the final chapter for its solution; but when the books came out in weekly numbers, as was the fashion forty years ago, we can fancy the regret with which a thrilling chapter was laid down and the impatience with which the next was waited for. Concerning this characteristic, Anthony Trollope says:

Of Wilkie Collins it is impossible not to speak with admiration, because he has excelled all his contemporaries in a certain most difficult branch of his art; but as it is a branch which I myself have not at all cultivated, it is not unnatural that his work should be very much lost upon me individually. When I sit down to write a novel I do not at all know, and I do not very much care, how it is to end.

This very clearly indicates the difference between the novel of intricate plot and the novel of the development of characters.

Collins was the intimate friend of Charles Dickens, and his co-worker in editing "All The Year Round" which he continued after the death of Dickens.

Anthony Trollope (1815–82), the most luminous and voluminous of English romancers, was born in London, of parents possessing ability, industry, bad judgment and bad luck. His childhood was passed at Harrow, at a farmhouse which he has described in "Orley Farm." He spent fifteen years in pursuit of an education, mostly in the great Harrow School and at Winchester College; an outcast among his cruel school-mates and brutal teachers by reason of his poverty of mind, body and purse; longing for love, esteem, popularity, and getting none. His delightful autobiography (published in 1883) tells the story of the family struggles and his own childish anguish, and is most pitiful. Nothing in all his wonderfully truthful pictures of fictitious life is more powerful in pathos than his simple story of the actual facts in the heroic self-sacrifice of his mother (Frances Milton Trollope) on the altar of family affection.

The last of the family's struggles (before they were forced to fly before creditors) was the strangely foolish experiment of establishing Henry Trollope in business as a merchant in Cincinnati. In furtherance of this plan Mrs. Trollope and her son came to America and built a "bazaar" in that city! Naturally the investment was a dead loss, and Mrs. Trollope's "Domestic Manners of the Americans"—a book compared with which Dickens's "American Notes" is almost flattering—was more a picture of what she felt than what she saw. Its only good result was the earning of £800 by that devoted and long-suffering woman; a success which turned her to travel-writing and novel-writing as a means of feeding her helpless flock, and perhaps indirectly led her son Anthony to that course which gave the world "Framly Parsonage," "The Small House at Allington" and all that delightful literature of English well-bred realism which forms, one may say, a new school of English fiction. As Anthony says, his mother, his brother and himself have written more books than any other family in the world.

In 1834, the elder Trollope fled to the continent to escape imprisonment for debt. Abroad, their home became a hospital, where died sister, brother and father, after lingering illnesses; the brave old mother always tending the sick and at the same time writing books for bread and burial expenses. She wrote in all *one hundred and fourteen* volumes; the first after she was fifty and the last after she was seventy - six. We forgive her caricature of the West — if indeed there was anything to forgive.

When, in his twentieth year, Anthony went to London and applied for a clerkship in the general post-office, it was shown that he could not write or spell common English, and did not know the multiplication-table, in spite of the so-called education of school and college! He got his clerkship, however, and made a very poor clerk for seven years —disliked, suspected, in debt, and somewhat dissipated, unconscious of any power and utterly hopeless. The post-office sent him away from his desk to do out-door work in Ireland, where he remained eighteen years and emerged from shiftless idleness into decency and manliness. His nature was evidently a sturdy plant, sour and uncouth while green, and late in ripening.

It was in Ireland that he began novel-writing. For the first three novels he received nothing. Then he wrote "The Warden," and "Barchester Towers," the first of that memorable series in which, as he says, he "added another county to England"—-Barsetshire—Salisbury with its cathedral sitting for the portrait of "Barchester." In his fortieth year he received the first money ever paid him for literary work — £9 8s. 8d.

Trollope visited America twice in his life, once during the

war for the Union.*   His second visit was in 1868, with the object of making a postal treaty, which happily succeeded, and with a further commission to make an effort in behalf of international copyright, which unhappily failed for that time, only to succeed a generation later.

He wrote a book embodying his first journey, and of it the autobiography says:

The book I wrote expressed an assured confidence—which never quavered in a page or in a line—that the North would win. This assurance was based on the merits of the Northern cause, on the superior strength of the Northern party, and on a conviction that England would never recognize the South and that France would be guided in her policy by England.   The South had provoked the quarrel . . . and had fought gallantly; and a feeling, based on misconception as to American character, that the Southerner is a better gentlemen than his Northern brother, did create sympathy here.

Trollope's statement of his literary method, in his autobiography, is one of the most curious disclosures ever made by any writer.   Writing, as he knew he was, from beyond the grave (for he left the book unpublished during life), he conducts his readers through his fiction-factory with a quiet humor, an unmistakable candor and frankness, unparalleled in the world of letters.   He says:

I was told that the surest aid to the writing of a book was a piece of cobbler's wax in my chair.   I certainly believe in the cobbler's wax much more than I do in inspiration.   I had long since convinced myself that in such work as mine the great secret consisted in acknowledging myself to be bound by rules of labor similar to those which an artisan or mechanic is forced to obey. . . . .
It had at this time become my custom to write with my watch before me, and to require from myself 250 words at least every quarter of an hour.   I have found that the 250 words have been forthcoming as regularly as my watch went.

Trollope criticises his own books with much severity and much naïve praise.   One thing he is ashamed of; his

---

* The writer chanced to meet him at this time; a hearty, kindly, short, stout, London gentleman, silent and observing.

many heedlessnesses of grammar and construction. But his industry can never be questioned. He wrote more book-pages of fiction than any other Englishman who ever lived. His published stories number fifty, while his other ten books—travels, biographies, etc.—bring his total pen-work up to 30,000 printed pages, or a million and a half of words!

He rates his novel-writing contemporaries in the following order as to merit: Thackeray, George Eliot, Dickens, Bulwer, Charles Lever, Charlotte Brontë, Charles Reade, Wilkie Collins, Anne Thackeray, and Rhoda Broughton. He also names Disraeli, but only to disparage him bitterly —unjustly. "Hair-oil and false jewels."

However readers may disagree regarding his relative place as to general eminence, all will admit that he stands at or near the head of the realistic school. He quotes with pride what Nathaniel Hawthorne said of his novels, before·they became generally known:

Have you ever read the novels of Anthony Trollope? They precisely suit my taste—just as real as if some giant had hewn a great lump out of the earth and and put it under a glass case, with all its inhabitants going about their daily business, and not suspecting that they are being made a show. . . . I should think that human nature would give them [the novels] success everywhere.

What would we not give for a Trollopean novel of the twelfth century or any earlier age? History itself tends toward becoming a life-like record of common folks' joys and sorrows, rather than of the result of wars and the succession of kings. So long as readers like to have romance made to seem like reality, and reality to seem like romance, so long will such novels as Trollope's be cherished. How long will that be? Judging the future by the past, no bound can be set, short of the day when words, written and spoken, shall perish in a perishing world.

CHAPTER LVI.

CHARLES KINGSLEY.   THE BRONTËS.   GEORGE ELIOT.

HARLES KINGSLEY (1819–75), clergyman, poet and novelist, was the son of an English clergyman, and on his mother's side a descendant of generations of West-Indian slave-holders. He was finely educated, and graduated (with high honors) at Magdalen College, Cambridge. After being eighteen years rector of the parish of Eversley, in Hampshire, he was appointed professor of modern history in Cambridge University. His culture was wide and varied and his powers great; he being (like Sydney Smith and many other Church-of-England clergymen) distinguished for wit as well as learning and piety; and for remarkable conversational powers.

His large-heartedness tended to make him sympathetic with the interests of the lower classes, and he was one of the few churchmen who espoused what was called "Christian Socialism;" which not only sided with the poor but attacked the rich and the system of social order which produced, or at least countenanced, the chasm that divides the two. He spent much time and strength in the effort to ameliorate and Christianize the working people, and to establish coöperative industry; that is, work wherein the laborer shall share the profit.

It was at this time that he wrote his most striking and memorable novels; "Yeast," and "Alton Locke, Tailor and Poet"; works which created the greatest interest and exercised immense influence; which interest and influence are still alive, and are impelling the minds of men to results which can not yet be fully foreseen or even guessed at. In one of his novels ("Two Years Ago") he shows knowledge of and sympathy with the negro race that may have had something to do with the slave-holding traditions of his family.

His next most marked book was "Hypatia;" a historical novel treating of the times of early Christianity in Egypt, and the martyrdom of a grand and lovely Greek Pagan woman forms the tragedy of the book.   In most of his novels the plot is very simple; and in all of them the reader has the impression that he had something to say for which the story serves only as a vehicle.   His book of travels in the West Indies, however, is charming and delightful for its own sake, giving a picture so lifelike as to place the reader in the midst of the scenes the writer describes.

Charlotte Brontë (1816–55) was the third child of a poor clergyman settled in Haworth in Yorkshire, and most of her early life was spent at that small country town.   She was one of six children, five girls and one boy.   Three of the girls, Charlotte (whose pseudonym was Currer Bell), Anne (Acton Bell), and Emily (Ellis Bell), afterward became writers.

The mother fell into ill-health, and the children were left to themselves, and so grew up rather quiet, delicate and reserved.   They were brought up on a vegetable diet, their father not considering flesh - meat, as he called it, to be good for them.   He had the theory, then very common, that exposure and privation made children grow up strong and hardy, and he enforced it with cruel and destructive determination.

Mrs. Brontë soon died, and the children lived more alone than ever, rarely meeting any one out of their own family. Each was sent, at about twelve years old, to a boarding-school, which Charlotte afterward described as "Lowood" in "Jane Eyre," and from the poor food and well - meant cruelties of which she suffered all her life. The girls walked two miles over a shelterless country to church, even in the coldest weather, carrying a cold dinner with them, and there attended morning and afternoon service in an utterly cold building. Charlotte's two elder sisters, delicate before they went to "Lowood," died within three years, in consequence of the treatment they received there. This left Charlotte the eldest of the family, and she devoted her life, with grave sweetness, to the care of the rest.

At fourteen we find her producing stories, essays, dramas and poems, which she wrote in an extremely minute hand in twenty-two small volumes of sixty to one hundred pages each. At fifteen she is described as a little, short-sighted, nervous, wise, beloved, set, antiquated girl, quiet in manner and quaint in dress. She was now sent to another school, Miss Wooler's, which was a delightful contrast to the dreadful place where she had suffered so much. She stayed there one happy year, then went home to educate her sisters. At nineteen she returned to Miss Wooler's as a teacher, and remained there several years. She next became a private governess, at the pitiful salary of £16 a year! All these experiences helped to mould the literary work which was to occupy herself and sisters, as did also her residence in Brussels, whither she and her sister Emily went to study in preparing themselves to set up a school of their own.

When Charlotte was twenty-eight, her father lost his sight for a time and (her brother having died a wretched drunkard) the entire care of the family fell upon her. At thirty she and her sisters published at the authors' cost a volume of poems by "Currer, Ellis and Acton Bell." They paid the entire expense of the publication and got back almost nothing. Then they published, on joint-account with the bookseller, three volumes containing three tales, one by each of them. This also failed to win popular favor. Next she offered "The Professor" for publication, but it was declined. Nothing daunted, she began and persevered in writing the book which was to bring to her fortune and lasting fame; the wonderful novel "Jane Eyre." She was thirty-one at this time.

The welcome to "Jane Eyre" was not sudden or tumultuous; but it was such as to yield a little money just when that was most sorely needed, and to call within a year for a second edition; in which its author wrote a dedication to Thackeray.

Emily Brontë, author of "Wuthering Heights," died in 1847, and Anne, author of "Agnes Grey" and "The Tenant of Wildfell Hall," in 1849. The deaths of her brother and both her sisters had occurred while Charlotte was writing "Shirley," and it was published in the latter year, when its brave writer was thirty-three. Up to this time the secret of authorship had been kept; now it became known and Charlotte might have been, if she had chosen, "a literary lion;" but she would none of it. She did go a little into London society, and there she met Thackeray, who gives an interesting account of the occurrence. For herself, she says she never could tell whether he was speaking in jest or earnest; and remarks; "I felt sufficiently at my ease with all but Thackeray; with him I was fearfully stupid." As to her supposed effect upon others, she says, "I believe most of them expected me to come out in a more marked, executive, striking light. They desired more to admire and more to blame." She returned to her country parsonage-home with relief and content. But her fame followed her and the post came loaded with letters. Other women had written books, but no woman books so *manly* as hers. "Mental Equality of the Sexes" was proclaimed by the reviews.

Her sisters' books are not without conspicuous ability; but scarcely comparable with Charlotte's, though she, in her sisterly love, was disposed to make them out her equals if not her superiors. Emily's "Wuthering Heights" may be called really great, but its atmosphere of gloom and horror is unnatural. In 1854, when thirty-eight years old, she married Mr. Nicholls, her father's curate, who had long loved her—as did every one who ever knew her. This was the happiest year of her life, and the last; for she died early in 1855.

Mary Ann Evans (Lewes) Cross, "George Eliot" (1819–80), the most distinguished of woman novelists, was the daughter of Robert Evans, in earlier life a carpenter, and at the time of her birth the agent or superintendent for the owner of an estate in Derbyshire. He is understood to be shadowed forth in several of the noble low-born characters which are marvellously depicted in the author's novels; "Adam Bede," "Caleb Garth," etc. The mother may also be traced in the daughter's fiction; not in portraits but in bits of portraiture wherein housewifely precision, industry and method are displayed. Her farm-work was done by nine in the morning, when she would sit down to her loom. Mrs. Poyser is a masterpiece of art. Her sharpness of speech is suggested as a memory of Mrs. Evans, and the probable origin of Mary Ann's own mother-wit and pointed plain speaking, but the novelist's "faculty of taking pains" which is an element of genius, is traceable to the father.

Mary Ann, or Marian, as she grew to be called, had as good education as the provincial neighborhood afforded, and early took on staid, womanly looks and ways, more like those of a teacher than a scholar, at the same time liking to have about her all the refinements and delicacies of luxurious appointments. Her culture was not limited to her school-days; she devoted herself to the more advanced studies as the years went on, and never found herself too old to learn. She continued to be a student, in every sense, to the end of her life.

When thirty years of age she lost her father; and, her mother having died many years before, she suffered much from her lonely position, though happy in the possession of many and valued friends. She made the tour of Europe, and spent about a year abroad. She had, before leaving home, translated Strauss's "Life of Jesus;" but her serious entry upon literary life may be said to date from her return, when she began to write for the "Westminster Review"; an early article being on Margaret Fuller, the American writer, of whom she says: "We are at a loss whether to regard her as the parent or child of New England transcendentalism." Another article, noteworthy in view of her later writings, is "Silly Novels by Lady Novelists."

Her first work of fiction, "Scenes of Clerical Life," of which "Amos Barton" was the opening tale, was published in Blackwood's Magazine, when she was thirty - eight years old. The success, though satisfactory, was not startling. The authorship was a secret, and, as a name was needed, George Eliot was adopted, and afforded room for much discussion as to the sex of the author; though Dickens expressed himself strongly in favor of the hypothesis of feminine authorship.

Two years later appeared "Adam Bede," which widened and strengthened the fame of its writer. It was accepted as the most perfect realism ever attained in fiction. People were continually recognizing in its characters the reproduction of living persons. It was said to hit the mark which Dickens only aimed at; he merely giving the outward shell of his low-life characters, while George Eliot pierced through flesh and blood and gave the heart and soul.

"The Mill on the Floss" kept up undimmed the name of George Eliot, and it also made her known in her real person; and a great joy was experienced by all advocates of the equality of the sexes on the revelation of the fact that a woman was doing such masculine work as this.

The well-known and almost unrivalled books which now flowed from this author's pen in rapid succession need only to be mentioned to recall them to the minds of all philanthropic readers of fiction. "Silas Marner," "Romola," "Felix Holt, the Radical," "Middlemarch," "Daniel Deronda," complete the marvellous list. Each had an object; but the story always carried on the object—not the object the story. Nowhere does there appear the sermonizing, didactic tone which says, "Be good, be brave, be kind, be true"; but one rises from reading each with a new love for goodness, courage, mercy and truthfulness.

"George Eliot" was also a poet; "The Spanish Gipsy," a drama, and some shorter poems in blank verse, bearing her name. These contain fine passages, but it is not as a poet that she will be longest remembered.

CHAPTER LVII.

THE BROWNINGS.

A WONDERFUL companionship is among the noteworthy events of the nineteenth century. Two great, poetic spirits whom nature seems to have intended for one another by their gifts, their tastes and their power of intense mutual affection. Robert Browning (1812–89), and Elizabeth Barrett Browning (1809–61), will go down to posterity linked together, and surrounded by a halo of admiration and love. Mr. Browning was born in London, of parents who were cultivated and accomplished, and were persons of unusual strength of character and mental ability. The elder Browning inherited from his mother a sugar-plantation in St. Kitts, but abandoned a residence there from hatred of slavery (which then existed in the British colonies), and became a clerk in the Bank of England. Robert Browning numbered among his immediate ancestors Germans, Scots, and West-Indian creoles, beside the English blood inherited from his father, which diversity of race may partly account for the variety and scope of his mental endowments. He had a careful school and home education, but did not take a university course, preferring to complete his studies by travel. After returning home, he devoted himself seriously to authorship (he was then about twenty-five) and published "Paracelsus," "Strafford" and "Sordello," all poems having the dramatic form. The last is said to have been its author's favorite. His "Bells and Pomegranates," a collection of poems which included "Pippa Passes," was the means of making him acquainted with Miss Elizabeth Barrett, who paid a tribute to his genius in her poem of "Lady Geraldine's Courtship."

> Or from Browning some "Pomegranate"
> Which if cut deep down the middle,
> Shows a heart within blood-tinctured,
> Of a veined humanity.

This led to a correspondence which, after two years, resulted in marriage, when she was in her thirty-seventh year and he in his thirty-fourth.

Elizabeth Barrett Browning was the daughter of an English country gentleman and seems to have always been marked out for a poet. She began to write when she was a mere child, having the good taste, however, never to wish her juvenile poems published, nor to have them seen by any one except her father, whom she calls "my public and my critic." Miss Mitford, who knew her well, speaks of her as having at this time "a slight, delicate figure, with a shower of dark curls falling on each side of a most expressive face, large, tender eyes, richly fringed by dark eye-lashes, and a smile like a sunbeam." Miss Barrett soon became a fine scholar, thoroughly acquainted with Latin and Greek, and, as a matter of course, with all the best literature of her own language. Her frail health obliged ·her to live very quietly, and added to her natural inclination for the seclusion which deep study requires. When she was twenty-six years old, the bursting of a blood-vessel in her lungs left her life hanging long by a slender thread. For seven years after this she was an invalid, confined to her couch, with the prospect of remaining so through life. During this long time of enforced retirement her sole resource was reading; and an amusing instance of her evading her physician's desire that she should discontinue her severe studies is shown in her having her Greek Plato bound to look like a novel that it might not excite his suspicions.

Her first volume of poems, containing "A Drama of Exile," "The Cry of the Children," "Lady Geraldine's Courtship," and other expressions of intense feeling and deep sympathy with humanity, established her position as a poet, and as has been said, resulted in her marriage with Robert Browning. The exquisite "Sonnets from the Portuguese," written during her engagement to him, though not published until long afterward, have never been surpassed for delicacy of tone combined with the utmost intensity of emotion.

Mr. Browning took his wife at once to Italy, where the mild climate undoubtedly did much to prolong her life. Both of them felt the deepest sympathy for the new Italy just rising into being under Victor Emanuel and Garibaldi, and many fine poems owed their inspiration to this source. At Florence (which they made their home), Mrs. Browning wrote her "Casa Guidi Windows," and her longest poem, "Aurora Leigh." The latter is partly of an autobiographical nature, and is very interesting as throwing light on her early life. A new translation of "Prometheus Bound," of which she had made a somewhat unsatisfactory one before her marriage, was also among her labors, and a volume of prose, "Essays on the Greek Christian Poets," and "Book of the Poets," the latter on English writers. Fifteen years of beautiful married life were passed in Italy, the last fourteen in Florence; then her health gradually failed, and she passed away calmly and without pain, in the very year (1861) and week which saw Victor Emanuel acknowledged king of a united Italy.

The house (called "Casa Guidi") occupied by the Brownings during their residence in Florence, has a tablet on the front, placed there by the city to her memory.

Mr. Browning published, during the fifteen years of their married life, several volumes of collected poems, one of which, entitled "Men and Women," contains a series of character-sketches, and some beautiful lyrics. After his wife's death he wrote "Dramatis Personæ," a work of the same nature; "The Ring and the Book," an epic poem, dealing with the passions; "Balaustion's Adventure," which includes a free translation of the "Alkestis" of Euripides, and many other books. His last volume "Asolando," a collection of short single poems, was happily completed just before his death.

It is needless here to attempt a criticism of Browning's writings. The "Browning Societies" scattered through our country show that a vast number of the poetry-loving people of the present day regard him as the greatest poet of the century. Another hundred years will decide his place among the writers of the world. His greatness is indisputable, his failings almost equally conspicuous. The former is chiefly in the thought expressed; the latter in the manner of expression, which is often obscure—almost incomprehensible — and sometimes grotesque, if not absurd. He might be called a Carlyle among poets; or turning to the sister art, be compared to a Wagner.

Mrs. Browning's gifts of lofty poetic feeling, thrilling tenderness, exquisite delicacy and fervency of expression combined with rare intellectual powers and great acquirements, are more easily expressed. Her defects are, too great fluency, occasioning an undue use of words, and a carelessness about rhyme which mars some of her finest rhymed work.

CHAPTER LVIII.

ALFRED TENNYSON.

T has been the plan, in preparing this brief account of England's noteworthy writers, to exclude from the list all the living. To this number belonged, until now, the poet-laureate, Alfred, Lord Tennyson. As the last sheets of our Short History are passing through the press, we hear of his death (October 6, 1892). Though it is a painful task to speak of one long and lately with us as having now no part in this busy life of ours, the work will not be complete without a few words on the man who for many years has filled so important a place in the hearts of his countrymen and of the English-speaking world.

Alfred Tennyson (born in 1809) was the third of a family of twelve children. His father, George Clayton Tennyson, was rector of Somersby in Lincolnshire, where the poet was born. After a home and school training under the superintendence of his father, Alfred went to Cambridge,* where he obtained his first laurels (1819) in the shape of the Chancellor's medal for a poem in blank verse called "Timbuctoo." This the laureate never acknowledged, or allowed to be printed among his works; but as it was unearthed and "pirated" by American publishers, we are enabled to judge from its lines whether any gleams appear in it of the genius which afterward made its author famous. The writer supposes himself to be standing on the heights of Gibraltar and gazing across "Calpe's Straits" into Africa; a region to which he gives the general name of "Timbuctoo:"

> I stood upon the Mountain which o'erlooks
> The narrow seas, whose rapid interval

---

* Like many other great authors, he left the university without taking a degree.

> Parts Afric from green Europe, when the sun
> Had fall'n below the Atlantic, and above
> The silent heavens were blench'd with fairy light,
> Uncertain whether fairy light or cloud,
> Flowing Southward, and the chasms of deep, deep blue
> Slumber'd unfathomable, and the stars
> Were flooded over with clear glory and pale.
>
> *   *   *   *   *   Then I raised
> My voice and cried, "Wild Afric, doth thy sun
> Lighten, thy hills enfold a city as fair
> As those which starred the night of the elder world?
> Or is the rumor of thy Timbuctoo
> A dream as frail as those of ancient time?"

It is not difficult to recognize in lines like these, the promise afterward fulfilled in "The Lotos Eaters," and "Œnone." They are certainly creditable to a young man of twenty. This, however, was not his first poetic effort. While still at school he had published, in connection with his brother Charles (who later added Turner to his family name), a volume of their joint composition entitled "Poems by Two Brothers." Little notice was taken of this youthful effort, though Coleridge said that the verses signed "A. T." gave promise of a coming poet. These also were ignored by the writer in later life.

In 1830, Tennyson put forth a volume called "Poems, Chiefly Lyrical." As successive editions were published he added new pieces, and omitted such of the old ones as he thought unworthy of preservation, until the volume contained all the poems we now find preceding "The Princess" in the general edition of his works. This collection placed him at once in the front rank of poets. The favorites among them are, perhaps, beside "Œnone" and "The Lotos Eaters," already mentioned, "Love and Death," "The Lady of Shalott," "The Palace of Art," "Lady Clara Vere de Vere," "The May-Queen," "A Dream of Fair Women," "Morte d'Arthur," "Locksley Hall," and " Break, break,

break." A fine specimen of his early manner is given in "The Deserted House:"

> Life and Thought have gone away
>   Side by side,
> Leaving door and windows wide:
>   Careless tenants they!
> All within is dark as night;
> In the windows is no light,
> And no murmur at the door,
> So frequent on its hinge before.
>   *   *   *
> Come away, for Life and Thought
>   Here no longer dwell:
>   But in a city glorious—
> A great and distant city—they have bought
>   A mansion incorruptible:
> Would they could have stayed with us!

It is difficult to characterize the charming poem called "The Princess, A Medley," on account of its inequality. In spite of unquestionable diffuseness, it contains passages which have been quoted until they are "household words," and some daintily-tender songs such as "The splendor falls," "Tears, idle tears," and others, which fasten themselves on our imagination as much by their music as by the thought contained in them.

> The splendor falls on castle walls,
> And snowy summits old in story,
> The long light shakes across the lakes,
> And the wild cataract leaps in glory.
> Blow, bugle, blow, set the wild echoes flying;
> Blow, bugle; answer echoes, dying, dying, dying.

Among other quotable passages are the following:

> Jewels five words long,
> That on the stretched forefinger of all time
> Sparkle forever.
>   *   *   *
> A rosebud set with little wilful thorns,
> And sweet as English air could make her.

25

> The moan of doves in immemorial elms,
> And murmuring of innumerable bees.

To these must be added the grand passage beginning:

> For woman is not undeveloped man,
> But diverse.

"In Memoriam," Tennyson's next separate work (published 1850), is rather a collection of short poems than one long one; being composed of groups of quatrains written at intervals, upon one subject, through a period of seventeen years. The whole was a tribute to his friend Arthur Henry Hallam (son of Hallam the historian), who died in Vienna in 1833, and whose loss the poet mourned with an unending regret. This, the most famous death-song in our language since Lycidas, is an elegy of wonderful grandeur and tenderness, coming from a full heart and inspired with the loftiest poetic sentiment. It has been called a journal of sorrows.

In 1851, on the death of Wordsworth, Tennyson was created poet-laureate; an office which the occupancy of Southey and Wordsworth had redeemed from the low estimation into which it had previously fallen. The first poetical effort the new laureate was called on to make was the "Ode on the Death of the Duke of Wellington." This poem, while containing much that is good and noble, appears labored, and is, to our thinking, inferior as a finished picture to the beautiful stanzas which our own Longfellow wrote on the same occasion.*

It is perhaps fortunate that modern custom does not require, of the laureate, verses made to order on each event that takes place in the royal family. The poet is allowed to use his own judgment as to the occasions when he shall call upon his muse for a contribution, and both Wordsworth

---

and Tennyson were exceedingly chary of this effort. In
"The Charge of the Light Brigade," Tennyson scored a
success. We may say of "A Welcome to Alexandra" (The
Princess of Wales), that the first lines are the best part of it:

> Sea - kings' daughter from over the sea,
> Alexandra!
> Saxon and Norman and Dane are we,
> But all of us Danes in our welcome of thee,
> Alexandra!

In 1845, appeared "Maud," a poem which puzzled the
critics not a little, and which does not even yet occupy a
fixed place in popular estimation. In meaning, though not
in diction, it is obscure, a fault so rare in Tennyson that
one is almost inclined to think the poem a sort of experiment; something to test the perspicacity of the public
mind. Be this as it may, "Maud" contains many passages
of rare beauty, and others of fervidly intense feeling.

Beside some pieces written in his capacity as laureate,
several other poems were published with "Maud," of which
"The Brook, an Idyl," and "Will," have remained the greatest favorites.

> Oh, well for him whose will is strong!
> He suffers, but he will not suffer long;
> He suffers, but he can not suffer wrong.

The "Idyls of the King," Enid, Vivien, Elaine, Gueni-
vere — supplemented in after years by "The Passing of
Arthur" and other poems on similar subjects, were named
by their author an "Arthurian Epic," but the title "epic"
seems questionable. The tales are fragmentary, and therefore
contrary in their nature to the idea of an epic; which, strictly
speaking, is a sustained and connected poem on one subject.
Individually, however, they are very beautiful.

"Enoch Arden" with its pathetic story of homely fidelity
and self - sacrifice, sprang instantly into general favor. In
1875 appeared the first of Tennyson's dramas—"Queen

Mary," which was followed by " Becket " and " Harold," and lastly, in the year of his death (the eighty-third of his life), " The Foresters." Seldom has a poet attempted, at such an age, so difficult a task as that of writing a play for acting ; more seldom still has the effort been crowned with success. "The Foresters" has not yet been published, but it has taken well upon the stage, and seems to have done no discredit to its author's fame.

Two more volumes, named respectively "Tiresias, and other Poems," and " Demeter and other Poems," close the list of Tennyson's collected works. A complete, uniform edition of his writings is still lacking.

In 1883, the poet was created Baron Tennyson of Ald-worth, in Sussex, and Freshwater, Isle of Wight; a clumsy title, which the short formula "Lord Tennyson" replaces for common use.

When Tennyson's first noteworthy book was published (1842), Wordsworth, then the greatest of living poets, had ceased to write. The latter had never been a poet of the people, his lofty strains reaching only minds raised above the ordinary level. But all could appreciate the warm humanity of the younger poet, the faultless music of his verse, his rich fancy, his glowing imagination. These sup-plied a need which till then had existed without being recognized. His exquisitely delicate observation of nature no poet has ever surpassed or perhaps even equalled. His moral is always of the highest, and he does not forget to emphasize it. For example, in speaking of the source of Wellington's eminence he desires that the great soldier's example may stand,

> Till in all lands and through all human story
> The path of duty be the way to glory.

Tennyson's poetic gifts are apt, at first sight, to throw into the shade the evidences of his wide reading and extensive acquaintance with classical and other literature. His poems are filled with allusions which show that what had been of old thought and written was as familiar to him as were the things about him. Never obtruding his learning, he makes use of it in a manner so unforced and natural that we do not even notice the proofs of it until, when our attention is called to it, we perceive how richly stored must have been the mind which could use its wealth of illustration with so lavish a hand.

Personally, the laureate was one of the most unapproachable of men. Unlike Scott, who considered it a part of his duty to receive with courtesy the hosts of "lion-hunters" who intruded on his privacy, Tennyson resented such curiosity, and pushed his resistance to it to the verge of rudeness. The friends to whom he was personally attached were devoted to him and he to them; but with the general public he had no patience. This habit of seclusion, which lasted many years, had the effect of withdrawing his interest somewhat from matters affecting the world's progress, and restricting it to a narrower field. It may also have produced the pessimistic tendency visible in his poem "Locksley Hall Sixty Years After." Here are some typical verses :

Chaos, Cosmos! Cosmos, Chaos! Who can tell how all will end?
Read the wide world's annals, you, and take their wisdom for your
        friend.

Hope the best, but hold the Present fatal daughter of the Past,
Shape your heart to front the hour, but dream not that the hour
        will last.

Ay, if dynamite and revolver leave you courage to be wise:
When was age so cramm'd with menace? madness? written, spoken
        lies?

The closing scene was ideal in its beauty. The dying poet lay at midnight in his lovely home (at Aldworth in Sussex), with no light in the room except from the moon which shone in at the open window, a volume of Shakespeare open in his hand at a page of "Cymbeline," and thus faded gently away, surrounded by his nearest and dearest, and perfectly conscious to almost the very end.

And so we must leave him,

As he stands on the heights of his life, with a glimpse of a height
that is higher. *

How he himself looked forward to his passing is best told in his own words when he wrote in anticipation of it:

CROSSING THE BAR.

Sunset and evening star,
  And one clear call for me!
And may there be no moaning of the bar,
  When I put out to sea.

But such a tide as moving seems asleep,
  Too full for sound and foam,
When that which drew from out the boundless deep,
  Turns again home.

Twilight and evening bell,
  And after that the dark!
And may there be no sadness of farewell
  When I embark.

For though from out our bourne of Time and Place
  The flood may bear me far,
I hope to see my pilot face to face
  When I have crossed the bar.

We bid farewell, for a time, to the immeasurable theme of English literature. From far-away old Gildas, almost invisible through the mist of ages and almost inaudible through the roar of events as the great world spins

Forever down the ringing grooves of change,

to Tennyson, the newly dead, the deeply mourned, who shone bright

In the white light that beats upon a throne,

we have followed, step by step, the wondrous story;

* "By an Evolutionist."—*Tennyson.*

more and more prone, as we go on, to think that England's splendor, after all, is not in her feats of arms, nor in her material progress, but in her moral and intellectual advance, of which her towering literature is at once cause and effect. Freedom, light, humanity, morality; all these and every other immaterial glory have climbed up hand in hand with the thought of her intellectual giants, made immortal in the words of their writings.

Is a greater height possible? It seems hard to believe it, yet before Chaucer and Spenser, Shakespeare and Milton, Tennyson and Browning, the world thought in each case that the summit had been gained. It may be that years will bring other revelations as startling as were these, but our imaginations fail to grasp the possibility. We can only wonder and wait.

INDEX.

Miss Kirkland's Works.

I.

A SHORT HISTORY OF ENGLISH LITERATURE. For Young People. Price, $1.25.

II.

A SHORT HISTORY OF ENGLAND. For Young People. Price, $1.25.

III.

A SHORT HISTORY OF FRANCE. For Young People. Price, $1.25.

IV.

SIX LITTLE COOKS, or Aunt Jane's Cooking Class. Price, 75 cents.

V.

DORA'S HOUSEKEEPING. Price, 75 cents.

VI.

SPEECH AND MANNERS. For Home and School. Price, 75 cents.

A. C. McCLURG & COMPANY, Publishers.